PILGRIMAGE AND AMBIGUITY

First published in 2017 by
Sean Kingston Publishing
www.seankingston.co.uk
Canon Pyon

In association with
The Centro Incontri Umani, Ascona

Text © Dionigi Albera, Isabelle Charleux, Jürgen Wasim Frembgen, Omar González, Angela Hobart, Carlos César Xavier Leal, Pierre-Jean Luizard, Manoël Penicaud, Yasushi Tonaga, Robin M. Wright, Thierry Zarcone
Images © Contributors and copyright holders named in the captions

British Library Cataloguing in Publication Data
A catalogue record for this book is available from the British Library.

This book is published under a Creative Commons Attribution Non-commercial Non-derivative 4.0 International license (CC BY-NC-ND 4.0). This license allows you to share, copy, distribute and transmit the work for personal and non-commercial use providing author and publisher attribution is clearly stated. Further details about CC BY licenses are available at http://creativecommons.org/ licenses/by/4.0

Printed by Lightning Source

Paperback ISBN 978-1-907774-77-5

Pilgrimage and Ambiguity

Sharing the Sacred

EDITED BY ANGELA HOBART AND THIERRY ZARCONE

Sean Kingston Publishing
www.seankingston.co.uk
Canon Pyon

In association with
The Centro Incontri Umani,
Ascona

From The Boy Who Was Afraid, *by Sperry Armstrong (illustrated by the author), 1942, William Heinemann Ltd. By kind permission of Random House.*

Acknowledgements

The conference on the theme of 'Pilgrimages and Ambiguity: Sharing the Sacred', which led to this book, was held at the Centro Incontri Umani, Ascona, overlooking Lake Maggiore, on the border between Switzerland and Italy. The Centre seeks to encourage cross-cultural understanding, respect and peace internationally. We want to express our gratitude to the participants for their stimulating and thought-provoking contributions and for the scientific support of the Groupe Sociétés, Religions, Laïcïtés of the Centre National de la Recherche Scientifique (based at the École Pratique des Haute Études) in Paris for their help in organizing the conference. We also thank Sean Kingston Publishing for the competent assistance in publishing the book.

We're living in an era of globalization, rapid technological development and far-reaching environmental and social changes, which often entail conflict, suffering and uncertainty. This is epitomized in recent years by perilous voyages of thousands of refugees leaving their destroyed and fragmented homelands to reach foreign shores for imagined safety. Where is the sacred, the light, in the turmoil of the night? (See illustration.)

This book is a modest attempt to explore questions confronting humans in their pilgrimages as they engage with multi-dimensional and ambiguous sites of worship and homage. In so doing, they expand their horizons of knowledge and experiences of different faiths and religious movements, perhaps to transcend them. This is beautifully expressed in the poem by the Indian saint, Kabir (d. 1518):

> Allah stays in the body of everyone,
> Try to understand this in your soul
> Allah is the same for the Hindu and for the Turk,
> This is what Kabir claims.
> (Kabir, 1959, *Au Cabaret de l'amour*, p. 70)

Angela Hobart and Thierry Zarcone

Contents

INTRODUCTION Why do pilgrims share a sanctuary?   1
Some hypotheses
ANGELA HOBART AND THIERRY ZARCONE

I
Ambiguous sacred places in the Mediterranean

CHAPTER 1 Towards a reappraisal of ambiguity   29
In the footsteps of Frederick W. Hasluck
DIONIGI ALBERA

CHAPTER 2 From the god Amon to Sufi *mawlids*   51
PIERRE-JEAN LUIZARD

CHAPTER 3 'Ambiguity in context' according to Islamic thought   69
Bridging theory and actuality relating to saints in Islam
YASUSHI TONAGA

II
Pilgrimages and sacred places in the Indo-Persian world and China

CHAPTER 4 Chinese, Tibetan and Mongol Buddhists on   87
Wutaishan (China) from the eighteenth to the
twenty-first century
ISABELLE CHARLEUX

CHAPTER 5 Betwixt and Between   119
Figures of ambiguity in the Sufi cult of Lāl Shāhbāz Qalandar (Pakistan)
JÜRGEN WASIM FREMBGEN

CHAPTER 6 Syncretism and the superimposition of Islam   131
on Buddhism in the Pamir
Mountain cults and saint veneration
THIERRY ZARCONE

III
Ambiguous sites cross-culturally

CHAPTER 7   **Monte Verita, the 'Mountain of Truth' in Ascona**   157
A pilgrimage site of paradoxes and contradiction
ANGELA HOBART

CHAPTER 8   **The Seven Sleepers pilgrimage in Brittany**   183
The ambiguity of a Christian-Muslim 'heterotopia'
MANOËL PÉNICAUD

CHAPTER 9   **Multi-centric mythscapes**   201
Sanctuaries and pilgrimages in north-west Amazonian Arawakan religious traditions
ROBIN M. WRIGHT, OMAR GONZÁLEZ NANEZ
and CARLOS CÉSAR XAVIER LEAL

LIST OF CONTRIBUTORS   233

INDEX   237

INTRODUCTION

Why do pilgrims share a sanctuary?
Some hypotheses

THIERRY ZARCONE AND ANGELA HOBART

We cannot kill the gods. Though we can knock them off their pedestals, they continue nevertheless to be present inside us, surviving in dark caverns, in the chambers that we thought to be closed up. From this unknown darkness, they speak once more.
(Roger Bastide 1975:222)

One of the main aims of the book was to question the expression 'ambiguous sanctuaries' that was coined by the historian William Hasluck (d. 1920), towards the end of the nineteenth century, with respect to Anatolian and Balkan sanctuaries, mausoleums and pilgrimages that were shared by Christian and Muslim pilgrims. An 'ambiguous' sanctuary, according to Hasluck (1973:94), represents a distinct stage of development – a point of transition between Christianity and a Sufi movement and vice versa (see Albera's chapter). The conference at the Centro Incontri Umani, in Ascona, on which this volume is based, set out to discuss the concept of 'ambiguity' and the question of sharing 'the sacred' from a wider global and spiritual perspective. In so doing, the resulting chapters examine 'ambiguous' sanctuaries in various parts of the world. Thus, they are not concerned only with sanctuaries in the Mediterranean but also with Middle Eastern (Egypt) and Asian sanctuaries (India, Central Asia, China); two others chapters deal with sanctuaries in Europe (France, Switzerland) and one in South America (Brazil). Furthermore, two participants of the Ascona converence, Dionigi Albera and Manoël Pénicaud, participated in organizing an international exhibition in Marseille from April to August 2015 called *Lieux saints partagés* (Shared Sanctuaries) at the Musée des Civilisations de l'Europe et de la Méditerranée in Marseille. The exhibition, as reflected in its title, dealt with the same subject matter as this book, but focused exclusively on the Mediterranean region. The catalogue, appropriately entitled *Lieux saints partagés* (MuCEM 2015) that accompanied the exhibition, includes several interesting articles.

The contributors to this book have investigated essentially two distinct categories of sanctuaries, although they are interrelated. The first category consists of sanctuaries or holy places that comprise mainly monasteries and mausoleums of saints. Till recently – implying at least one or two centuries ago – different religious groups visited them, although nowadays they are linked to one religion only (see chapters of Luizard and Zarcone). In the past, however, two or several religions were either superimposed at these sanctuaries, or existed simultaneously or successively to one another. In these instances ambiguity is reflected by the legacy of previous religions movements on the devotions, rituals, symbols or narratives (hagiographies) associated with these sanctuaries, which echo the past in subtle ways. Ambiguity may also arise because the authentic identity of these holy places is often far from clear.

The second category, by contrast, concerns sanctuaries which were in the past and are still nowadays visited by pilgrims of different faiths (see chapters of Charleux and Frembgen). They are for the most part atypical pilgrims who cultivate 'interreligious', or what is often referred to as 'perennialist' faiths (see chapters of Pénicaud and Hobart). It is evident that two or more religions have in the course of time left their imprint on some of these sanctuaries. The main difference between these two categories is that in the first the ambiguity of a sanctuary relates to the hybridization of the oral and/or written narratives associated with it. The narratives may also reflect the religious orientations of the people presently in control of the sanctuary; in some cases earlier narratives may have been recycled.

Finally, we want to draw attention in this section to the chapter by Wright *et al.* on the Arawak-speaking peoples of the north-west Amazon and their traditions of sacred geographies, creation narratives, ancestral spirits and places of shamanic protection. The authors' discussion of these themes in the local context is intriguing and important, as it highlights a different problematic in relation to the notion of ambiguity. In this way another perspective is given on ambiguity that extends our horizon on the subject.

'Pre-religious sacredness'

The main question raised by the authors is: why people from different faiths, who may be in conflict or rivalry with one another, are attracted to the same sanctuary – particularly a tomb – and share with ease its sacredness. In the eyes of Hasluck this feature makes these sanctuaries 'ambiguous'. This implies that the religion associated with them is often not readily identifiable. Even in cases where the religion is well known, the pilgrims' own religious orientation may be vague. Ambiguity when used in mainstream religious contexts often has a negative connotation because a juxtaposition, mixing or syncretization of cults, devotions and rituals indicates impurity. Impurity here refers to an illicit amalgam that affects dangerously the cohesion of the religions involved. By contrast, as explained in detail by Albera in this volume, ambiguity can have positive connotations when it suggests great sanctity and power. It is then a sacred place open to many meanings and interpretations.

Another important question relating to the sharing of a sacred site by two or more distinct religions turns on what is meant by the 'main character' of the sacred, and whether it is universally perceived as such. Although we believe it is universal, other scholars or lay people may disagree with our approach. This is not the place to attempt an all-encompassing definition of the sacred. Yet it is necessary to say a few words about what may constitute its universality. It is initially relevant to recognize that sites reputed to be sacred are found almost everywhere and throughout time. Moreover, many religions regard them as sacred. The site may even have been taken over by a rival religion after the collapse of the former, or taken by force, or shared by two or more religions. Additionally, the narratives and rituals associated with a holy site, as well as its symbolic artefacts, are often reused and recycled. In these cases a temple, shrine and sanctuary is not only a symbol of victory of one religion over another through appropriation of the old, but the new religion absorbs the 'spirit' of the sacred *locus*. This also applies if a former religious building has been knocked down and a new one built at the same place. It is as if the sacred nature of the site had the capacity to expel its non-essential qualities (i.e. those linked to a particular religion). So, a sanctuary, in its widest sense is neither an 'hollow' place (see D. Albera in this volume) ready to accept any symbol or meaning brought by a new religion, nor 'full', i.e. replete with symbols and meanings (according to Durkheim and Turner, see Albera 2005:370). Essentially, the site is 'neutral' – implicit being that it embodies a 'non-religious' sacredness, and has not yet been adopted or reinterpreted by any institutionalized or established religion. And all the main religions – Zoroastrism, Judaism, Hinduism, Buddhism, Christianity or Islam that still flourish – can be considered institutionalized. In other words, the sacredness experienced can be labelled 'pre-religious sacredness'.

How do we define pre-religious sacredness? First and foremost, the sites imbued by the sacred are usually places where men can encounter the creatures, deities and spirits of the unseen world. In other words, they act as thresholds that mediate between the visible and invisible realms of human existence, the world of men and the world of spirits. Hence, these places must

Figure 1   *A black stone (meteorite?) venerated at the shrine of the Compagnons of the Cave or Seven Sleepers (Ashāb al-Kahf) in the Nakhichevan district of Azerbaijan (photograph: T. Zarcone, 2013)*

be exceptional *loci*, more precisely sites that terrify (*tremendum*) or fascinate (*fascinant*) people (Otto 1923). The most powerful among these *loci* are caves and mountains. Mountains are the gateways to the upper world (Potapov 1946) that allow 'communication' with the sky' (Stein 1987:211–17), whereas caves are thresholds to the chthonic spirits of the land (Ogudin 2003; Tátar 1996) or to the 'monde invisible' (Dermenghem 1954:43–4). Interestingly, grottos are often matrix-caves for rebirth rituals, *regressus ad uterum* (Bizot 1980; Bouillier 2008; Stein 1988).

There are other places that are impregnated with 'pre-religious sacredness', for example unusual and exceptional rocks, stones and majestic trees, hot springs etc. In many cultures spirits are thought to dwell in special stones and trees. (Boomgaard 1995; Popovska 2012, 2014; Tanyu 1968). Singular and enigmatic stones, due to their unusual shapes or colours, are often venerated. Outstanding among them are meteorites, as evidenced by the black stone at Mecca, that was one among many others meteorites (*betyl*) adorned by the Arabs before Islam (Lammens 1920:72–5). All places where such trees or stones tend to be found have welcomed later buildings linked to specific religions – usually mausoleums of their saints, their monasteries and shrines. Pre-religious sites, caves, rocks, trees, stones, although they may be completely integrated to religious sanctuaries or situated near them,

Why do pilgrims share a sanctuary?

Figure 2   Pilgrims venerating a tree at the Bektashi shrine of Merdivenköy, Istanbul (photograph: T. Zarcone, 2013).

still continue to attract pilgrims, as is the case at Wutaishan (Charleux in this volume) and many other holy places. Even if a human adheres to a mainstream religion, he may experience astonishment in coming across such an object that may still be the focus of a pre-religious cult. For example, in the nineteenth century, an official envoy of the Ottoman sultan was impressed by the fact that people from Anatolia were worshipping 'the great trees and monumental rocks when touched by the first rays of the rising sun' (Zarcone 2005:35). Nowadays homage is still given in the Pamir ranges (Tajikistan) and in Kirghizstan, to pre-religious sanctuaries marked by trees and collection of stones, although referred to as Muslim or Ismailian. They constitute, in the eyes of the local population, a category, or an *oston* (threshold) that is distinct from the sanctuaries that comprise the tombs of Prophets, kings or Sufi figures (Mock 2011:124–8; Vasil'tov 2013).

It is important to emphasize that sacred sites or objects called 'pre-religious' provide space where rituals or ritual acts can take place. Dwelling in the space between cosmic spheres, what Arnold van Gennep and Victor Turner called the 'liminal', can inspire and fill a human with awe and wonder. It is an indeterminate, magical space as rebirth ceremonies mentioned later in the introduction foretell. The liminal is like a dream where all possibilities can be conjured up by the creative imagination of the human. It is noteworthy that imagination is activated in all sacred places. Imagination to the medieval Sufi

Figure 3 Veneration of a sacred tree at the Buddhist shrine of Kurama, Kyoto, Japan (photograph: T. Zarcone, 2015).

mystic Ibn 'Arabî is intrinsic to the intermediate sphere and between 'being' and 'nothing'. In the philosopher's evocative terms, the between is 'something that separates two things, while never going to one side, as, for example, the line which separates shadow from light' (see Crapanzano 2004:58). As such, imagination is ambiguous and appropriate to be alluded to in this work in the discussion of pilgrimages and sacred sanctuaries, irrespective of whether they are conceived of as pre-religious or not, as are the 'pre-religious saint' figures to which we next turn.

The 'pre-religious saint'

Exceptional natural settings are not the only places impregnated by pre-religious sacredness. Also places where an ascetic, a hermit or shaman – i.e. people in search of an encounter with the supernatural or invisible world –

Why do pilgrims share a sanctuary? 7

lived and died have always attracted pilgrims of all faiths. The dwelling place was often remote, in the desert or mountains. As intercessors between the visible and the invisible, regardless of their religious affiliation, these ascetics may assist, give advice or heal pilgrim. Such a figure may be portrayed as a 'pre-religious saint'. Sacredness derives in this case from an experience of transcendence, as the ascetic is able to perform in both the visible and invisible realms. Alfred Métraux, in his book on Haitian voodoo clearly illustrated this: 'the initiates to voodoo' are supposed to obtain a *nanm* (spiritual principle, sacredness) at the end of their initiation ritual, i.e. after coming out of their retirement cell, the liminal space. In other words, they are 'impregnated with emanations from the sacred' (Métraux 1958:136).

It is a common phenomenon that sanctuaries or caves inhabited by ascetics belonging to a particular religion were re-utilized by ascetics of other religions. This is the case with the Sufi Sharaf al-Dīn Yahyā Manerī, at Rajgir (d. 1381), who started meditating at a *samadhi*, actually a place where a Hindu ascetic had died, after having performed spiritual exercises. Here, the *samadhi* was that of Devadatta, a cousin of the Buddha (Servan-Schreiber 1997:155). Similarly, inside the Muztagh Ata Mountain located in Xinjiang, the place of meditation of an Indian saint (*arhat*), was succeeded by an Ismaili *pīr* (see Zarcone in this volume). This is also the case at the Kohmari grotto (Khotan district, Xinjiang), a Buddhist site inhabited by a hermit who was succeeded by a Sufi shaykh (Stein 1921,vol. I:95). It is nowadays the focus of a Muslim pilgrimage (Davut 2001:123-5; personally observed in 2011). Thus a man who had died in a specific place, usually a cave and whose body didn't decompose while his hair and nails continued to grow, is regarded as a saint or a man with miraculous powers (as is the case of the Seven Sleepers, a site venerated by both Christians and Muslims). We have some contemporary examples of the sacred initiation of such deceased humans in the Mongol autonomous district of Northern Xinjiang, where Buddhist and Muslims lived (Hamada 2004:1035). It is worth noting here that the origin of one of the most ambiguous sanctuaries, the tomb complex of Shaykh 'Adī, the founder of the Yazidi syncretic religion in northern Iraq, was a grotto formerly occupied by Christian ascetics and Zoroastrian priests (Açıkyıldız 2009:328).

The appeal of these saint figures is intensified when they are seers, healers or magicians (though shamans in general and many ascetics have such competencies). This is supported by the fact that a sick person who visits a healer at a sanctuary in order to be cured, is generally not concerned about the religion of either the place or healer. It is well known, for instance, that Christians priests and monks who are reputed to be powerful therapists and exorcists, are frequently consulted by Muslims in Turkey and in the Middle East – a situation T. Zarcone has witnessed at Istanbul in the last decade of the twentieth century (at the Greek church of Çengelköy). The same applies to Hindus visiting Sufi tombs in India (Servan-Schreiber 1997:150). T. Zarcone has observed the same occurrence at Kashgar, Xinjiang, in 2013, when a Chinese (Han) women attended a ritual for acquiring magical protection at a Muslim Uyghur mausoleum (Arslankhan mausoleum). Magic has no frontiers, and any sanctuary operated by a seer or an ascetic is visited by pilgrims of all religions.

The 'dual saint'

A pre-religious saint is an ideal type and has rarely existed in pure form. However, there are several Muslim, Buddhist, Hindu, Taoist saints etc. who more or less fit this type. These saints show limited respect for their specific faith and are open to other religions. In cases when they consider themselves to have transcended their own religion, though still respectful of it – which is rare – they belong to a category we designate as the 'supra-confessional saint' (see below).

Generally, it is more common to find that a saint associated with a shared sanctuary is a 'dual saint', implying that he embodies two identities. The dual saint may be in the process of becoming syncretized, but he is not a syncretic saint, because his two identities have not yet intermingled. The process whereby humans reinterpret a religion so that it transforms into another religion takes time. This is evidenced by a dual saint: his sanctuary is still shared by two distinct holy figures whose religions are clearly identified; they are not associated through a logic of cohabitation (I follow here Roger Bastide's 1954 criteria on syncreticism).

Let us look at some examples of dual saints. In Anatolia and in the Balkans some of these figures are either Muslim or Christian, though interchangeably (only the syncretic saint is both). We might mention Hacı Bektâsh alias Saint Charalambos in Central Anatolia; Akyazılı alias S. Athanasius in Bulgaria (Eyice 1967:575–6; Hasluck 1973, vol. II:90–2); Khidr or Elias alias Saint George (Hasluck 1973, vol. II:319–36; Ocak 2007; Popovic 1996:100–2). In Morocco, dual saints are known under an Arabic and a Hebrew name: Daniel Hashomer Ashkenazi alias Sidi Denil and R. David Alshqar alias Moulay Ighi, both found at Casablanca (Ben-Ami 1990:154–8). Catholic and African dual saints are numerous in South America and in the Caribbean, as seen in the list of saints who have a double identity published by Bastide (1967): for example Notre-Dame du Rosaire alias Yemanjá in Brazil, Sainte Barba alias Yansan at Cuba, Mater Dolorosa alias Ezili at Haiti (Bastide 1967:163). In general, cults to these dual saints are juxtaposed and not intertwined. Although the sanctuary is shared it retains a precise boundary. The rituals are rarely mixed, and when they are, this is due to the similarity of the elements used in them. This emerges, for instance, in the offering of lights, luminaries, in Anatolia and in South America, or in the offerings of flowers or banners/flags in Central Asia and India etc. (see below). A final example from the island of Lampedusa, south of Sicily, is particularly intriguing. Here a cave welcomes an image of the Virgin and the tomb of a Turkish saint (called *marabout*). People who survived a shipwreck and came to the cave might find food in it which tallied with their faith and its interdictions (wine and pork for Christians and other meat for Muslims). According to the local legends, the cave was inhabited by a hermit who supposedly changed his faith in line with the religion of the visitors and hence was regarded as a man with double faith (*doppia fede*) (Kaiser 2015:106–7).

Likewise, the orally transmitted hagiographies of miracle-maker saints are easily transferable to the mausoleum of the saint who inherited the site. This is the case of Ja'far Tayran ('the flying Ja'far'), whose tomb is located near Khotan, in Xinjiang. Ja'far Tayran's hagiography is inspired by a tradition that goes back to the time when the shrine was Buddhist. According to the tradition, a Buddhist statue flew from India after the death of Buddha, and reached the place where it is now, at the Ja'far Tayran's tomb. Similarly, it is told that this Muslim saint flew from Mecca to China (Dutreuil de Rhins 1898:240). For the Muslims and Hindus who visited the sanctuary of Baba Qalandar Shāh in South India, at Mysore, and currently the shrine to Dattatreya and Anasiiyii, the site retains Hindu mythological significance (Bharati 1963:142). Likewise, the image of a saint riding a lion with a serpent as whip in his hand, is well known in Indian Sufism, and probably inspired by Tibetan Buddhism. It has been adopted by many hagiographies of Muslim saints across the whole of Central Asia, Iran and Anatolia. Because of its prestige, it was even welcomed by members of the Christian and Judaic faiths (Danik 2004; Digby 1994; Slyomovics 1993:84–5; van Bruinessen 1991). There are pictorial representations of this hagiographic motif at Muslim mausoleums, shrines and even on the tomb of the Jewish saint Rabbi Ephraïm al-Naqava at Tlemcen, Algeria (Slyomovics 2000:82–3, 88).

In South American myths about the deities, for instance, the myth of the African god Omulû, are intertwined with parables of the Gospel, one of which referred to the prodigal son (Bastide 1967:162). There are some examples in this volume of such processes of hagiographical transfer or mingling. This is the case in Egypt, with the adoption by the Muslims of pharaonic myths (Luizard), or amongst the Himalayan Pamirs, where a Buddhist legend of an hidden kingdom was Islamized (Zarcone).

Figure 4 Printed poster of the Jewish saint Rabbi Ephraïm al-Naqava at Tlemcen, Algeria, beginning of twentieth century (private collection, Paris).

The syncretic and 'supra-confessional' saint

The reinterpretation of one saint by a saint from another religion is epitomized by the 'syncretic saint' whose hagiographies, and in some cases devotions performed at their tombs, intermingle. In Anatolia and in the Balkans the model of the syncretic saint is from Sarı Saltuk alias Saint Nicholas or Ilyas alias Saint Spiridon (d. 1293). The saint is usually depicted as Saltuk the wizard (Saltık-ı sāhir) and was portrayed in the sixteenth century by the highest religious authority in the Ottoman Empire as a Christian monk performing intense asceticism (Anetshofer 2011; Ocak 2002:46, 71–6; Zarcone 1992:2–4). His hagiography is partly inspired by the Gospel. Many miracles performed by Jesus Christ are also attributed to Sarı Saltuk (Yüce 1987:139–40). Surprisingly, Sarı Saltuk's figure was revered in the early twentieth century by a Christian

Why do pilgrims share a sanctuary?

Figure 5   *Miniature of the Sufi Saʻīd Sarmad (right, d. 1659) with his disciple Dārā Shikūh (left), eighteen century (d. 1661) (Museum of Lucknow, India).*

who was initiated into the Bektashi Sufi order without apostatizing his own religion (Zarcone 2015). A sanctuary and a grotto dedicated to this saint in Albania (among many others in Turkey and the Balkans) are nowadays shared by Muslims and Christians.

Another example of a syncretic saint is Khānifnāth (called Shāh Ramjām Mahi Sanvar by Muslims). His mausoleum is located in the Ahmednagar district in India. Trained as a Hindu ascetic, Khānifnāth converted later to Islam. However, according to the hagiographic tradition, the saint was perceived as playing the flute while being accompanied by a cow, like the Hindu deity Krishna. The animal was killed by one of his spiritual masters, and by magic Khānifnāth brought the cow back to life (Burman 2002:37–9). Surprisingly, Khānifnāth was buried alive in 1360. After his death two persons, a Muslim and a Hindu respectively, each with specific attributions, were appointed by the local king to take care of his tomb. Although primarily their descendants carried out 'syncretic rites' at the shrine, they also competed over who controlled the place (Burman 2002:40–1). A second remarkable Indian syncretic saint is the Sufi Saʻīd Sarmad (d. 1659), whose mausoleum is at Delhi. Although he was born a Jew, Sarmad was considered by his contemporaries to be neither a Jew nor a Muslim, but a conniving atheist. In fact, Sarmad adapted to the faith of the people he lived among, and presented himself as a Hindu, adopting the custom of Hindu ascetics of walking naked (Katz 2000:144;

Tortel 1997:444–5, 455–6). He is known to most present-day Indians as a Muslim saint (Troll 1991).

Another intriguing holy figure in Central Asia is Dede Qorqut, who was both a Muslim saint and the patron saint of Islamized shamans (*baksy*). Qorqut, according to the tradition, was buried with his customary musical instrument (*qobuz*) in a mausoleum situated near the Sir Darya river. Undoubtedly, this saint was a shaman in the garb of a Muslim (Garrone 2000:175–81, 2013:42–3; Reichl 2001:72–3). Many of the pilgrims who visited his tomb sought his intercession as a Muslim saint in order to be cured by him. Other people, who had greater faith in shamanism, came to the tomb as they desired to tap the forces in the invisible realm, or to become shamans themselves.

To some extant a syncretic saint can appear as a 'supra-confessional' saint when he transcends any religious dispute. He considers that all religions are similar and that there is only one truth. This is the case of both Sarı Saltuk and Sa'īd Sarmad. A poem by the latter illustrates almost perfectly this disposition: 'I adapt to the Quran, I am a priest and a monk at the same time, and also a Jewish rabbi, an idolator and a Muslim.' (Tortel 1997:446). The best example, however, of a supra-confessional saint is the Indian Kabīr (d. 1518), who was regarded by Indian Muslims as a Sufi, and as a yogi by Hindus. Yet Kabīr criticized all the manifest practices of both Islam and Hinduism. After his death, the mausoleum built over his body was visited by both Hindus and Muslim, who later quarrelled and fought one another. Consequently, a second shrine was erected near the first one; ultimately the two religions erected their own independent sanctuaries (Kabir 1959:15–16, 26). Another of his poems nonetheless indicates that he stood above all the different religious confessions:

> Allah stays unseen in the body of every one,
> Try to understand this in your soul
> Allah is the same for the Hindu and for the Turk,
> This is what Kabīr claims.
> (Kabīr 1959:70)

There are many analogies between mausoleums occupied by a 'supra-confessional' saint and 'perennial pilgrimages' found in Europe in the twentieth century. (Two of them are studied in this volume: the pilgrimage to Monte Verità at Ascona and the Seven Sleepers pilgrimage in Brittany). Sacredness at Monte Verità does not favour one religion over another and suggests that 'truth' has many perspectives. But the neutrality of such sanctuaries does not signify shallowness; on the contrary, their pilgrims seem intent on rediscovering the pre-religious sacred, usually through expressing reverence to nature (Hobart in this volume). The Islamic-Christian pilgrimage of the Seven Sleepers in Brittany, when performed as an 'ecumenical pilgrimage' attracted Judaic, Christian and Muslim pilgrims; later, when the site was visited by perennials, atheist etc., it became essentially an 'empty locus', these new pilgrims being free to fill it with any feelings that may emerge (Pénicaud in this volume).

Ultimately, ambiguity does not stem from dual, syncretic or supra-confessional saints only, but also from another type of holy figure, as explained by J. Frembgen in this volume: a person who incarnates a third gender who is neither a man nor a woman, but is two in one, i.e. a transsexual, hermaphroditic, eunuch transvestite. Such saints are possible, as Frembgem demonstrates, thanks to the tolerance cultivated at some sanctuaries, like the Lāl Shahbāz Qalandar shrine in Pakistan.

Transposable rituals

Ambiguity also relates to components of the rituals that are performed at a shared sanctuary. Their special characteristics comes to the fore when rituals that belong to two distinct religions are performed side by side, or when elements foreign to the religion associated with a particular sanctuary are reused, as illustrated in Egypt (Luizard in this study). The analysis, by Charleux, in this volume, of the Taoist and Buddhist rituals performed at the Wutaishan complex can be compared to the rituals performed during the pilgrimage of Damballahwèdo in Haiti, where Catholicism and voodoo share certain rituals – for instance, the bath of purification in sacred waters inhabited by deities, and the sacred forest where the Virgin under the name of Notre-Dame of the Carmel is venerated and heals the sick (Métraux 1958:292–4).

Moreover, if a sanctuary is shared by two religions, the rituals of both religions may be juxtaposed. More intriguing is the presence of a common ritual in which the elements of former rituals are intermingled with later ones. In many cases, the hybridization of rituals is facilitated by the presence of specific ceremonials and gestures that appear to be universal, making them 'pre-religious'. This is the case of the ritual of encircling or circumambulating around a sacred place, a building or an artefact. Shamans, Buddhists, Muslims, African animists etc. perform this ritual during their procession. It is relevant here to keep in mind that a procession is frequently a circular movement (for example, the Arabic term for 'procession' in Egypt is *dawra*, circuit – Luizard in this volume); also the ritual of crawling through holes in the earth (Charleux in this volume). All these rituals qualify to be called universal or pre-religious rituals. They can easily be transferred from one religion to another or they can be shared by pilgrims of different faiths who visit a shrine.

Figure 6 A Chinese (Han) performing circumambulation at the Muslim Uyghur mausoleum of Arslankhan, Kashgar, Xinjiang (photograph: T. Zarcone, 2014).

In focusing on the ritual of circling or circumambulation it emerges that performing such a ritual is more than just showing respect to the sacred. It is said to either protect the holy place or the sacred object encircled, or destroy it. In Judaism, the paradigmatic model of the encircling points to the seven circles made by Josuah and the Hebrews around the city of Jericho intended to destroy its walls (Fenton 1996:163). However, in pre-Islamic Arabia, the devotional act of circling one artefact was interpreted as a 'rite of union with a deity' (Gaudefroy-Demombynes 1969:40). Besides, it is of interest to notice that, according to Turner, to 'encircle' in the context of African Ndembu ritual has the general meaning 'to sacralize'. Hence a hut after being encircled is considered a sacred site (Turner 1975:53, 80-1). To quote some other examples that demonstrate the universality of this ritual, shamans in Central Asia and Eastern Turkestan encircle a pole during one of their main rituals with the intent to heal (Zarcone 2013:184-5). Similarly, nowadays, if an Uyghur cook wants his earth oven to produce good bread and bring him money, he encircles it early in the morning before opening it (personal observation by T. Zarcone at Artush, Xinjiang, China, 2013). Other religions have welcomed circling rituals. They are found in Hinduism and Buddhism, where circumambulation (*pradaksina*) is invariably observed during the pilgrimage

Why do pilgrims share a sanctuary?

Figure 7 Drawing of Hāji Bektāsh, nineteenth century (private collection, Paris).

to the mausoleums (Bharati 1963:138). The circumambulation ritual (tawaf) performed by Muslims around the Ka'aba at Mecca is found at the tombs of saints everywhere in the Islamic world. Furthermore, we know that in ancient China the K'ouen-Louen, the sacred mountain which symbolized the centre of the universe, had a revolving stone room (or grotto) or a room around which pilgrims walked (Stein 1987:213, 220).

The processions manifest at a sanctuary are frequently interpreted as circular in movement. This is the case with 'processions circulaires' in Catholic Brittany (Passais district). The procession actually encircled a space or a territory – the movement from its beginning to its end constituting a circle (Bertin 1993:70–3). As mentioned by Charleux in this volume, the Tibetan term for pilgrimage is *nékor*, 'circuiting, going around a place', and it is *ergil mörgül* in Mongolian, 'circumambulating while praying/and bowing'.

Another widespread ritual is when a human crawls or creeps though a hole in the ground, sometimes referred to as 'pulling through', during the liminal phase of the ritual. Usually such a ritual is given for sick people or female pilgrims who want to find a husband or wish for a child. This is described at Wutaishan, in the chapter by Charleux. At this place, the ritual is performed by both Chinese and Tibetan pilgrims. This ritual exists also at Yarkand, in Xinjiang: Uyghurs pilgrims pass the hole of a stone seven times in order that their children shall not die (Jarring 1946–51, vol. IV:174–5). It was witnessed in Europe, but condemned by the Church (Wayland 1968:387). In Central Anatolia, pilgrims used to be 'pulled through' a hole in a cave that was situated near the sanctuary of the saint Hacı Bektash (Noyan 1964:64–5). Similar

Figure 8   Offering of candles at the shrine of Lourdes, France (photograph: T. Zarcone, 2014).

Figure 9   Offering of candles by a Tibetan monk at a Chinese Buddhist shrine, Guangdong (photograph: T. Zarcone, 2015).

Why do pilgrims share a sanctuary?

Figure 10   Chinese Muslim (Hui) pilgrims offering incense sticks at a shrine in Lingxia, Gansu, China (photograph: T. Zarcone, 2015).

Figure 11   Offering of candles at the Bektashi shrine of Merdivenköy, Istanbul (photograph: T. Zarcone, 2013).

Figure 11 Poster with instructions about a rebirth ritual performed when Mongol and Tibetan pilgrims enter a matrix-cave at the Fomudong monastery, Wutaishan, China (photograph: Isabelle Charleux).

rituals exist in Macedonia and are attended by Christians and Muslims alike; the stone is often compared to a mosque or a church (Popovska 2012:98–100).

The ritual of crawling through the holes of rocks is similar to an initiation ceremonial. The dynamic of the ritual brings about a transformation when the pilgrim is considered 'reborn' (Popovska 2014:68; Wayland 1968:401–2). Concomitantly, it is interesting that holes in the rocks or caves are comparable to the female reproductive organ and that the stones may be called 'vulvic' or 'phallic stones'. A similar ritual is carried out in Cambodia in a cave designated 'cave of birth': the pilgrims are convinced that they will die and then be resurrected (Bizot 1980:233–4). Such a ritual can be observed in a few sacred mountains in Japan, where some pilgrims and ascetics crawl through 'vagina-like tunnels' in order to be reborn (Schattschneider 2000). It is especially noteworthy that this ritual of death and re-birth is performed at the shared sanctuary of Khānifnāth/Shāh Ramjām in India (quoted above): the devotees of the saint descend into a shaft near the tomb of Khānifnāth and then start crawling laterally through the mountain underneath the tomb in order to reach a linga-like shrine where the saint is said to have practised yoga (Skyhawk 1999:195).

There are other rituals that welcome the sharing of a sacred site. This comes to the fore in rituals that are easily transposable from one sanctuary to another. The tradition of offering lights, candles, incenses and flowers to tombs is intended to please the dead saint or the deity. Offering of lights, lamps and candles during a pilgrimage seems to be a universal feature of rituals and hence cross-cuts borders. Light is a powerful symbol that frequently refers to a deity (Melikian-Chirvani 1987; Omidsalar 1990; Ray 1994:334–5). Additionally, incense is offered at Taoist temples in China – an act that was adopted later by Chinese Muslims at mausoleums of Sufi saints, and even at some Uyghur mausoleums visited by Hui pilgrims (personal observation by T. Zarcone at the Tuyuq mausoleum, Turfan district, Xinjiang, 2013). Offering flowers is performed at many sacred sites throughout the world. Flowers, for instance, are used in rituals that are originally Hindu in India. Later flowers were offered in significant rituals at Sufi tombs (Moini 1989:64–73).

Ambiguous architecture

It is worth pointing out that religious buildings erected at such sacred sites as a mausoleum or sanctuary may manifest ambiguity, i.e. the architecture reflects two influences. The best examples of such phenomenon are seen in India. Mention here can be made of the mausoleum of Malīk Ibrāhīm Bayyu, in Biharsharif, which is composed of the tomb of a Sufi saint covered with an Islamic cupola and a square platform of brick which is the basement of an Indian stupa (Burman 2001:1230; Servan-Schreiber 1997:153). Likewise, the mausoleum of the saint Gogā, a site shared by Hindus and Muslims alike, is depicted as a 'temple-tomb' (*samādhi-mandin*) 'in the shape of a mosque' (*masjid ka rūp*) (Bouillier 2004:258). Gogā is a dual saint, a 'composite figure', or 'paradoxical' according to Bouillier, who portrays him as a *pīr* (a Muslim saint) or as a *vīr* (hero for Hindus) (ibid.:260, 265).

It is also clear that meanings of symbols may intermingle – especially apparent of symbolic images and artefacts found at the same sanctuary, though they originate from distinct religions. We need but think of the presence of the Buddhist svastikā depicted in the architecture of the Muslim Sufi mausoleum (*dargāh*) in India (Bouillier 2004:256). This is also the case at Uyghur sanctuaries, for example, at the great complex of Afāq Khwāja at Kashgar (personal observation by T. Zarcone in 2008). In Iraq, at Lalish, a monumental portal of the mausoleum of Shaykh 'Adī, centre of Yazidism, is decorated with a peacock that symbolises Ahriman, the Zoroastrian principle of evil (Açıkyıldız 2009:313), in tune with a syncretic religion in which elements from Zoroastrianism, Sufism and Islam are intertwined,

In China, Charleux (in this volume) shows that Chinese and Buddhist monasteries have voluntarily adopted a syncretic architecture to adapt to the aims of the pilgrims. Syncretic architecture is well represented also in Chinese Islam, for instance, at the Ershilipu mausoleum (*gongbei*) and lodge (Ningxia, Gansu district) that are linked to the Jiucaiping branch of the Qādirī Sufi lineage. The architectural style of this site – that was supposedly once a Tibetan Buddhism monastery – is highly syncretic. The mausoleum is a hexagonal building, inspired by the Chinese Eight Diagrams' (*bagua*) doctrine. The site is nowadays occupied by two co-existing Han and Hui Chinese cults (oral communication by Eloisa Concetti). In addition, some specificities of the Chinese religious architecture have inspired both Chinese and Uyghur Islam. This is the case of the pagoda-shaped mausoleums and mosques, with particular reference to Gansu. It is also striking that the big incense pot used in Taoist devotions has been introduced in pilgrimage rituals at Sufi mausoleums in northern China, a feature that prevails also in Uyghur tombs in Xinjiang (personal observation by T. Zarcone at Kashgar in 2008 and at Turfan in 2013). It should also be noted that the traditional moon-gate (in the form of half moon) was integrated into the architecture of an Uyghur Muslim mausoleum (Sögäl Khojam Maziri – personal observation by T. Zarcone, Turfan 2008).

The pilgrimage site of Monte Verita in Ascona, which developed its own architecture and special structure, is replete with paradoxical imagery (Hobart, in this volume). This comes to the fore these days in the trekking path through the forest leading to Celtic stones, the Japanese Tea House and the serpent path to the Buddhist mandala in front of the main building. Can we give it the label of perennialist architecture? Similarly, in the newly created pilgrimage of the Seven Sleepers that Penicaud analyzes in this volume, it is worth noting that extraneous Muslim artefacts (banner, icon) are integrated with the former Catholic shrine, making it an Islamic-Christian site. Unfortunately, the attitudes of the locals to this ambiguous combination have become mainly one of curiosity and aloofness (see also Pénicaud 2014:136).

Shared, disputed and manipulated sacredness

Two chapters in this volume (Charleux and Albera) draw attention to the fact that shared sanctuaries may be places for competition and disputes between two or three religions, involving the curators of the site, the pilgrims and the local populations. Albera argues that the competition is strongest among the Abrahamic religions, which are all exclusive. This is less marked among Asiatic religions (for example, in Buddhism and Taoism). We know of many sites in Anatolia and the Balkans that Christians and Muslims shared peacefully in the nineteenth and early twentieth centuries and which were later fiercely disputed. A significant contemporary example is the tomb of Rachel in Israel, a site that Jews, Christians and Moslems formerly shared together in peace, but which later they disputed over. Now radical Jews with the help of the

Israeli State have seized the sanctuary by force, although it was placed under the control of the Palestinian Authority from 1993–5. Since 2007 the wall of separation encircles the sanctuary so that is only accessible from the Israeli side (Bowman 2015:73).

It is well known that ambiguity is not only the consequence of a natural or spontaneous process, it is also created by humans deliberately. Curators of shrine or tombs, too, are instrumental in manipulating what is conceived of as sacred, as well as the symbols and rituals connected with the sanctuary. Thereby curators ensure that the place is sufficiently ambiguous to serve their interests, i.e. to attract more pilgrims, or to persuade some of them who belong to another religion to change their beliefs.

Another reason to encourage ambiguity at a sacred site can be cultural, i.e. to adapt harmoniously to a foreign context. Zoroastrians, for example, may have imitated Muslim gestures, elements or names at their sanctuary in order to be more acceptable to the latter. Mention can here be made of the Zoroastrian temple named *pīr* after the Muslim Shi'i mausoleum; at the same time the Zoroastrian pilgrimage was called *ziārat* (an Arabic word that has the same meaning) (Vivier-Muresan 2007:458). Generally, many Sufis want to adapt to the context of a site, even if it is culturally impregnated by another faith. In India, at Vaishali in Bihar, the keepers of a Sufi sanctuary of the Shattariyya order took over an ancient site that had been linked to Buddhism, Jainism and Vishnuism with the intention to please Hindus and share several festivals with them. During one of these festivals effigies of serpents and a Hindu deity at the saint's tomb were venerated by both Muslims and Hindus (Servan-Schreiber 1997:149).

Economic factors may also determine the reasons for manipulating the sacred in order to create ambiguity, as demonstrated by Charleux in this study: the Taoist and Buddhist sanctuaries at Wutaishan compete to attract more pilgrims to visit them. This was also the case in the nineteenth and twentieth centuries at the Bektashi sites in Anatolia, which embraced Christian legends in order to welcome Christian pilgrims for financial gain (Albera in this volume).

By focusing on the notion of pre-religious sacredness, pilgrimage sanctuaries, and pre-religious saints we seek to isolate what might be interpreted as the core features of the 'sacred'. We initially linked the concept to topology (a mountain, cave etc.) and human behaviour (asceticism, divination or healing rites etc.) – all factors that contribute to the pristine identity of a site, making it essentially neutral. Yet pre-religious sacredness and pre-religious saints are rarely found in their pure form. Both usually comprise elements of diverse religions. Intriguingly, the more a sacred site is marked by signs indicative of its pre-religious sacredness, the more it will appear ambiguous, uncertain, unclear, obscure and difficult to pin down in the eyes of the representatives of the mainstream religions. This also applies to the attitude of a site's curator towards a pre-religious saint. The term 'paradoxical' is also used by several scholars mentioned in the introduction to characterize such sacred sites or the saint himself (Bouillier 2004:260; Lory 1985:177). This term is appropriate, as etymologically it refers to what is contrary to expectation (in the opinion of adherents of mainstream religions). Thus the sacredness perceived by some humans when encountering paradoxical sanctuaries does not accord to religious opinions that are commonly adhered to. This is also the case of sites that have been recently created, as, for example, in Monte Verita in Ascona – referred to as a pilgrimage 'site of paradox' (Hobart in this volume). Irrespective of whether a particular site is considered ambiguous or paradoxical, all the sanctuaries investigated in this book are syncretic or hybrid and all tend to respect more or less the norms of the religions to which they are linked. At the same time, these sanctuaries retain the quality of 'pre-religious sacredness', as defined here. This applies also to models of pre-religious figures. This book is a modest attempt to explore questions that confront humans who seek to expand their understanding of such multi-dimensional and ambiguous sanctuaries, pre-religious figures or saints, and of the sacred.

References

Açıkyıldız, B. 2009. 'The sanctuary of Shaykh 'Adî at Lalish: centre of pilgrimage of the Yazidis'. *Bulletin of the School of Oriental and African Studies* 72(2):301–33.

Albera, D. 2005. 'Pèlerinages mixtes et sanctuaires 'ambigus' en Méditerranée'. In S. Chiffoleau and A. Madœuf, (eds) *Les Pèlerinages au Maghreb et au Moyen-Orient: Espaces publics, espaces du public,* pp. 347–78. Beyrouth: Institut Français du Proche-Orient.

Anetshofer, H. 2011. 'Legends of Sarı Saltık in the Seyahat nâme and the bektashi oral tradition'. In V. Tezcan, S. Tezcan, R. Dankoff (eds) *Evliya Çelebi: Studies and Essays Commemorating the 400th Anniversary of his Birth,* pp. 292–300. Ankara: Republic of Turkey Ministry of Culture and Tourism.

Bastide, R. 1954. 'Le principe de coupure et le comportement afro-brésilien'. *Anais de XXXV Congresso Internacional des Americanistas, vol. 1.* São Paulo : Anhembivol.

——— 1975. *Images du nordeste mystique en noir et blanc.* Clamecy: Pandora / Ses Sociétés.

——— 1967. *Les Amériques noires.* Paris: Payot.

Ben-Ami, I. 1990. *Culte des saints et pèlerinages judéo-musulmans au Maroc.* Paris: Maisonneuve et Larose.

Bertin, G. 1993. 'Les Processions circulaires du Passais'. *Galaxie anthropologique* 2–3 (July):70–3.
Bharati, A. 1963. 'Pilgrimage in the Indian tradition'. *History of Religions* 3(1):135–67.
Bizot, F. 1980. 'La Grotte de la naissance. Recherches sur le bouddhisme Kmer II'. *Bulletin de l'Ecole Française d'Extrême-Orient* 67:221–74.
Boomgaard, P. 1995. 'Sacred trees and haunted forests in Indonesia, particularly Java, nineteenth and twentieth centuries'. In O. Bruun and A. Kalland (ed.) *Asian Perceptions of Nature. A Critical Approach*, pp. 47–62. London: Curzon.
Bouillier, V. 2004. 'Samâdhi et dargâh: hindouisme et islam dans le Shekhavati'. In V. Bouillier and C. Servan-Schreiber (eds) *De l'Arabie à l'Himalaya. Chemins croisés en hommage à Marc Gaborieau*, pp. 251–71. Paris: Maisonneuve et Larose.
——— 2008. 'Grottes et tombes: les affiliations des nâth yogis avec le monde souterrain'. *Rivista di studi sudasiatici* 3:33–48.
Bowman, G. 2015. 'A l'ombre de Rachel'. In *Lieux saints partagés. International exibition hell at Marseille, MuCEM, April 29th – August 31th 2015*, pp. 70–3. Marseille: MuCEM - Actes Sud.
Burman, J.J.R. 2002. *Hindu-Muslim Syncretic Shrines and Communities*. New Delhi: Mittal.
Burman, R. 2001. 'Shivaji's myth and Maharashtra's syncretic traditions'. *Economic and Political Weekly* 14(April):1226–34.
Capranzano, V. 2004. *Imaginative Horizons: An Essay in Literary-Philosophical Anthropology*. Chicago: The University of Chicago Press.
Danık, E. 2004. 'Alevi ve bektaşi mitolojisinde aslana binenler, yılanı kamçı yapanlar ve duvar yürütenler' [Men riding lion with a serpent crop in the hand and men moving wall]. In İ. Engin and H. Engin (eds) *Alevilik*, pp. 101–19. Istanbul: Kitap Yayinevi.
Davut, R. 2001. *Uyghur Mazarliri* [Uyghur Mausoleums]. Ürümchi: Shinjang Khälq Näshriyati.
Dermenghem, E. 1954. *Le Culte des saints dans l'islam maghrébin*. Paris: Gallimard.
Digby, S. 1994. 'To ride a tiger or a wall ? Strategies of prestige in Indian Sufi legend'. In M.W. Callewaert and S. Rupert (eds) *According to Tradition. Hagiographical Writing in India*, pp. 99–129. Wiesbaden: Harrassowitz V.
Dutreuil de Rhins. 1898. *Mission scientifique dans la Haute-Asie, 1890–1895*, 3 vols. Paris: Ernest Leroux.
Eyice, S. 1967. 'Varna ile Balçık arasında Akyazılı Sultan Tekkesi' [The convent of Akyazılı Sultan between Varna and Balçık]. *Belleten* 124:551–600.
Fenton, P.B. 1996. 'Le Symbolisme du rite de la circumambulation dans le judaïsme et dans l'islam'. *Revue de l'histoire des religions* 213(2):161–89.
Garrone, P. 2000. *Chamanisme et Islam and Asie centrale*. Paris: Jean Maisonneuve.

——— 2013. 'Healing in Central Asia: syncretism and acculturation'. In T. Zarcone and A. Hobart (eds) *Shamanism and Islam. Sufism, Healing Rituals and Spirits in the Muslim World*, pp. 17–46. London: I.B. Tauris.

Gaudefroy-Demombynes, M. 1969 [1957]. *Mahomet*. Paris: Albin Michel.

Hamada, M. 2004. 'Le Pouvoir des lieux saints dans le Turkestan oriental'. *Annales, Histoire, Sciences sociales* 5–6:1019–40.

Hasluck, F.W. 1973 [1929]. *Christianity and Islam Under the Sultans* (ed. M.M. Hasluck), 2 vols. New York: Octagon Press.

Hayden, R.M. 2002. 'Antagonistic tolerance: comparative sharing of religious sites in South Asia and the Balkans'. *Current anthropology* 43(2):205–31.

Jarring, G. 1946–51. *Materials to the Knowledge of Eastern Turki. Tales, Poetry, Proverbs, Riddles, Ethnological and Historical Texts from the Southern Parts of Eastern Turkestan*, 4 vols. Lund: Lund Universitets Årsskrift.

Kabir 1959. *Au Cabaret de l'amour* (introd. and trans. C. Vaudeville). Paris: Gallimard.

Kaiser, W. 2015. 'La Madone et le marabout'. In *Lieux saints partagés. International exibition hell at Marseille, MuCEM, April 29th – August 31th 2015*, pp. 104–7. Marseille: MuCEM - Actes Sud.

Katz, N. 2000. 'The identity of a mystic: the case of Sa'id Sarmad, a Jewish-Yogi-Sufi courtier of the Mughals'. *Numen* 47:142–60.

Lammens, H. 1920. 'Le culte des bétyles et les processions religieuses chez les Arabes préislamiques'. *Bulletin de l'Institut Français d'Archéologie orientale* 17:30–101.

Lieux saints partagés. 2015. *Lieux saints partagés. International exibition hell at Marseille, MuCEM, April 29th – August 31th 2015*. Marseille: MuCEM - Actes Sud.

Lory, Bernard. 1985. *Le Sort de l'héritage ottoman en Bulgarie*. Istanbul: Isis.

Melikian-Chirvani, A.S. 1987. 'The lights of Sufi shrines'. *Islamic Art* 2:17–47.

Métraux, A. 1958. *Le Vaudou haïtien*. Paris: Gallimard.

Mock, J. 2011. 'Shrine traditions of Wakhan Afghanistan'. *Journal of Persianate Studies* 4(2):117–45.

Moini, S.L.H. 1989. 'Rituals and customary practices at the dargah of Ajmer'. In C.W. Troll (ed.) *Muslim Shrines in India*, pp. 60–75. Delhi: Oxford University Press.

Noyan, B. 1964. *Hacıbektaş'ta Pîrevi ve Diğer Ziyaret Yerleri* [The lodge of the master and other pilgrimage sites at Hacıbektaş]. İzmir: Ticaret Mat.

Ocak, A.Y. 2002. *Sarı Saltık. Popüler İslam'ın Balkanlar'daki Destanî öncüsü* [Sarı Saltık, an epic narrative from popular Islam in the Balkans]. Ankara, Türk Tarih Kurumu.

——— 2007. *Hızır-İlyas Kültü* [The cult of Khidr-Elias]. Istanbul: Kabalcı.

Ogudin, V.L. 2003. 'Kul't pesher v narodnom islame' [The cult of cave in popular Islam]. *Etnograficheskoe obozrenie* 1:69–86.

Omidsalar, M. 1990. 'Candle'. *Encyclopaedia Iranica* IV(7):748–51.
Otto, R. 1923. *The Idea of the Holy*. Oxford: Oxford University Press.
Pénicaud, M. 2014. *Le Réveil des Sept Dormants. Un pèlerinage islamo-chrétien en Bretagne*. Paris: Cerf.
Popovic, A. 1996. 'Morts de saints et tombeaux miraculeux chez les derviches des Balkans'. In G. Veinstein (ed.) *Les Ottomans et la mort. Permanences et mutations*, pp. 97–115. Leiden: Brill.
Popovska, D. 2012. 'A Flow of ideas through symbolic images of the sacred stones in Macedonian folk traditions'. *Croatian Journal of Ethnology and Folklore Research* 49(1):95–110.
––– 2014. 'Macedonian sacred stones sites as pilgrimage and tourist attractions'. In M. Katić, T. Klarin and M. McDonald (eds) *Pilgrimage and Sacred Places in Southeast Europe. History, Religious Tourism and Contemporary Trends*, pp. 65–78. Wien: Lit Verlag.
Poptapov, L.P. 1946. 'Kul't gor na Altae' (The Cult of the mountain in Altaï). *Sovetskaja Etnografija*. 2:145-160.
Ray, R.A. 1994. *Buddhist Saints in India. A Study in Buddhist Values and Orientation*. New Yor : Oxford University Press.
Reichl, K. 2001. 'L'Epopée orale turque d'Asie centrale'. Dans *Etudes mongoles et sibériennes* 32:7–162.
Schattschneider, E. 2000. 'My mother's garden: transitional phenomena on a Japanese sacred mountain'. *Ethos* 28(2):147–73.
Servan-Schreiber, C. 1997. 'Partage de sites et partage de textes. Un modèle d'acculturation de l'islam au Bihar'. In J. Assayag and G. Tarabout (eds) *Altérité et Identité. Islam et Christianisme en Inde*, pp. 143–69. Paris: EHESS.
Skyhawk, H. van. 1999. 'A note on death and the holy man in South Asia'. In E. Schömbucher and C.P. Zoller (eds) *Ways of Dying: Death and its Meaning in South Asia*, pp. 190–202. New Delhi: Manohar.
Slyomovics, S. 1993. 'The pilgrimage of Rabbi Ephraïm al-Naqava, Tlemcen, Algeria'. *Jewish Folklore and Ethnology Review* 15(2):84–8.
––– 2000. 'Geographies of Jewish Tlemcen'. *The Journal of North African Studies* 5(4):81–96.
Stein, A. 1921. *Serindia. Detailed Report of Explorations in Central Asia and Westernmost Asia*, 5 vols. Oxford: Clarendon Press.
Stein, R.A. 1987. *Le Monde en petit. Jardins en miniature et habitations dans la pensée religieuse d'Extrême-Orient*. Paris: Flammarion.
––– 1988. *Grottes-matrices et lieux saints de la Déesse en Asie orientale*. Paris: Ecole Française d'Extrême-Orient.
Tanyu, H. 1968. *Türklerde Taşla İlgili İnançlar* [Beliefs about stone among the Turks]. Ankara: Ankara Üniversite.

Tátar, M.M. 1996. 'Mythology as an areal problem in the Altai-Sayan area: the sacred holes and caves'. In J. Pentikäinen (ed.) *Shamanism and Northern Ecology*, pp. 267–77. Berlin: Mouton de Gruyter.

Tortel, C. 1997. 'Loi islamique et haine impériale. Sarmad Shahîd Kashânî, poète mystique et martyr (m. 1659)'. *Revue de l'histoire des religions* 214(4):431–66.

Troll, C.W. 1991. 'Abul Kalâm Âzâd's Sarmad the Marthyr'. In C. Shackle (ed.) *Urdu and Muslim South Asia. Studies in Honour of Ralph Russel*, pp. 113–28. Delhi: Oxford University Press.

Turner, V. 1975. *Revelation and Divination in Ndemdu Rituals*. Ithaca: Cornell University Press.

van Bruinessen, M. 1991. 'Hadji Bektash, Sultan Sahak, Shah Mina Sahib and Various Avatars of a Running Wall'. *Turcica* 21–3:55–70.

Vasil'tov, K.S. 2013. 'Svjashchennye gory i Svjashchennye kamni: predanija o musul'manskikh auliya' na Pamire i ikh rol' v sozdanii sakral'nykh prostranstv' [Sacred mountains and sacred stones: the stories of the saints in Pamir and their role in the sacralization of the space]. *Pax Islamica* 1(10):123–36.

Vivier-Muresan, A.-S. 2007. 'Sanctuaires et sainteté chez les zoroastriens d'Iran'. *Revue de l'histoire des religions* 224(4):435–60.

Wayland, D.H. 1968. 'Passing through: folk medical magic and symbolism'. *Proceedings of the American Philosophical Society* 112(6):379–402.

Yüce, K. 1987. *Saltûknâme: Tarihî, Dinî ve Efsanevî Unsurlar* [The Saltûknâme: historical, religious and legendary elements). Ankara: Kültür ve Turizm B. Y.

Zarcone, T. 1992. 'Nouvelles perspectives dans les recherches sur les Kızılbas-Alévis et les bektachis de la Dobroudja, de Deli Orman et de la Thrace orientale'. *Anatolia Moderna* 4:1–11.

——— 2005. 'Stone people, tree people and animal people in Turkic Asia and Eastern Europe'. *Diogenes* 207(52):35–46.

——— 2013. 'Shamanism in Turkey: bards, masters of the jinns, and healers'. In T. Zarcone and A. Hobart (eds) *Shamanism and Islam: Sufism, Healing Rituals and Spirits in the Muslim World*, pp. 169–201. London: Tauris.

——— 2015. 'Christians and Bektashis: cults and legends shared, double membership'. Presentation at the MuCEM Conference on 'Lieux saints en Méditerranée, entre partage et partition', Marseille, June 2015.

I

Ambiguous sacred places in the Mediterranean

CHAPTER 1

Towards a reappraisal of ambiguity
In the footsteps of Frederick W. Hasluck

DIONIGI ALBERA

The notion of ambiguity has been outstandingly propelled in religious studies by the work carried out by the English scholar Frederick William Hasluck at the beginning of the twentieth century, since the publication of his key article on 'Ambiguous sanctuaries and Bektashi propaganda' in the 1913/14 issue of the *Annual of the British School of Athens*. In the framework of a growing interest in multi-faith attendance at holy sites, a number of authors have recently resumed his notion of 'ambiguous sanctuaries' in order to portray situations in which pilgrims belonging to different religious groups are attracted by the same shrine (Albera 2005, 2008; Albera and Couroucli 2012; Bowman 2013; Duijzings 2001; Hayden 2002; Hayden et al. 2011; Hayden and Walker 2013). Here, I would like to take some further steps in the exploration of Hasluck's legacy with regard to the notion of 'ambiguity' in religious behaviour. Then I will try to point out some theoretical directions that can be built from a consideration of his seminal reflections.

I

The influential work of Frederick William Hasluck (1878–1920) on the interchange between Christianity and Islam occupied the last years of his short life. After his education in Cambridge, where he became Fellow of the King's College, Hasluck left for Greece, where he was affiliated to the British School of Archaeology in Athens. For several years he researched on numerous subjects, including archaeology of ancient Greece, medieval and modern history of Smyrna, Greek and Turkish folklore, accounts of travel to the Levant, and Genoese and Venetian numismatics and heraldry found in the Near East. In spring 1913, he sojourned in Konya with his wife, for their honeymoon, and according to the latter's account, this experience was pivotal, because Hasluck developed from this point a strong interest in the interplay between Christians and Muslims in the Turkish world. This became the almost exclusive subject of his subsequent work. He started extensive historical and ethnographic comparisons, focusing on the Ottoman Empire. This research was hampered by the outbreak of the First World War and then by a disease that Hasluck tried in vain to cure in Switzerland. Despite a declining health, he tenaciously continued to collect data, until his death in 1920, at the age of forty-two. On the theme that captivated his attention during the last period of his lifespan, he left a few published articles, some manuscripts and a large amount of notes. His wife Margaret revised and collected this material in a book, *Christianity and Islam under the Sultans*, published in 1929. If Hasluck's work has been rather neglected in the following period, it has been recently rediscovered and its influence has been considerably invigorated during the last decades.[1]

The main semantic context in which Hasluck employs the terms 'ambiguous' or 'ambiguity' is associated with his discussion of 'sanctuaries' whose religious affiliation is somewhat blurred. His seminal article that analyses 'ambiguous sanctuaries' in connection with Bektashi propaganda is the *locus classicus* of this discussion.[2] In his introduction, Hasluck proposes an often-quoted definition of such a phenomenon:

> The 'ambiguous' sanctuary, claimed and frequented by both religions, seems to represent a distinct stage of development – the period of equipoise, as it were – in the transition both from Christianity to Bektashism and, in the rare cases where political and other circumstances are favourable, from Bektashism to Christianity.
>
> (Hasluck 1913–14:94)

As a matter of fact, Hasluck analysis is far more complex that this definition suggests, and it is quite far from a mechanical view of the transference of holy

---

1 In the following, I will refer to the 2000 edition of *Christianity and Islam under the Sultans*. Biographical information is essentially derived from the 'Editor's note' that Margaret M. Hasluck wrote for this book (Hasluck 2000:11–3). For an evaluation of Hasluck's contribution see the important interdisciplinary work directed by David Shankland (2004–13).
2 This article has been published, in an abridged form, in *Christianity and Islam under the Sultans* (Hasluck 2000, vol. II: 454–77).

places from one religion to the other that one may infer from this quotation. As we will see, in numerous cases documented by Hasluck, it is a Bektashi *tekke* that is made 'ambiguous' by introducing Christian symbolic elements, in order to attire a Christian clientele. Hasluck pays attention to the multifaceted organization of the Bektashi, which include laymen along with professed dervishes who live in the convent (*tekke*) under the authority of a *baba*:

> The religious doctrines of the Bektashi are devised to cater for all intellects and temperaments: their system includes, like other mystic religions, a gradual initiation to secret knowledge by a number of grades: these form a series of steps between a crude and popular religion, in which saint-worship play an important part, to a very emancipated, and in some respects enlightened, philosophy.
>
> (Hasluck 1913–14: 95)

Bektashism incorporates several Christian elements and professes respect for non-Muslims, who may also have been admitted to the order without asking them to convert to Islam. According to Hasluck, from the beginning, the spread of Bektashism has repeatedly implied the usurpation of tribal shrines or of sanctuaries belonging to other Islamic mystic orders, through a diversified strategy going from the dissemination of legends and accounts of miracles for common people, to initiation into secret knowledge for more learned persons. The same procedure was applied to Christian churches and saints' tombs, as Hasluck shows by taking into account several examples spread over Anatolia and the Balkans.

According to his analysis, sanctuaries are made ambiguous between Christianity and Bektashism through three main mechanisms: conversion, intrusion and identification. The circulation of a series of legends may suggest that a saint belonging to one religion was in fact secretly converted to another religion; that the mausoleum also houses the tomb of a saint of a different religion; that the holy person is actually the transfiguration of a saint of the other religion. Even in these cases, the attitudes vary according to the culture and the religion of the persons who are involved:

> The educated Bektashi, to whom the ideas of pantheism and metempsychosis are familiar, find it easy and natural to identify the Christian saints with their own; for simpler souls, if indeed the efficacy of the miracles does not suffice them, fables like the 'disguise' of Sari Saltik in the robe of 'Svity Nikola' may be used to bridge the gap. Christians, having before them numerous examples of churches usurped by the Moslem conqueror, accept rather the assumption that the Baktashi sanctuary

occupies a site already consecrated by Christian tradition, though their act of worship is made in the actual tomb-chamber of the Moslem saint, and conforms to the custom of the Moslem sanctuary.

(Hasluck 1913–14:112)

As one can see, Hasluck's concrete analysis displays a complex picture. The examples he examines show that ambiguous sanctuaries do not result only, or principally, from usurpation of Christian sites. In several occasions, it is rather a Bektashi place that is made attractive for Christians by its occupiers. If Hasluck documents various examples in which Christian sanctuaries adopt fictitious Baktashi legends and are thus made accessible to Bektashi pilgrims, he also clearly shows that in other circumstances Bektashi sites embrace Christian legends in order to receive Christian pilgrims. The material interests of the personnel in charge of these holy sites are similar and, according to Hasluck, they play an important part in these processes:

The occupiers of the ambiguous sanctuary, be they Christian or Bektashi, find their *clientèle*, and consequently their revenues, increased, while the frequenters receive the less tangible but not less appreciated benefits of miraculous healing and intercession.

(Hasluck 1913–14:112)

Hasluck insists on the multifaceted nature of the interplay between religions. One of the main aims of his work was to reject simplistic theories based on assumptions centred on theories of survivals. For example, he firmly contests that the frequentation of a Muslim sanctuary by Christians may be seen as a proof that the sanctuary in question was originally Christian (2000:104, 108). His notion of 'ambiguous sanctuaries' puts an emphasis on multilayered processes that involved different actors and depended on the crucial involvement of religious specialists.

In his pages the notion of ambiguity is also associated to that of 'cults'. In these cases a saint figure is made the object of distinct identifications by different religious groups, becoming a Christian saint for some, a Muslim holy person for the others. Sometimes these 'ambiguous cults' are simply refraction of the devotions present at the 'ambiguous sanctuaries'. Yet in some circumstances Hasluck employs the term with a less specialized meaning. Thus some 'ambiguous cults' are not visibly the result of the propaganda by religious specialists, but seem created in a rather spontaneous way, without political and economic interests at stake, as in the case of 'ambiguous cults' linked to natural settings, like springs (2000:125).

Therefore it is possible to perceive another dimension of ambiguity, which remains implicit in Hasluck's work. This dimension makes reference to practices that cross religious borders in situations in which interfaith attendance is relatively independent from the stratagems of religious specialists, and is not significantly connected to the issue of the control of the shrine. This occurs when shared sites of worship are located in natural settings – on mountaintops or in the vicinity of trees or wells – which often escape the control of religious corporations. In other cases, mixed attendance is simply related to the power attributed to the sanctuary, as manifested by miracles and other extraordinary phenomena. What I am suggesting here is that it is possible to enlarge the scope of the notion of ambiguity to include these phenomena. Along with its stronger meaning (which denotes an ambiguous sanctuary experiencing an overlap of claims, symbolic elements and strategies of annexation of a clientele of worshippers), it is possible to speak of ambiguity with a weaker connotation.

Drawing on a huge literature, Hasluck described a widespread disposition for crossing religious borders in a quest for supernatural assistance. With a remarkable erudition, he gleaned hundreds of examples distributed over several centuries, especially in Anatolia and the Balkans, of interfaith frequentation of sacred sites, where people of different religions share the search for well-being and often practice the same rites. He strongly suggests that the relations between religious groups within the Ottoman Empire had symbiotic aspects. In this context, the frequentation of shrines of another religion appears as a common, almost banal phenomenon (Hasluck 2000:97) and 'practically any of the religions of Turkey may share the use of a sanctuary administered by another, if this sanctuary has a sufficient reputation for beneficent miracles, among which miracles of healing play a predominant part' (2000:100). For Hasluck, these forms of devotional mixing were particularly pronounced at the popular level, as the 'popular religious thought' and the ritual practice of Oriental Christendom have much in common with those of Islam. Thus 'in the case of saints the attraction of healing miracles goes far to overcome all scruples, and Greek no less than Turk admits the ideas that, if his own saints fail him, an alien may be invoked' (2000:105). Regular participation in the shrine of another religion did not generally imply a desire of annexation or a wish to convert. The clergy and certain mystical orders could take advantage of this indefinite interfaith attendance to support their strategies (2000:101), thus giving birth to forms of religious ambiguity in a stronger sense. Yet low intensity ambiguity is, so to say, the raw material, which allows all forms of religious interchange. This is the phenomenon that lies at the basis, which permeates more elaborate forms of religious interrelationship. And it is also the most difficult to explain.

To sum up, it seems possible to describe a continuum of cross-border situations that materialize in ambiguous *practices, cults* and *sanctuaries*. These situations are linked to slightly different, and complementary, definitions of the term 'ambiguous'. The practices accomplished in order to gain the help of 'foreign' saints, including through the use of the cultic infrastructures of another religion, may be seen as ambiguous because they lack clearness and definiteness in terms of religious membership of the worshippers. The cults that attribute a double identity to some holy figures are ambiguous because the latter have several possible meanings and interpretations. The frequentation of a sanctuary by people of distinct faiths makes it ambiguous, that is to say of uncertain nature, and this ambiguity becomes stronger when there is the explicit presence of a double cult (and in some rare cases of celebrants of both religions) that makes difficult to classify precisely the holy site from the point of view of its religious affiliation.

I think that it is important to expand the scrutiny of the notion of ambiguity in order to avoid too narrow interpretations of these phenomena. This is the case of the model of 'antagonist tolerance' recently developed by Robert Hayden and his collaborators (Hayden 2002; Hayden *et al.* 2011; Hayden and Walker 2013), which has been inspired by a quite abridged reading of Hasluck's work on ambiguous sanctuaries. This model posits the existence of monolithic religious groups, which are defined through a rather primordialist approach. Hayden suggests that sharing of a shrine among faithful of different religions is but a temporary manifestation, bound to be erased by the innate tendency of religious groups to compete and differentiate. The presence of the 'other' in its sanctuaries is only tolerated as long as a group is clearly dominant. Reconsidering ambiguity may help to undertake less mechanical interpretations. Moreover, this notion may possibly be useful as a more general analytical tool. This is at least the hypothesis that I will explore in the next parts of this chapter.

II

By collecting hundreds of examples of how religions have overlapped since the Middle Ages, Hasluck has clearly indicated that these interfaith explorations were important in the Mediterranean region. Both historical and contemporary sources showed that relations between religious groups in the Ottoman Empire tended to be symbiotic. Christians and Muslims were ready to address their requests to shrines administered by the other religion, provided that they had a reputation for being efficacious. Even if the focus of his work concerned the interplay between Christians and Muslims, Hasluck also documented several examples in which interreligious attendance of the same shrine concerned the Jews[3]. On the whole, the Mediterranean's religious landscape displayed an 'overcrowding' that resulted from the everlasting presence within the same space of different branches of the three monotheisms and their countless followers. In this context, ordinary religious practices deviated quite often from the canons of institutionalized religions, and this clearly contrasted with the strength of the religious clashes so present in the history of the Mediterranean region. In spite of the exclusivist tendencies typical of a monotheistic milieu, and of the fears of pollution deriving by the contact with the 'other', ordinary devotional practices often blurred religious distinctions, sometimes with the connivance of mystical orders and local clergy.

Hasluck's research was carried out in a period when the Ottoman Empire was approaching its end. The clash of bellicose nationalisms has since then changed the ethnic and religious profile of broad sectors of the eastern and southern Mediterranean. A process of homogenization has often put an end to centuries of coexistence. In spite of this generally hostile socio-political environment, interfaith porosity in devotional attitudes and practices has not disappeared, as has been documented by several recent studies (Albera and Couroucli 2012; Barkan and Barkey 2014; Bowman 2012; Depret and Dye 2012; Valtchinova 2010). The powerful drive to homogenize both territories and identities has not completely destroyed local specificities. Even now religious ambiguity is often socially acceptable, and there is room for interfaith convergences. If in some regions there appears to have been a decline in religious mixing as a result of the combined aggressiveness of nationalism and of a religious reformism with rigorist and scriptural overtones, in other cases religious pluralism is nowadays becoming more common, as, for example, in some post-socialist countries.

On the basis of this firm continuity, some very general questions lead to the heart of the issue of the ambiguity in religious practices, cults and sanctuaries. Why, over the centuries, did the faithful of a particular religion not hesitate to visit the holy place of another religion? How could they so easily overcome obstacles and barriers in the exclusivist context of the Mediterranean faiths? How can they continue to do so even today, as it has been shown by a number of studies that have pursued Hasluck's investigations? Indeed, when people frequent a holy place managed by specialists of another religion, they generally adapt to material foundations of devotion and symbolic infrastructures that are a priori unfamiliar. Would it not be easier, more 'natural', to limit oneself to familiar religious spaces, which certainly are not lacking, given the wealth of religious offers?

---

3   On this see also the work done by Voinot (1948) and Ben-Ami (1990).

Hasluck's arguments are of little help in answering these questions. For him, the impetus of interfaith attendance comes essentially from the superstition and the credulity of the masses, resulting mainly from their ignorance. Yet the notion of ambiguity may suggest a way to render intelligible these apparently bizarre comportments. The use of the concept should nevertheless be divested of its demeaning connotations in the common language, in which it is seen as synonymous with contradiction and as a symptom of a lack of consistency, clarity and truthfulness. The attribution of a character of ambiguity to religious actions or beliefs depends clearly on the perspective from which the statement is made. It supposes, in a more or less explicit way, an idea of what is clear, non-ambiguous.

Even scholarly use of the notion of ambiguity may be derivative of a Christian vision, which has been so often integrated and somewhat naturalized in the scientific language. Thus, when a shrine contains the symbols of a plurality of faiths, or a supernatural figure becomes the object of multiple identifications by the faithful, this is easily perceived as 'strange' and 'unnatural'. A double nature for a saint figure is seen as an index of 'confusion'. Moreover, a pious pilgrimage to the shrine of another religion may easily be perceived as an equivocal practice, because it is in contrast with the internal image of the religious group, promoted by the authorities, which tends to consider the religion as an uniform set of practices, beliefs and norms, where the same spiritual 'essence' is evenly distributed, and stems almost naturally from a series of premises that are contained in the founding episodes and texts. What stays outside is the realm of deviance and rebellion, arising from malice, ignorance or the weakness of human beings.

In order to attain a more balanced apprehension of places, behaviours and beliefs labelled as 'ambiguous', we should not limit ourselves to a vision of 'ambiguity' conceived in a 'negative' way as a deficiency (of clarity, intelligibility, and coherence) and as the reversal of what is univocal, well defined and distinct. What disappears in this perspective is, so to say, the positive aspect of 'ambiguity'. Therefore it may be useful to draw a distinction between the emic perspective, internal to any social or religious group, and the etic perspective of the social analyst. An etic account should adopt a 'positive' conception of 'ambiguity', by privileging its objective meaning, that to say a property of things or beings that admit more than one interpretation or explanation. Moreover the meaning of this expression may also refer to the field of practice. From this point of view, the etymology suggests some interesting inferences. Ambiguity derives from the Latin *amb* and *agere*, namely 'to move, to drive, to push on both or many sides'. It denotes at the origin an action that takes several directions, exploring different possibilities without stopping at a single dimension. If we put this in a religious setting, the etymological background can help to understand the processes by which some of the faithful abandon the linear clarity of the path traced by their religious affiliation and take the back roads of ambiguous sanctuaries and cults.

More generally, the notion of 'ambiguity' may prove useful, provided that we reverse the perspective. In other words, I suggest that we should regard 'ambiguity' as an element situated at the foundation, and not at the margins, of religious attitudes. Instead of considering ambiguity as a synonym of defective order and coherence, it would be possible to conceive it as evidence for another logic, which is animated by a wealth of meanings and interpretations, and by the tendency 'to push on many sides' the quest for supernatural benefit. Such sensibleness, based on a semantic of overabundance, has been undergoing a process of reduction due to the action of a different order that superimposes its principles. Thus, if at the end the profusion of symbols, beliefs and practices is perceived as synonymous of wandering, inaccuracy, obscurity, and hesitation, this is only because an external law imposes by now its stricter requirements. But to advance on this line of inquiry demands that we broaden the perspective, venturing in a detour in the *'longue durée'*.

III

In its objective meaning, ambiguity is an essential property of language (whether from a lexical, syntactic or semantic point of view). It animates many rhetorical figures and feeds artistic expression. More generally, as recalled by Simone De Beauvoir (1976), ambiguity is inherent to human existence, which is suspended between mind and matter, interiority and exteriority, instant and eternity.

Since ancient Greece, philosophy has tried to counter ambiguity, or at least to delimit its range of action, in the field of logic as well as in that of ethics. The search for precise definitions of entities like beauty, goodness or virtue in Plato's dialogues is symptomatic of this development. In its quest for absolute truth, philosophical research detaches itself from the *doxa*, that is to say, from opinion, which is fatally ambiguous and likely to be true as well as false. The philosophical operation may be seen as the passage from the indefinite opinion ('they say', 'it is said'), to definite statements formulated by a subject that isolates and coordinates his assertions ('I say', 'you say') (de Certeau 1983:257).

The rise of Greek philosophy is part of the breakthrough that the philosopher Karl Jaspers has identified with the term 'Axial Age'. It is a period from roughly 800 to 200 BC during which there were major changes in different Euro-Asian cultural systems.[4] These changes imply an increased reflexivity; an amplification of the consciousness that human existence is located in time and space; the development of the intuition of the malleability of individual experience and of the potential of human action; the creation of a more elaborate cosmology, which often involves the recognition of a transcendent order, detached from the worldly order; a radical questioning of schemes regulating the social order; and the condensation in the texts of these new visions, with the development of a set of principles for the codification and the interpretation of these writings. This movement is accompanied by a broadening of horizons, with the opening of potentially universal perspectives, the establishment of an ontological distinction between upper and lower levels of reality, and the attempt to translate the principles of higher order in human behaviour. The protagonists of this revolution were influential minorities (often mentioned among the paradigmatic cases are the prophets of ancient Judaism, the Greek philosophers, Hindu Brahmins, Buddhist monks, Chinese literati). These new figures of religious and cultural specialists had a strong impact on their civilizations. The Axial Age produced a crystallization of intellectual resources that were crucial for successive revivals, with periodic returns to the source. This permitted the development of both power structures and contestations of these structures, originating from the same cognitive, ethical and spiritual basis. Universal religions are derived, directly or indirectly, and sometimes centuries away, from this crucial turning point, drawing on cultural reservoirs formed during the Axial Age.

This transformation may be conceived as a process of differentiation. In Eric Voegelin's terms, this means a conceptual transition from 'compactness' to 'differentiatedness'. As it has been put by Ian Assmann, 'conceptual compactness results not so much from an inability to differentiate [...] but from a will to connect and to integrate, to establish alliances, equations, and identities' (2012:372). The movement initiated with the Axial Age involves instead the establishment of distinctions through a radical questioning of tradition and a critical examination of accepted ideas and customs. This antagonistic second-order thinking affirms its legitimacy against what already exists.

The ethical and cognitive rationalization that accompanies the development of world religions had major implications on religious behaviour. The dynamic is parallel to that which marks the detachment of philosophical knowledge from the indefinite realm of the 'opinion' (*doxa*). Like the latter, believing can also be seen as indefinite. On these aspects, Michel de Certeau's

---

4   For recent overviews on this topic, see Arnason, Eisenstadt and Wittrock 2005; Bellah and Joas 2012.

reflections (1981, 1983) offer challenging pathways. In his perspective, believing means to 'give credit' to a recipient. It is an act that poses both a different partner and a deferred repayment; it creates a reference to the other and to the future. Believing produces a relational commitment, whereby something is given to someone 'other', pending a reward from him. This requires that the latter recognize his obligation and be able to do what is asked. Therefore, the deployment of belief is padded with uncertainties. Without ever being assured of his bet, the believer is brought to multiply the transactions with the supra-mundane partners who could meet his demands. Consequently, according to de Certeau, mobility is a dominant feature of the act of believing. In the search of a respondent, the believer tends to compensate for his uncertainty by an endless reference to a multiplicity of supernatural 'others'. Moreover, in the absence of any certainty, the believer is brought to rely on the fact that other people believe in the action of some supra-mundane guarantors. Even from this point of view, the process of believing proceeds from an indefinite plurality, very much like 'opinion' does. This is the domain designated by expressions like 'it is believed', 'they believe'. Hence emerges a general, neutral authorization of the belief. De Certeau defines this dimension as that of 'plausibility', whose subject remains undetermined.

The neutral and anonymous sphere of believing pointed out by de Certeau overlaps with the etymological meaning of 'ambiguity' that I have underlined before. It corresponds to 'moving on both or many sides', through a multiplication of respondents who could meet the demands of the faithful. The process of ethical and cognitive rationalization associated to the growth of universal religions has resulted in a trend towards the disenchantment of the world, to use Max Weber's formula. This movement could also be described as a 'disambiguation', which replaces the indeterminate and versatile realm of what is credible by limiting the number of the supernatural interlocutors, by identifying distinct beliefs and ritual actions, and by ensuring their coherence.

De Certeau is describing this process when he points to the action of the institution, which isolates specific contents (like 'the Church decrees') in the global sphere of what is credible. The institution selects and refines the assertions, gives them the form of a doctrine, and organizes them into allowed practice, which is put under its control. A new domain (labelled by the statement: 'we believe') replace the anonymous sphere designated by the expression 'it is believed'. The institution defines the sphere of a new plausibility, by introducing determinations, by producing order and by setting the conditions for operability. Even if de Certeau does not take in account this aspect, it could be added that the religiosity of virtuosi (to use a well-known Weberian category) tends in its turn to escape to the indefinite, general plausibility of believing. Virtuosi are more concentrated on soteriology, search for transcendence and requirement of coherence, and focus mainly on the consequences of the beliefs in terms of individual behaviour and spiritual tension.[5]

IV

There are substantial differences between world religions from the point of view of the implementation of this second-order religious perspective in the concrete life of people. In Eastern Asia, for instance, religious elites and virtuosi pursued certainly strong personal goals of spiritual elevation and ethical development, but they quite easily made substantial accommodations with other forms of religiosity, more interested in material requests and the effectiveness of the rites. They also show little interest in building barriers among religious traditions (Sharot 2001). This situation emerges clearly in the Chinese Empire, in which for a long time there has been a conglomerate of religious traditions. Buddhism and Taoism had priesthood, a liturgy, a canon and training centres, but religious membership was restricted to the clergy and a very limited circle of laity. Correspondingly, Confucianism was limited to a narrow environment of literati. The vast majority of Chinese people had no religious affiliation, and they could not be defined as Confucians, Buddhists or Taoists. They were organized in worship communities of very disparate nature, had recourse to the services of different clergies according to circumstances and phases of the lifespan, and drew from the symbols and texts of the three religious traditions (Goossaert 2004:12). The Chinese landscape was punctuated by an impressive number of temples, which in their vast majority did not have an exclusive religious identity (Goossaert 2000). The shrines were rarely confined to one religious group and there was also considerable heterogeneity among pilgrims (Naquin and Yü 1992:8–9). Pluralistic and composite pilgrimage sites were a reflection of a Chinese preference for the merger, rather than the distinction of religious identities, expressed also in the ideal of the 'three religions being one' (*san-ho-chiao i*) (Naquin and Yü 1992:10). Likewise, since the introduction of Buddhism in the sixth century, and until the second half of the nineteenth century, in Japan there was a close link between Shinto and Buddhist practices, sites and beliefs. For centuries, the faithful went to the same shrines to worship both *kami* and *bodhisattvas*. These pilgrimages were marked by a confessional fuziness,

---

5   Max Weber stressed that religious competencies of human beings are unevenly distributed (as are musical aptitudes). From this point of view, the intensive religiosity of virtuosi stays in opposition with the religiosity of the masses (that to say people who are religiously unmusical) and often with the hierocratic powers.

making it difficult to attribute them to either tradition (Thal 2005). It was only after the Meiji Restoration (1868), in fact, that the two religions were officially separated – or rather, that they were identified as separate religions (Grapard 1984; Sekimori 2005).

Developments have been very different in the monotheisms. Like other Axial Age's movements, at their origin there is a demarcation from existing religious ideas and practices, which are seen as empty, formalistic and lacking ethical tension and spiritual value. The antagonism is here particularly strong, and qualifiers such as 'superstition' and 'idolatry' are typical of this derogatory attitude. Monotheisms are indeed based on a tough dichotomy between truth and falsehood. It is what Ian Assmann (2010) has described as 'Mosaic distinction'. The 'true' religion is opposed to false religions that preceded it and surround it. Exclusivism and controversy dominate, far removed from the mutual translatability of beliefs and gods that was present in the Mediterranean religions during Antiquity, and also from the religious interweaving in East Asian societies. This irreconcilable antagonism between a real God (our God) and all the others (which are only false gods or demons in disguise) characterizes monotheism, much more than the mere assertion of the existence of a single deity. As a matter of fact, polytheisms can serenely accept the principle of the existence of a supreme deity, which copes quite well with the existence of a variety of minor deities.

If a certain amount of competition between religious enterprises may be present everywhere (it is, so to speak, physiological, in order to consolidate a position in the 'market' of supernatural goods), for the monotheisms the antagonism is constitutive. Either one belongs to the true religion, or one is in a dangerous superstition. The competition is not only external but also (and above all) internal. A constant effort is devoted to fighting against release and compromise. Vacillations and adulterations are even more reprehensible than the simple mistake of enrolling in the 'wrong' religious system. One sees the triumph of what Sigmund Freud called the narcissism of minor differences: between the three monotheistic religions, between denominations, between 'orthodoxy' and 'heterodoxy'. The history of monotheisms is dotted with episodes where the champions of monotheistic intransigence become the protagonists of a struggle for the return to the purity of the sources, for the affirmation of the 'true' faith, for the triumph of orthodoxy and orthopraxis against any 'deviation'.

Monotheisms are marked by a strong effort to inculcate the principles of second-order thinking (that form the theological nucleus of the faith) in the community. Indoctrination is linked to a consistent interest in building barriers with other religious traditions and to instil a generalized respect of ritual obligations and prohibitions. Monotheistic religions inaugurated a particular vision of religious affiliation, based on the constitution of bonded faith communities. People adhere to a religion, granting belief to the revelation that is at its origin, subscribing to its basic principles, respecting its laws and accomplishing a series of mandatory rites. One becomes a 'faithful' – a 'Christian', a 'Jew' or a 'Muslim' – in a way that is completely extraneous to the ancient religions' experience or, until recent developments, that of East Asian religions.[6] The same principle is true for holy places, which in a monotheistic context are expected to 'belong' to only one religion (or denomination).

The catechizing of the masses had important consequences in terms of ritual behaviour. Monotheisms are inhabited by a tension between ritual observance on one side, and ethical rationalization and spiritualization on the other. This tension often took the form of reaction and reform movements that, to ensure the pure divine transcendence and to enforce ethical behaviour, condemned the materiality and formalism of the rites, their exteriority in relation to moral imperatives, as well as harmful consequences in terms of idolatry and magical aberrations. As a consequence, many doctrinal debates arose, with their share of mutual condemnations, schisms and strong antagonism. However, even the most anti-ritualistic currents cannot do without rites if they want to structure and to stabilize themselves over time. Driven out by the door, rites often came back in through the window.

Another outcome of the constitutive tension around ritual was the development of a set of crucial rites with a low intensity from the point of view of supernatural efficacy. Several fundamental rites of monotheistic faiths (such as liturgical prayer or fasting), which became canonical and compulsory for all the faithful, put a damper on the compelling force of ritual – its autonomous capacity to communicate with the supernatural and to influence or constrain it – and instead emphasize an ethical and symbolic dimension. In many cases one is witnessing a disarticulation of the three basic elements – speech, gesture and object – whose conjunction in a particular space-time, associated to procedures of fragmentation and repetition of acts and phrases, confers operational power to the ritual. Both opposition to, and reform of, ritual implied a process of disenchantment of the world and of disambiguation of human practices and beliefs. Moreover, the same aim of clarity and transparency also produced another form of disambiguation,

---

6 One should add that this aspect is less univocal in Judaism, which has also kept a fidelity to an ethnic principle of religious affiliation. On the other hand, Christianity and Islam are not entirely alien, at least on a symbolic level, to an ethnic principle, and tend in their turn to create 'peoples' that are united by their faith.

through the written fixation of the script of the rites that should be repeated in a uniform and immutable manner.

By borrowing some conceptual tools of Jacques Lacan and Claude Levi-Strauss, I have suggested elsewhere (Albera 2013) that monotheisms experiment with an internal opposition between a ritual syntax based on metonymy and another based on metaphor. The former tries to establish, by a principle of successive adjacencies, a relationship with an immanent presence of the supernatural. The second puts the accent on symbolism and similarity, and keeps a separation from the divine, thus ensuring the latter's transcendence. Rituals tend to become, so to speak, symbolic acts that are conscious of themselves, and of their limits. They do not claim a performativity, nor do they pretend to act directly on the supernatural. Often they materialize the memory of a founding event. The tendency towards ethical rationalization and the disenchantment of the world, which is inscribed in the theological core of monotheistic religions, has propelled the metaphorical syntax to the centre of the stage, manifesting a strong opposition to the rituals of the religions of Antiquity, which emphasized the metonymical aspect. This new syntax is a direct emanation of second-order religiosity, with its emphasis on transcendence, its criticism of mundane order and empty ritualism, and its exigencies of inner spirituality.

Naturally the substitution of metonymy has never been complete. Moreover, from this point of view there exist differences between religions and, within these, between denominations. There is no doubt that Christianity was the more inclined to recognize the intrinsic efficiency of rites. The sacraments, for example, combine the proclamation of divine transcendence with performative gestures, which discreetly externalize the relationship with the supernatural, by objectifying it in speech, gestures and sacralized objects. But this tendency, which was often seen as idolatrous and magical deviation by Jewish and Muslim polemicists, regularly provoked resistance and internal opposition within Christianity. The substitution of the Catholic Eucharistic sacrifice by the Protestant Lord's Supper expresses well the transition from metonymy to metaphor, which is also evident in the institution of Abrahamic sacrifice in Islam. Similarly, the ritualism that punctuates the daily life of pious Jews is not intended to perform effective actions aimed at directly influencing the supernatural dimension. Rather, it follows a legal requirement and is animated by a metaphorical vocation. In fulfilling the commandments, the practitioner scrutinizes the symbolic meaning of the ritual gestures through a hermeneutic work extensively elucidated by rabbinic teaching.

The implementation of a metaphorical syntax has always been an incomplete success, and several rituals have kept a metonymic content. In other words, all monotheistic religions (and not only Catholicism or Orthodoxy) have made significant concessions to the materialization of the sacred. A supernatural immanent action is clearly manifested in sacred landscapes, miraculous hierophanies, objects and images with prodigious properties, and performative gestures. While generally promoting a more austere piety, religious authorities accommodated these manifestations. In its constantly renewed battle for the disenchantment of the world, the ethical-religious rationalization promoted by radical groups has been constantly striving to reduce this space, with varying results, according to regions and periods. But generally this metonymic orientation has maintained a considerable strength, mainly among lay people, the illiterate masses that for centuries constituted the overwhelming majority of believers. This subaltern world, while accepting the precepts conveyed by religious specialists, conceived religious activity in relation to concrete needs of life. Yet the processes of ethical rationalization, disenchantment and disambiguation of the world created a divide that does not only run on sociological lines. It could be said that the contradiction is present, one way or another, in every soul, thus creating intimate room for another dimension of ambiguity.

The theological stance of monotheistic religions shows a specialization of belief. It proposes a unique guarantor/respondent (God), and an extreme horizon of expectation (the final reward after death). This tendency had to compete, in different contexts and times, with the compactness and the metonymic syntax that stress the immanence of the divine, and more generally with the rebel ocean of a 'belief' that is diffuse and unorganized, being based on a multiplicity of interlocutors and a combination of gifts and debts, an interlacing of operations linked to particular aims and dispersed in time and in space. Such a colourful set contrasts with the monochrome world that the champions of rigorist monotheism have tried to create on the earth. It has been designated by various epithets, all inevitably inadequate and all more or less biased, like superstition or popular religion. The cult of the saints, which has flourished in the three monotheisms despite sweeping assertions about the uniqueness God, also reports to this form of believing, which is diffuse, mobile and looking for partial and concrete responses. Sharply opposed by the purists, it has only been contained by institutional religion, which has often viewed its manifestations with suspicion.

Transgressions of religious borders that occur in shared holy sites only amplify a trend that is internal to each religious group. The act of 'believing' reflects the ambiguous richness and complexity of human life. It implies a wandering quest that multiplies the possible referents in the transactions with the supernatural. Therefore it transcends rather easily the borders drawn by the institutions, obeying the call of a 'credible' domain of belief that is diffuse, indeterminate and neutral. 'It is believed', 'others believe': this is a sufficient

Towards a reappraisal of ambiguity 45

legitimacy for ambiguous practices that 'push on both or many sides' the quest for soteriological and thaumaturgical goals, with the aim of profiting from the spiritual offer linked to holy places that, according to the semantics of monotheisms, 'belong' to another religion.

V

Following Hasluck's footsteps, it has been possible to identify a large domain in which religious behaviours are not constrained by the borders separating monotheistic religions, and which may thus be described, one way or another, as ambiguous. I have tried to take this notion away from a narrow 'emic' perspective, which depends too heavily on historical and ideological context, and to promote a more objective 'etic' viewpoint, in order to take a few steps towards a comparative perspective.[7]

Hasluck's work on the interplay between Christianity and Islam profited from his vast competences in classical culture and history, which provided him with an important comparative background. Thus, when studying the transfer of cults in the Ottoman world, he was establishing parallels with Antiquity. He was planning a companion volume, with this perspective, on the transferences from paganism to Christianity in the West, which his untimely death prevented him from writing. Furthermore, he considered that the methods and processes of transfer of the cults that he had identified for Bektashism and Christianity were analogous to those operating in the pagan context. He even suggested that the study of these more recent phenomena could help elucidate the mechanisms generating the stratification of cults in the sanctuaries of the ancient world, on which researchers are limited to conjectures. Should we conclude that these ancient sanctuaries were 'ambiguous' too?

We could say 'yes' from an 'etic' standpoint, but not certainly on the 'emic' side. In Latin 'ambiguous' could be used to indicate beings that, like the centaurs, had a double nature. For instance in a passage from Ovid's *Amores*, these are designated as *ambiguos uiros* (*Am.* I:4, 8).[8] There is as an analogy with the use of this designation by Hasluck for the sanctuaries or cults that appear to have a dual character. This understanding, however, depends

---

7   No doubt, my exploration is far from being complete. There are other dimensions to the discussion of ambiguity that I have not pursued in this chapter. I would at least mention, among the more relevant, the issue of the tolerance of ambiguity in the exegesis of sacred texts, which has recently been examined by Thomas Bauer (2011) in relation to the Islam.
8   It is impossible to pursue here a more developed discussion of the use of this term in Antiquity. A rich synthesis on this is offered by Moussy and Orlandini (2007).

strongly on the parameters by which what is the 'normal' state of the thing or being is judged. In Classical Antiquity the multiplicity of cultic references would not appear linked to a double nature (and therefore ambiguous), but rather as the manifestation of the multifaceted sacredness of a sanctuary. In a similar way, the multiple identifications of the same divine figure would appear as richness and not as ambiguity. It is the criterion of uniqueness, typical of the monolithic conception of monotheistic religions, which leads internal observers to consider that plural cults and shrines are 'ambiguous'.

In spite of these distinctions, there is no doubt that there exist significant similarities between the processes identified by Hasluck and those that generated a superposition of cults in Antiquity. As he suggested, there is an analogy between the mechanism of the *intrusion* of a saint in the Ottoman context and the 'reception' of a new god by the old in the ancient world. Furthermore, *identification* operates along the same lines in the two contexts. On the contrary the third mechanism identified by Hasluck, that of *conversion*, is deeply embedded in the semantics of the monotheisms, with their idea of 'belonging' to a faith, and would have been inconceivable in a pagan milieu.

This clearly shows that we are not in presence of a survival, a phenomenon that moreover Hasluck would have strongly denied. Rather, we are confronted with the acclimatization in a monotheistic milieu of symbolic processes animated by a will to connect and to establish associations and equivalences. It is a form of religiosity that certainly found a coherent systematization in the religions of Antiquity, notably thanks to the principle of 'translatability' of gods, but is not specific to this setting. It is present in other areas of the world, and has not been obliterated by the growth of universal religions. In Eastern Asia the multidirectional quest for supramondane assistance is directed to specialists of different faiths, and the blurring of saint figures' and shrines' religious identities has long been an ordinary phenomenon, perfectly accepted by the hierarchies of official religions. On the contrary, the monotheistic context has been particularly unfavourable to its expressions, though even in this case there have been substantial accommodations and margins for manoeuvre. Along with that of ambiguity, a number of notions (like compactness, metonymic ritual syntax, indeterminate believing) that I have discussed in this chapter could help capture the frothy sea of such a religious experience.

The notion of ambiguity is tributary of the monotheistic experience and, more particularly, of that of Christianity. The parameters that permit the perception of ambiguity in certain practices, ideas, beliefs or shrines are embedded within this particular history, and are marked by a strong effort to install a univocal order in religious behaviours and conceptions. This transfer of concepts from a particular emic conception to the scholarly discourse is far from exceptional. Many crucial notions in religious studies (starting from the very notion of 'religion') derive from Christian history. The only, partial, escape from this antinomy may reside in a reflexive effort devoted to build a more neutral etic perspective. The preliminary attempt I have made in this chapter suggests that it may be analytically fruitful to reassess the notion of ambiguity by considering it not as synonymous of lack, but in a positive way, as abundance and mobility of references. In other words, once it is deprived of some derogatory meanings that are present in a European emic perspective, ambiguity seems able to express a tendency that is at the basis of the act of believing.

A number of features that I have designated under the umbrella of ambiguity are often referred to by resorting to the notion of syncretism. The latter has been ruminated by a huge amount of scholarly works, which without any doubt have offered important intellectual stimuli, but have also resulted in convoluted and contrasting arguments. The notion of ambiguity puts the accent on the mechanisms that generate multifarious and apparently contradictory practices and beliefs, more than on the production of a discernable synthesis. An often-identified problem related to the use of the notion of syncretism (as well as that of some of its companion words, like hybridity and *métissage*) is that it risks being conceived of as the result of a merging of traditions that before were autonomous. No doubt, real processes are more complex and stratified. The notions of ambiguity and disambiguation may help to reverse the perspective and to focus the attention on developments that go in the opposite direction, that to say from an entrenched plurality towards clarification, normalization and distinction.

References

Albera, D. 2005. 'Pèlerinages mixtes et sanctuaires 'ambigus' en Méditerranée'.
    In S. Chiffoleau et A. Madoeuf (eds). *Les Pèlerinages au Moyen-Orient: espaces public, espaces du public*, 347–68. Beyrouth: Institut Français du Proche-Orient.
——— 2008. "Why are you mixing what cannot be mixed?' Shared devotions in the monotheisms'. *History and Anthropology* 19(1):37–59.
——— 2013. "Jacob offrit un sacrifice à la montagne' (Genèse, 31): rites et rituels'.
    In D. Albera and K. Berthelot (eds). *Dieu, une enquête. Judaïsme, christianisme, islam: ce qui les distingue, ce qui les rapproche*, 457–554. Paris: Flammarion.
Albera, D. and Couroucli, M. (eds) (2012). *Sharing Sacred Spaces in the Mediterranean. Christians, Muslims, and Jews at Shrines and Sanctuaries*. Bloomington: Indiana University Press.

Arnason, J.P., Eisenstadt, S.N. and Wittrock, B. (eds) 2005. *Axial Civilizations and World History*. Leiden and Boston: Brill.

Assmann, J. 2010. *The Price of Monotheism*. Stanford, California: Stanford University Press.

——— 2012. 'Cultural memory and the myth of the Axial Age'. In R.N. Bellah and H. Joas (eds). *The Axial Age and its Consequences*, 366–407. Harvard: Harvard University Press.

Barkan, E. and Barkey, K. (eds) 2014. *Choreographies of Shared Sacred Sites. Religion and Conflict Resolution*. New York: Columbia University Press.

Bauer, T. 2011. *Die Kultur der Ambiguität. Eine andere Geschichte des Islams*. Berlin: Verlag der Weltreligionen.

Bellah, R.N. and Joas, H. (eds) 2012. *The Axial Age and its Consequences*. Harvard: Harvard University Press.

Ben-Ami, I. 1990. *Culte des saints et pèlerinages judéo-musulmans au Maroc*. Paris: Maisonneuve et Larose.

Bowman, G. (ed) 2012. *Sharing the Sacra. The Politics and Pragmatics of Intercommunal Relations around Holy Places*. Oxford: Berghahn Books.

Bowman, G.W. 2013. 'Hasluck redux: contemporary sharing of shrines in Macedonia'. In D. Shankland (ed.). *Archaeology, Anthropology and Heritage in the Balkans and Anatolia: the Life and Times of F. W. Hasluck, 1878–1920*. Vol. III, 229–46. Istanbul: Isis Press.

de Certeau, M. 1981. 'Une pratique sociale de la différence: croire'. In *Faire croire. Modalités de la diffusion et de la réception des messages religieux du XIIe au XVe siècle. Actes de table ronde de Rome (22–23 juin 1979)*. Rome: École Française de Rome, 363–83.

(1983). 'L'institution du croire : note de travail'. *Recherches de Science Religieuse*, 71:61–80.

de Beauvoir, S. 1976 [1949]. *The Ethics of Ambiguity*. New York: Citadel Press.

Dépret, I. and Dye, G. (eds.) (2012). *Partage du sacré. Transferts, dévotions mixtes, rivalités interconfessionnelles*. Bruxelles: E.M.E.

Duijzings, G. 2001. *Religion and the Politics of Identity in Kosovo*. New York: Columbia University Press.

Goossaert, V. 2000. *Dans les temples de la Chine. Histoire des cultes, vie des communautés*. Paris: Albin Michel.

——— 2004. 'Le concept de religion en Chine et l'Occident'. *Diogène* 205:11–21.

Grapard, A.G. 1984. 'Japan's ignored cultural revolution: the separation of Shinto and Buddhist divinities in Meiji (Shimbutsu Bunri) and a case study: Tnomine'. *History of Religions* 23–3:240–65.

Hasluck, F.W. 1913–14. 'Ambiguous sanctuaries and Bektashi propaganda'. *Annual of the British School at Athens* 20:94–119.

——— 2000. *Christianity and Islam Under the Sultans* (ed. M.M. Hasluck). Istanbul: The Isis Press [first edn: New York: Clarendon Press, 1929].

Hayden, R.M. 2002. 'Antagonistic tolerance: competitive sharing of religions sites in South Asia and Balkans'. *Current Anthropology* 43(2):205–31.

Hayden, R.M., Sözer, H., Tanyeri-Erdemir, T. and Erdemir, A. 2011. 'The Byzantine mosque at Trilye: a processual analysis of dominance, sharing, transformation and tolerance'. *History & Anthropology* 22(1):1–17.

Hayden, R.M. and Walker, T.D. 2013. 'Intersecting religioscapes: A comparative approach to trajectories of change, scale, and competitive sharing of religious spaces'. *Journal of American Academy of Religion* 81(2):399–426.

Moussy, C. and Orlandini, A. (eds.) 2007. *L'Ambiguité en Grèce et à Rome. Approche linguistique*. Paris: Presses de l'Université Paris-Sorbonne.

Naquin, S. and Yü, C. (eds.) 1992. *Pilgrims and Sacred Sites in China*. Berkeley: University of California Press.

Sekimori, G. 2005. 'Paper fowl and wooden fish. the separation of Kami and Buddha worship in Haguro Shugendo, 1869–1875'. *Japanese Journal of Religious Studies* 32(2):197–234.

Shankland, D. (ed.) 2004–13. *Archaeology, Anthropology and Heritage in the Balkans and Anatolia: The Life and Times of F.W. Hasluck, 1878–1920* (3 vols). Istanbul: The Isis Press.

Sharot, S. 2001. *A Comparative Sociology of World Religions: Virtuosi, Priests, and Popular Religions*. New York and London: New York University Press.

Thal, S. 2005. *Rearranging the Landscape of the Gods. The Politics of a Pilgrimage Site in Japan, 1573–1912*. Chicago-London: Chicago University Press.

Valtchinova, G. (ed.) 2010. *Religion and Boundaries. Studies from the Balkans, Eastern Europe and Turkey*. Istanbul: The Isis Press.

Voinot, L. 1948. *Pèlerinages judéo-musulmans du Maroc*. Paris: Editions Larose.

CHAPTER 2

From the god Amon to Sufi *mawlids*

PIERRE-JEAN LUIZARD

Pharaonic reminiscences, inventions of Egyptologists craving for romanticism, expressions of the urban and village communities of Upper Egypt and the Nile Delta...? Several current commemorations of Muslim saints in Egypt are giving rise to these questions through rituals implicitly evoking ancient Egypt. Beyond the element of truth of each of these three proposals, it can be clearly seen how the exploitation of the past is a central factor in the legend of a saint, whether or not he is a Muslim. The legend of the saint refers first to the time when it was 'in force', which makes it difficult to disentangle its portion of historical accuracy. And as with any legend, it is not surprising if it evolves over the years.

Three saints and their three *mawlids* (commemorations of their birth) illustrate better than anything else the comings and goings between the challenges of the moment and a past constantly reinvented: Abū al-Hajjāj in Luxor in Upper Egypt, Aḥmad al-Badawī in Tanta and Ibrāhīm al-Dīsūqī in Disuq in the Nile Delta.

In the city of Amon
Certain *mawlid*s attract an impressive number of pilgrims. This is the case of the very popular patron saint of Luxor, Shaykh Sayyid Yūsuf Abū al-Hajjāj al-Uqsurī (d. 1258). The tomb of this venerated saint of Upper Egypt (the *Ṣaʿīd*) is situated in the mosque that bears his name in Luxor. This mosque is of particular interest. Not because of its architecture, which is without great originality, but because of its site: built on the debris which largely covered the columns of the peristyle hall of the temple of Amon and overlooked by the

Large Pylon, the mosque has in turn overlooked Luxor for more than seven centuries. The Abū al-Hajjāj mosque seems to have set the round and white softness of its cupola and of one of its minarets over the temple of Luxor. As for the other minaret, constructed in mud bricks, it dates back to the Fatimid era and seems to have been flirting for centuries with the pylon and the obelisk of the temple of Amon.

This mosque was built in 1244 (year 632 of Hijra) by the local saint, Abū al-Hajjāj – or by his son according to some sources – on the courtyard of Ramses II. This location was previously occupied by a Christian church. The mosque is erected on the 'medieval level', which is located seven metres above the level of the Pharaonic era. Over the centuries, the ground of the temple has been covered with debris and sand. This explains the very strange presence of the door situated very high that can be noticed during a visit of the temple. After the clearing of the temple by Gaston Maspero at the end of the nineteenth century, this opening had to be blocked. The Egyptologist Georges Daressy relates the following:

> For many long years, the Service des Antiquités, desirous of clearing up the temple of Amon of Luxor, negotiated the expropriation and the displacement of the mosque of Abū al-Hajjāj which occupies the north-eastern part. It was widely predicted that, should the transfer of the relics of Abū al-Hajjāj and his companions occur, the earth would then open up to swallow either Mr. Maspero, or any other European official belonging to the Services des Antiquités.
>
> (Legrain 1914:80)

The mosque therefore remained untouched and a new entry, preceded by a flight of stairs, was built on the eastern side. The capitals of the columns, and the lintels carrying the cartouche of Ramses II, are located in the interior of the mosque. Two of the columns were even hollowed out in order to make *mihrāb*s. The local legend thus prevailed. The Egyptologists were in effect attacking one of the most popular saints of Upper Egypt, Abū al-Hajjāj, who was in his lifetime the Supreme Pole (*Qutb*) of Egypt, the protection (*madad*) of Muslims, a Sufi who performed many miracles and who surrounded himself with many disciples. Abū al-Hajjāj has therefore been the object of a great devotion for seven centuries: his *mawlid*, which is held each year during the Muslim month of *sha'bān*, attracts thousands of pilgrims (Chih 1993:67–77; Serdiuk: 2015).

Of uncertain origin, the shaykh is an Iraqi or Maghrebi *sharīf* (a descendant of the Prophet by Husayn). He came to settle in the *Sa'īd* in the thirteenth century (seventh century of Hijra), where he contributed to the development of Sufism and to the revival of the Sunni faith after the Shiite interlude of the Fatimid caliphate in Egypt. Though the *mawlid* of Abū Al-Hajjāj constitutes an attractive centre for the local population, the religious celebration of the saint was also the subject of various scientific researches.

Indeed, Abū al-Hajjāj was, by adoption, from Luxor, which he became the patron saint of, but everything that happened before his arrival in Egypt remains in fact a mystery. The biographer of the saints, Ibn Mulaqqin, reported in his *Tabaqāt al-Awliyā'* that Abū al-Hajjāj is from Maghrebi origin, settled in the *Sa'īd*. We also know that later, during his mystical initiation, he essentially surrounded himself with Maghrebi masters. Georges Legrain, who, at the beginning of the twentieth century, collected legends on Luxor, gave the partial translation of a text known only by the descendants of the saint, the *Hajjājiyya*. Abū al-Hajjāj would be a *sharīf* who reportedly left Baghdad for the Hijaz in 619 of Hijra, in the company of his four sons and a slave. After residing in the holy places during one year, having learned that the graves of his ancestors were located in al-Mansura, al-Marg and Cairo, he left Mecca and made his way toward Egypt in the company of other *sharīf*s. He made stops in several cities before settling permanently in Luxor, formerly called al-Uqsurayn, the city with the two palaces (in reference to the temples of Luxor and Karnak).

The cult of a saint is based on the belief in his *baraka* (divine gift). His tomb is the place where it abounds; certain days of the week or at the time of his *mawlid* are the times when it is the most influential. Abū al-Hajjāj knew how to bequeath an important legacy to his descendants. During his lifetime, he wore the marks of the divine election, but his *baraka* would probably have remained personal if his descendants had failed to create a place to transmit it. One of his sons, Najm al-Dīn (685/1296) had a tomb erected in the mosque that overlooks the temple of Amon, to keep alive the memory of his holiness. His descendants have inherited, by genealogical relationship, the *baraka* of their ancestor, who himself, had inherited it from the Prophet as it is recalled in his *nasab* (family tree), which is inside the tomb.

The *mawlid* is therefore the key moment of the cult rendered to Abū al-Hajjāj. During the *mawlid*, the trade of holy pictures is profitable: portraits of shaykhs (still alive or deceased during the past twenty years) are sold in frames or as key-holders, photographs in black and white or in colour that sometimes appear in the tombs, but that most often adorn houses and shops. The photograph is, too, a source of *baraka*, because it protects the family of the place from misfortunes and the evil eye. A lot of disciples carry with them a photo ID of their shaykh. Saints who died in the thirteenth century, such as Abū al-Hasan al-Shādhilī, are represented in blurred photos, in which they appear with long white beards and turbans. The image of Abū al-Hajjāj – a photo of Sayyid Yūsuf who died in 1914, originally a black and white photo, but which was coloured afterwards – is reproduced as a calendar. For the Sufi brotherhoods too, photography is a significant support: it is used to maintain the legend of the saint, in particular for the younger disciples who did not know him when he was alive (Chih 1993:73–4).

Today, the Hajjājiyya are one of the most powerful and influential families of Luxor. At the beginning of the century, one of its members, Sayyid Yūsuf (1842–1914), an Azharī and Sufi worshipper, was the object of general veneration:

> The sins of whoever touches his clothes shall be forgiven. It is claimed that he is sometimes animated by the spirit of divination, by knowing immediately what is happening and being said in the distance. Therefore, each and everyone bows to him.
>
> (Legrain 1914: 83).

His tomb, at Karnak, is still visited, especially by women.

But, let us come to the *mawlid*. The flow of pilgrims moves toward the mosque of Abū al-Hajjāj. The crowd around the tomb is so dense that worshippers are sometimes trampled. Every evening, a group of worshippers sitting around the cenotaph of the saint recites the *Dalā'il al-Khayrāt* (guide to good works), that is an anthology of prayers in honour of the Prophet, authored by 'Abd Allāh Muhammad al-Gazûlī (870/1465–6).

Inside the Abū al-Hajjāj mosque, a series of rites specific to Sufism is performed by the Hajjājiyya (the 'Sufi brotherhood', which it is preferable to consider as a lineage composing the descendants of Abū al-Hajjāj rather than as a conventional initiatory brotherhood). These rites, performed during the holy week of the *mawlid* of Luxor, constitute the religious dimension of the celebration. During the evenings of the *mawlid*, the opening ritual (*al-dāyim*, meaning the limitlessness of the divine presence on the universe), is followed by Quran readings (*al-muqra*), songs of praises (*al-madīh*) to the Prophet Muhammad, a *wird* (all the additional prayers) composed of the recitation of a poem (*shi'r*) that is addressed to Shaykh Abū al-Hajjāj (where his nature of Pole – *Qutb* – is praised, as a saint at the top of the hierarchy of holiness) and the recitation of the *Dalā'il al-Khayrāt* of al-Gazūlī. This *wird* precedes and prepares the rite which closes every ritual evening, the *dhikr*, the 'remembrance of God' that aims at the realization of divine uniqueness (*tawhīd*) as well as the purification of hearts. Over the ritual evenings, the rites, instruments of sacred time, are subject to reiteration and intensification, and this constitute ways of fighting and resisting the profane time, a time that distances the worshipper from the purity of the origins, from the purity of the beginnings of the Islamic era (Serdiuk 2015).

This is how every evening progresses, until the big night preceding the processional day. During this night of the full moon, the lineage invites the population and the important representatives (political, economical, religious) of the city of Luxor in order to formalize the party and to assert their authority as a social and religious elite. Outside the mosque, a huge tent was set up to celebrate officially the feast of the saint: on the evening of the great night (*al-layla al-akbar*) that marks the climax and the last night of the festival, the representatives of the government, the governor of Qina, the mayor of Luxor, the chief of police, the representatives of the Coptic Church arrive to attend the preaching of the shaykh. The latter explicitly links the cult of the Muslim saint with the site, 'the city of Amon'. At least, this is how it was under the regime of Mubarak. Since 2011, when the Muslim Brotherhood came to power, the *mawlid* no longer has government officials attending, and some of its rites, considered contrary to the Islam upheld by the Brotherhood, have been abandoned. The allusions to Amon have disappeared from speeches.

Added to this political dimension is a social dimension, for the *mawlid* contributes to the reinforcement of the social links between the members of the lineage, between the latter and the members of the different families of Luxor and between the pilgrims who visit and give their love to Shaykh Abū al-Hajjāj. The *mawlid*s also include an economic dimension and are often compared to trade fairs. Commerce and shops make good business, and a range of street vendors and 'wild' small shops take advantage of the windfall provided by the *mawlid* of Luxor.

Finally, a playful dimension can also be observed when, during the afternoons of the holy week, before sunset, many men engage in traditional games of Upper Egypt: the *tahtīb*, a kind of stick fighting that engages two duellists in a game of attack and counter-attack, or the *murmah*, a series of equestrian games, such as a race or a dance, that submits the rider to his mount.

To bring an end to the holy week, on the day after the great night, at the date of the 15 *sha'bān*, during the first hours of the day, a first procession (*zeffa*), more specifically named *dawra* (lit. 'circuit') is formed in the locality of Luxor. During the procession, the *mahmal*s (sort of litters adorned with fabrics symbolizing a holy figure mounted on a camel) of the patron saint of the city and his sons will be taken out of the mosque of Abū al-Hajjāj , as well as a camel fitted with large percussion instruments that will mark the rhythm of the processional march. The purpose of this morning outing is to visit the holy figures at the dwelling places of their descendants – both the major figures and the newborns of the lineage – in order to provide them with their *baraka*.

At the end of this first procession the sun is at its zenith. The surrounding area of the mosque is packed. The leading figures of Luxor are in the streets and a large number of the inhabitants of the city have moved up to the mosque to attend the rising of the camels that will depart for a second *dawra*, the circuit of the afternoon. The *mahmal* of the saint is waiting for departure, the pious persons are in direct contact with him and take advantage of this precious moment to charge his *baraka*.

After the Friday prayer the *khalīfa*, descendant of Abū al-Hajjāj, goes out of the mosque with many acclamations, amidst shouts of 'God is great!' and 'There is no other god but God'. Doves are freed amidst a cloud of incense, and the crowd is moved: it is the saint in person who goes out of the mosque! The Hajjājiyya, dressed in white and gathered around the leader of lineage, goes out of the mosque while singing the verses of the *Qutbiyya*. Mounted on his horse, the *khalīfa* leads the procession, followed by the cortege, composed of a *mahmal*, representing a litter of camels adorned with colourful fabrics that usually cover the cenotaphs of the different saints. Some carry flags on which are embroidered the name of the saint or verses from the Quran. The *mahmal*s of Abū al-Hajjāj and his sons will be lifted and these will now be accompanied by many other *mahmal*s, those of the shaykhs of Luxor and its periphery. This procession has quite a different stature to the previous one that took place in the morning, for many other actors are present and are taking part in this procession. Barques follow slowly, hauled by dozens of worshippers, and then horse-drawn carriages (*hantūr*) garlanded with flowers and trucks representing different trades close the procession.

The procession moves off among cheers from the crowd. We find again, in order, the *khalīfa* on a mount and opening the procession, the head of the lineage in a car, the banners of the Hajjājiyya, the *mahmal*s of Abū al-Hajjāj and of his sons, those of the local saints and a set of barques (the large green, steel barque of the corporation of the boatmen of the Nile, named Abū al-Hajjāj, and a set of smaller, wooden barques) and, finally, the floats of different corporations (mechanics, cooks, bakers, railway workers, the floats of different youth associations or neighbourhood associations, drivers of horse-drawn carriages etc.) (Serdiuk 2015).

This custom of procession, once performed three times a year, when it marked the end of the month of *ramadān*, the *mawlid* of the Prophet and the *mawlid* of Shaykh Abū al-Hajjāj, is nowadays performed only for the latter occasion. This procession, ritually marking the territory, actually constitutes a remembrance of the political ownership of the city of Luxor by Shaykh Abū al-Hajjāj. Indeed, the oral tradition of Luxor actually provided a justification for this appropriation by giving to the city a founding legend that would enable it to establish the beginning of its Muslim history. According to this oral tradition, Abū al-Hajjāj solicited Tharzah, the Coptic virgin who then governed Luxor, so that she allowed him to spend one night in the city. Tharzah and her counsellors granted him, in writing, the authorization to occupy what could be contained on a buffalo skin which was given to him. By nightfall, the saint, armed with a razor, began to cut the buffalo skin into fine strips. Attached end to end, these formed a long rope of leather that, at dawn, would enable the saint to encircle the city. Today, as in the past, just as the shaykh turned to the left in order to implement his plan, the procession follows the same direction (Serdiuk 2015).

Over the years, at mid *sha'bān*, the procession updates the hagiographic narrative and, thus, the Hajjājiyya perpetuates the gesture of their eponymous ancestor, asserting by doing so the ancient Islamic settlement in the thousand-year-old city of Luxor; materially marking in space the legitimacy of its presence and, through ritual practices, focusing on the claim of its identity, on the claim of the memory of the saint, the 'Friend of God', Shaykh Abū al- Hajjāj.

At the end of the day, tired, the *khalīfa* returns home, alone. The people in the street do not recognize him. The *mawlid* is over.

Over a long period, some Western researchers have interpreted the popular rites and traditions of the Egyptians of today as the survival of Pharaonic and Christian rites. Thus, it seems that during the last century, French Egyptologists suggested introducing into the procession an element of Pharaonic origin: a barque which stayed throughout the year inside the tomb, to be taken out on the day of the procession. The European observers who studied the origins of this barque provided the following elements:

> A European is rarely allowed to enter the mosque of Abū al-Hajjāj, visit the tombs or see the barque of the saint. Because the latter, having supplanted Amon by lodging in a part of his temple, has inherited his fertilizing qualities, charges and attributes. And, as Amon once, Abū al-Hajjāj makes, once a year, in a barque, a tour around his good town of Luxor ... At the time of the procession, the barque is lifted onto a four-wheeled frame and covered with the large multicoloured piece of fabric which, during the year, conceals the tomb of the saint. Hauled by the worshippers, adorned with flags, the barque of the saint moves slowly among the songs, cheers, prayers and shots of the excited crowd that gathers to touch the veil of the saint, under which some privileged children are crouching.
>
> (Legrain 1914:87)

However, no archaeological record attests to the Pharaonic origins of the presence of this barque. According to a Muslim legend, this barque would have carried Abū al-Hajjāj to the different villages of the region where he went to preach. Here, the barque would rather be the symbol of the spread of Islam through Upper Egypt.

Yet, during the 1930s English magazines published photos of it, accompanied by a legend according to which the procession of Abū al-Hajjāj was the survival of the former feasts of Opet, during which the Theban triad – Amon, Mout and Khounsou – performed a procession by barque from the temple of Karnak to the temple of Luxor (McPherson 1941:307). The Beautiful Festival of the Valley was a ceremony of ancient Egypt that was celebrated annually in Thebes from the Middle Empire era. During this festival the sacred barques of Amon-Re, his wife Mout and his son Khounsou left the temple of Karnak to visit the funerary temples of the late kings on the west bank of the Nile, and their sanctuaries in the Theban necropolis (Davies and Friedman 1998; Strudwick and Strudwick 1999).

Having made a special trip to attend the *mawlid* of 'Abd al-Rahīm al-Qinā'ī in 1938 to see the famous barque, Joseph Williams McPherson was very disappointed to learn that it had been banned by the government. 'Nowadays, no barque remains in the tomb of the saint but, probably due to folklore, several barques full of children continue to be part of the procession.' (McPherson 1941:307).

Also called the 'Beautiful Festival of Opet', *heb nefer en Ipet*, during which the Amon-Re of Karnak visited the Amon-Min of Luxor, it was one of the most sumptuous religious feasts of Pharaonic Egypt. These magazines added that 'today, there is still a survival of the Festival of Opet through the Muslim festival of Abu Haggag, which is celebrated every year in Luxor': the festivities of the present day culminate in a cortege of small boats that are taken in a procession around the enclosure of the temple of Luxor. The starting point of the ancient procession was the temple of Karnak, where the king, 'Lord to do things', performed the appropriate rites. Then, shaven-headed Ouab priests carried the sacred barques on their shoulders to the Nile, while dancers, singers, acrobats and musicians animated the party in front of the local population and the soldiers gathered along the ceremonial avenue lined with sphinxes. On their arrival at the bank of the Nile, the barques were laid on vessels, the largest of which, the *Ouserhet* ('powerful prow') of Amon, made of Lebanese cedar wood, measured one hundred and thirty cubits. The hull of the *Ouserhet* was plated with gold, with embossed designs featuring the king officiating before the god. The ram's head of Amon, adorned with necklaces and splendid pectorals, decorated the prow and the stern. After the embarkation of the deities, the sacred fleet was hauled toward Luxor, against

From the god Amon to Sufi mawlids

the current, by haulers and teams of bargemen encouraged by the worshippers gathered on the wharf and along the banks.

When the heavy vessels finally moored at Luxor, the sacred barques would be unloaded, with extreme care, and taken cross the sacred precinct of the Opet of the south. Priests would deposit them in the chapel of repose so that the 'living pictures of the gods' could be revitalized by offerings of crystal-clear water, fruits, meats, freshly picked flowers and incense, 'all good and pure things'. Once these solemn rites had been accomplished, the divine procession would move into the colonnade of Amenhotep III, cross the solar court and enter the penumbra of the sanctuary, where the king would welcome them, surrounded by the highest dignitaries (Posener 1960; Kemp 2004).

Seeing in the rituals of the *mawlid* of Abū al-Hajjāj at Luxor a reminiscence of 'The Beautiful Festival of Opet' is obviously most tempting.

The *mawlid* of Sayyid Ahmad al-Badawī at Tanta, a recurrence of the festivals of Busiris and Bubastis?

Outside of Cairo, Ahmad al-Badawī (1200–76) and Ibrāhīm al-Disūqī (1246–88), buried at Tanta and Disuq in the Delta, respectively, are among the holy founders of the most popular brotherhoods in Egypt. And, again with the exception of the Egyptian capital, the two greatest pilgrimages are those of Tanta and Disuq. The tomb of Shaykh 'Abd al-'Al, one of the first shaykhs of the Ahmadiyya order, a brotherhood that appeared after the death of Ahmad al-Badawī, is also in the mausoleum of Sayyid al-Badawī.

But who was this saint revered by the Egyptians? Sayyid Ahmad al-Badawī was born in Fez, Morocco. He lived during a period of a general decline of Islam, which was facing the invasions of the Christians of the *Reconquista*, the Crusaders in Egypt and the Mongolians in the East. He departed with his family for Mecca, where his father was to die. During a mystical crisis he went to Iraq, and later came to settle in the Nile Delta. At Tanta he chose to live on the Terrace, an elevated place from which he enjoyed a position of isolation and elevation. For a long time, Sayyid al-Badawī was presented in the *mawlid*s as a fighter of the faith facing the crusade led by Saint-Louis in Egypt.

There were, traditionally, three *mawlid*s of Sayyid al-Badawī at Tanta, held on fixed dates each year according to the Coptic calendar. Distinctions were made between *al-mawlid al-sughayyar*, on the tenth of the month of Coptic *tūba*, that is to say around January 17–18; the second one, at the spring equinox, *al-mawlid al-wasit*, linked to Sayyid 'Abd al-'Al, which always fell in *barmūda* (9 April – 8 May); and the third, *al-mawlid al-kabīr*, the most important, a month and a half after the summer solstice, held in the middle of the month of *abīb*, at the beginning of August, at the time of the annual flooding of the Nile. Each *mawlid* lasted one week and one day, beginning on Friday and ending on the following Friday. Today, the three *mawlid*s have been grouped into a single event, held after the harvest of cotton in the Delta, during the month of *bābih*, at a date which corresponds to mid-October. The previous date of the great *mawlid* of Sayyid al-Badawī, in summer, emphasized the close relationship between the saint and the water.[1] Indeed, it fell just at the time of the flooding of the Nile. The construction of several dams in the Delta and in Aswan put an end to this intimate relationship between the saint and the water, and the *mawlid* has therefore been held, for a little more than a century, at the end of October, at the time of harvest. Actually, al-Badawī is the patron saint of harvests: he turns barley into wheat and foresees the price of grain.

The Pharaonic influences in the *mawlid* of Sayyid al-Badawī are not limited to the choices of dates according to the Coptic calendar. Many alleged reminiscences of ancient Egypt are to be found in the rites and manner of celebrating the dead. In the traditional Vulgate, al-Badawī frees his first disciple, 'Abd al-'Al, from the horns of a furious bull. His virility turns out to be greater than that of the bull. In the Egyptian legends collected by the nineteenth century, the bull is depicted as supporting the Earth on its horns. This is perhaps the remembrance of Mīn, Hathor's husband, both a bull god and an ithyphallic form of Amon, one of whose attributes is lightning. The bull, a symbol of power, is the image of fertility. It is therefore not a coincidence that its trace can be found in the images of Sayyid al-Badawī. In the miracle of Infant 'Abd al-'Al, we have the image of a child wrapped in swaddling clothes taken for a ride by a bull: the representation is too accurate not to allude to Osiris wearing his strips and brought by a bull. The Egyptologists were more than happy to discover in al-Badawī the heir of the ancient cults of the Delta.

Is the *mawlid* a recurrence of the pilgrimages of Busiris and Bubastis? Confronted by the gatherings of male and female prostitutes, and the obscene fertility rituals (a remembrance of the sacred prostitution of ancient paganism) that can be found in the *mawlid* of Tanta, the comparison comes immediately to mind. This is how Olympe Audouard, who published *Les Mystères de l'Egypte dévoilés* in 1865, described the *mawlid*, quoting Herodotus, and asserting that the *mawlid* evokes the feasts of Bubastis and Busiris: 'Tanta is perhaps the only city in the world where prostitution is put on public display, freely and proudly, where Venus is celebrated without the slightest shame' (Audouard 1865:259–78). The great Hungarian Islamic scholar, Ignace

---

1   The history of the holiness of Sayyid al-Badawī has been admirably recounted and analysed by Mayeur-Jaouen 1994. The *mawlid* of the saint was also described by the same author in Mayeur-Jaouen 2004, 2005a. See also Pagès-El Karaoui 2005; Mayeur-Jaouen 2005b, and Luizard 1990.

Goldziher (1850–1921) concludes: 'The best explanation of this remarkable feast, is that the tomb of the saint Ahmad al-Badawī has replaced, as a place of pilgrimage, that of the Artemis of Bubastis.' (Goldziher 1880:303). Maspero himself expresses the same thoughts: 'the fair has emigrated into the next city of Tanta, where the Egyptian Muslims pay the same tribute of prayers and disorders to the sheikh Sidi-Ahmad-El-Bedaoui as their pagan ancestors paid to Bastit, the cat goddess' (Maspero 1914:40).

Let's recall that Busiris is the Greek name of Djedu, the city of antique Egypt. Its name may originate from a deformation of the name Per-Osiris, 'the house of Osiris', another name of the city. The city of Busiris was located in the centre of the Nile Delta, on the site which today bears the Arab name of Abūsîr. All that remains of the temple mentioned by Herodotus are scattered stones. Busiris was one of the main places of cult of the god Osiris. Great feasts in honour of the mourning of Osiris were celebrated there. The Osirian myth relates that Isis buried the remains of her male consort (brother and husband) at Busiris.

As for Bubastis, it was, successively, a capital of province, then the capital of Egypt under the kings of the 22nd dynasty. Herodotus tells us that the goddess Bastet, with the head of a cat, was venerated there. Her temple, surrounded by the water of two wide canals, except at the entrance, had the appearance of an island. The festival of Bastet was, according to Herodotus, the most important of the annual feasts. Crowds from all Egypt used to gather there. The numerous sacrifices that were made were pretexts for extraordinary feasts during which, according to Herodotus, more wine was drunk than during the rest of the year. Today, hashish, the scent of which embalms the city of Tanta at the time of the *mawlid*, has visibly replaced the wine.

The *mawlid* in Tanta is also the opportunity for a huge trade fair, while the city is invaded by a dense crowd. Merry-go-rounds, performing conjurers, sellers of knick-knacks, pastries and sweets provide the city with the atmosphere of popular bazaar. Here and there, some lotteries (*yā nasīb*, assimilated to games of chance and, consequently, considered as illicit) can be found next to places of devotion. Tents, erected throughout the city for each of the numerous brotherhoods, that organize there sessions of *dhikr*, increase the indescribable turmoil of the city. The governor of the province of Gharbiyya, representing the president of the republic, as well as all the members of the Higher Sufi Council, used to regularly attend the *mawlid* of Tanta. Festivities end with several Sufi processions. It is estimated that prior to 2011 the number of pilgrims for the *mawlid* of Sayyid al-Badawī used to exceed two million. With the fall of the regime of Mubarak and the accession to power of the Muslim Brotherhood, a modest veil has been thrown over a demonstration judged as not really compliant with the Brothers' reformist

Islam. The official representatives were scarcer at the time of the *mawlid* and even the attendance was a lot less dense than before.

The veneration of Ibrāhīm al-Disūqī

One or two weeks after the end of the *mawlid* of Tanta, the *mawlid* of Sīdī Ibrāhīm al-Disūqī begins at Disuq. The *mawlid* of Disuq has been far less studied than that of Tanta, with which it shares a lot of features, probably because it closely follows the latter.[2] As with the other *mawlid*s, it lasts a week and a day. Just as in Tanta, this commemoration is a pretext for a huge funfair that spreads from the mosque where the saint is buried to the shores of the Nile. Pilgrims and sayyids arrive in boats on the Nile and moor near the mosque. The sayyids of the Burhāmiyya (the Sufi brotherhood that appeared after the death of Ibrāhīm al-Disūqī) have, of course, a leading role, but the Ahmadiyya, Rifā'iyya and Shādhiliyya are also very present. The shaykh of the Magāhidiyya Burhāmiyya Brotherhood, riding a white horse, leads the Sufi procession, on the last Friday after the noon prayer. As during the major *mawlid*s, in that of Disuq there is a role for civilian and religious representatives of the state, in this case the governor of the province of Kafr al-Shaykh, and other who mark the presence of the Ministry of *Waqf* and the mufti of the Republic. This *mawlid* gathers a lot of people, in 1989 the municipality of Disuq announced that it was ready to welcome two million pilgrims.

According to the legend of the saint, the shores of the western branch of the Nile where Disuq is built would have sheltered a gigantic crocodile that the saint would have tamed. In the mosque, they may show you the forty-cm wide vertebra of the monster. The crocodiles disappeared from the Delta more than 170 years ago, and the miracle accomplished by the saint is still surprising.

During the Pharaonic era the crocodile was feared and dreaded, and was perceived as an ambivalent animal of the forces of good and evil. In order to win the favour of this ruthless predator, the Egyptians turned it into a very popular god: Sobek, the animal of Seth, the god of evil. They also assimilated it to almost all other gods: Re, Osiris, Horus etc. The crocodile frequently appears on healing steles that evoke Seth, and crocodile-shaped amulets are very appreciated. When it is associated with Osiris, the crocodile evokes rebirth, the revival of the floods of the Nile and the resurrection of nature.

In some cities the crocodile enjoys a genuine veneration (Kom Ombo, Gebelayn, Crocodilopolis in Fayoum). Herodotus relates how, in the temple of Thebes, the sacred crocodile was fed with geese, fish and carefully prepared dishes, and how it was adorned with collars, golden rings and precious stones. In certain temples the sacred crocodile would live in sumptuous tiled and

---

2   We can however quote Schielke 2008.

decorated pools. On its death, the sacred crocodile was embalmed and buried according to the same rituals as humans. Necropolises containing hundreds of mummified crocodiles have been discovered.

Again, how can one not associate the Muslim saint tamer of the crocodile with the rites of Ancient Egypt?

Pharaonic reminiscences or an Islamic brand?

There exists no text that forbids the commemoration of the birth of a saint or of a member of the family of the Prophet. But sometimes the nature of these commemorations is more that of social rejoicing than that of religious demonstration. And often, they happen to be the occasion of rites qualified as anti-Islamic by European visitors, as in Luxor, Tanta or Disūq. Are these Pharaonic reminiscences or an Islamic brand? There are differing points of view.

Indeed, since the nineteenth century the *mawlid* of Abū al-Hajjāj at Luxor has attracted travellers and Egyptologists. The first to be interested was the English Lucy Duff-Gordon, who had elected to reside in the temple of Luxor, from where she observed the *mawlid* of Abū al-Hajjāj over several years (Duff Gordon 1983). After this first testimony, we have to wait until the twentieth century to rediscover the *mawlid* in scientific literature, particularly in the work of the Egyptologist Georges Legrain, who described the celebration of the *mawlid* in *Louqsor sans les pharaons* (Legrain 1914). Later, James Hornell (1938) wrote an article published in the journal *Man* and McPherson (1941) devoted, for his part, a chapter to the *mawlid* of Luxor in his book *The Moulids of Egypt*. More recently, the works of Rachida Chih (1993) and Shelley Wachsmann (Wachsmann 2002a, 2002b) provide a more current testimony on the evolution of the *mawlid*.

These different authors focused their works on the procession that marks the end of the holy week and during which barques are hauled into the city. For a long time, this procession remained the main topic in studies of the *mawlid* of Abū al-Hajjāj, and, according to these authors, it embodies with certainty the survival of antique rites of the Theban region, in particular the decadal celebrations: the Beautiful Feast of the Valley and the Festival of Opet.

This approach, which can be qualified as Egyptological, has apparently been taken over since the time of Georges Legrain by a local discourse, in this case by some members of the Hajjājiyya, a lineage of the patron saint of Luxor. Catherine Mayeur-Jaouen questions this Pharaonic relationship, as she puts forward the distorting effect of focusing on the final procession of the *mawlid*. According to her, many assumptions of deterministic and Islamic nature allow us to assert that the generalizations arising from this perspective are not well founded, and that these assumptions can thus constitute new pathways to understanding the rituals (Mayeur-Jaouen 1994:96–106).

Since Egyptian Antiquity, any sacred event has always moved on water. Thus, formerly, the gods visited the divinities that were their neighbours by waterway. These sacred displacements therefore have their foundation in a natural determinism. The Nile constitutes the ideal communication path and accordingly induces the use of a typical and local symbolism, the one of the barque.

The boat is one of the former means of transportation for pilgrimage to Mecca. A few decades ago, the crossing of the Red Sea by boat was the most popular way to go to the Hijaz. In this sense, the barques can be envisaged as the symbolic means that the procession gives itself to evoke the pilgrimage to Mecca. The boat could also symbolize the remembrance of a *karāma* (miracle of a saint) of Abū al-Hajjāj:

> Youssef was returning from Mecca in a small fleet of boats of pilgrims. A big storm arose and the boat of Youssef was in imminent danger of sinking. In response to his prayers, it crossed the sea safely while all the other vessels that sailed with it were lost. Impressed by the miracle, the survivors promoted their saviour to the rank of holiness and at his death, they erected a tomb above his remains in Luxor.
>
> (Hornell 1938:145)

According to oral tradition, Abū al-Hajjāj would initiate and teach Islamic doctrine in the villages of the region of Luxor. He would sail on the Nile and on the channels connected to it in his own boat in order to go preaching from village to village.

> Abd al-Rahīm al-Qināʾī, the saint of Qina, also used a boat as a means of transportation in order to preach. Besides, the *mawlid* of Qina shows a processional activity similar to that of Luxor. Therefore, the barque seems to be the symbol of the spread of Islam (and more precisely that of Sunnism) through Upper Egypt.
>
> (Chih 1993:77)

Mayeur-Jaouen (2005a:236) also notes that 'there is nothing exceptional about the barque in the *mawlid*s of the banks of the Nile and that other processional boats parade, for example during the mouleds of Rifāʿi in Cairo, Disudisq in the Delta'. This observation intends thus to indicate to researchers that it is not relevant to establish such links between the procession of the patron saint of Luxor and old processional traditions. Still according to

Mayeur-Jaouen, 'Western researchers focused on the barques of Abū al-Hajjāj because of Luxor and its temples'. It cannot be denied that the representation of Amon, Mout and Khounsou travelling on their respective small barques is a strong image within the divine and funerary temples of the Theban region, but for any researcher, exclusively considering the local reality involves risks. Broadening the scientific approach (using social facts belonging to Islam) and considering the phenomenon of the small processional barques at the global level of Egypt would enable, according to the researcher, a better understanding of the phenomenon.

With regard to Tanta, Mayeur-Jaouen puts forward a fashionable view of Egyptologists. The birth of the ethnography of the Egyptian cults and of the recording of its stories, from the beginning of the nineteenth century, often echoes the relationship between ancient Egypt and modern Muslim cults. Maspero, who led the first archaeological mission in Egypt, (1881–6/1899–1914), not to be outdone and keen of folklore, saw in the contemporary Egyptian tales many reminiscences of the past. Apart from Ignace Goldziher (1880) and the German Orientalist Enno Littman (1875–1958) (Vollers and Littman 1969), no Arabist, however, adds convincing elements to the mythical origin of the cult of Ahmad al-Badawī (Mayeur-Jaouen 1994:96–106).

Mayeur-Jaouen lists the 'assumptions to put aside': al-Badawī as a bubastite, al-Badawī as a founder of brotherhood, al-Badawī as a Christian monk, al-Badawī as a crusader and fighter of faith (*mujāhid*), al-Badawī as a Shi'ite, and so on. However, she agrees to consider other assumptions: al-Badawī as a Bedouin, al-Badawī as a militant of the great Sufi order Rifā'iyya and al-Badawī as the successor of a Coptic saint (Mayeur-Jaouen 1994:257–62).

Thus, the Pharaonic reminiscences in certain *mawlid*s of Egypt would only be, in the eyes of the majority of the researchers of the latest generation, a trope belonging to the taste for folklore of preceding generations of visitors and/or scientists. More than any other, the history of popular piety is inspired by the fashion of the moment. Successively, during the twentieth century, researchers were very interested in popular Muslim piety, before predicting its decline in the face of reformist Islam, and then again recognizing its force. If the legend of the saints is constantly reinvented, cannot the same be said about history? All the more so since the latter legend refers directly to the corpus of scientists. Isn't the holy biography of 'Umar ibn al-Farid (d. 1235) in his mausoleum in the City of the Dead in Cairo the very notice written by Massignon on this great mystical poet (Luizard 1993)?

Since this work is about shared cults, it would not be presumptuous to think that the first sharing is with the past... reconsidered in the light of the present day.

References

Audouard, A. 1865. *Les Mystères de l'Egypte dévoilés*. Paris: E. Dentu.

Chih, R. 1993. 'Abu-al-Hajjāj al-Uqsuri, patron saint of Luxor'. *Egypte/Monde arabe* 14(2nd quarter):67–78.

Davies, V. and Friedman, R. 1998. *Egypt*. London: British Museum Press.

Duff-Gordon, L. 1983. *Letters from Egypt*. London: Virago Travellers.

Goldziher, I. 1880. 'Le Culte des saints chez les Musulmans'. *Revue de l'histoire des religions* 2:257–351.

Hornell, J. 'Boat processions in Egypt'. *Man, A Monthly Record of Anthropological Science* 38:145–6.

Kemp, B.J. 2004. *Ancient Egypt: Anatomy of a Civilization*. Abingdon: Routledge.

Legrain, G. 1914. *Louqsor sans les pharaons*. Lille, Paris: Vromant.

Luizard, P.-J. 1990. 'Le Soufisme égyptien contemporain'. *Egypte/Monde arabe* 2:35–94.

——— 1993. 'Un *mawlid* particulier'. *Egypte/Monde arabe* 14:79–102.

Maspero, G. 1914. 'Chansons populaires recueillies dans la Haute-Égypte de 1900 à 1914 pendant les inspections du Service des Antiquités'. *Annales du Service des Antiquités de l'Egypte* 14:97–200.

Mayeur-Jaouen, C. 1994. *Al-Sayyid al-Badawī, A Great Saint of the Egyptian Islam*. Cairo: IFAO.

——— 2004. *Histoire d'un pèlerinage légendaire en islam: le mouled de Tanta*. Paris: Aubier.

——— 2005a. *Pèlerinages d'Egypte. Histoire de la piété copte et musulmane XVe–XXe siècles*. Paris: EHESS.

——— 2005b. 'Les Processions pèlerines en Egypte : pratiques carnavalesques et itinéraires politiques, les inventions successives d'une tradition'. In Sylvia Chiffoleau and Anna Madœuf (eds). *Les Pèlerinages au Maghreb et au Moyen-Orient. Espaces publics espaces du public*, 217–32. Paris: IFPO.

McPherson, J.W. 1941. *The Moulids of Egypt, Egyptian-Saints days*. Le Caire: N. M. Press.

Pagès-El Karaoui, D. 2005. 'Le mouled of Sayyid al-Badawī à Tantâ: logiques spatiales et production d'une identité urbaine'. In Sylvia Chiffoleau and Anna Madœuf (eds). *Les Pèlerinages au Maghreb et au Moyen-Orient. Espaces publics espaces du public*, 237–64. Paris: IFPO.

Posener, G. 1960. *De la divinité du Pharaon*. Paris: Imprimerie nationale.

Schielke, S. 2008. 'Policing ambiguity: moslem saints-day festivals and the moral geography of public space in Egypt'. *American Ethnologist* 35(4):539–52.

Serdiuk, E. 2015. 'The mawlid of the shaykh Abû al-Hajjāj, patron saint of Luxor'. egyptologica.be, accessed February 2015.

Strudwick, N. and Strudwick, H. 1999. *Thebes in Egypt*. New York: Cornell University Press.

Vollers, K, and Littman, E. 1969. 'Ahmad al-Badawī'. *The Encyclopaedia of Islam, vol.* 2. Leiden: Brill.

Wachsmann, S. 2002a. 'Sailing into Egypt's past, does a celebration of Luxor patron saint echo ancient pharaonic traditions'. *Archaeology Magazine* 55(4):36–9.

——— 2002b. 'The moulid of Abu el-Haggag: A contemporary Boat Festival in Egypt'. In *Tropis VII (7th International Symposium on Ship Construction in Antiquity. Pylos, August 25–30, 1999*, 821–35. Athens: Harry Tzalas and Hellenic Institute for the Preservation of Nautical Tradition.

CHAPTER 3

'Ambiguity in context' according to Islamic thought

Bridging theory and actuality in relating to saints in Islam

Yasushi Tonaga

People often think that there is enormous gap between the theories developed about Islamic saints, which are often related to Sufism, and the practices of saint cults, which often derive from non-Islamic origins. The latter practices are often considered to be representative of the little tradition.¹ This chapter tries to bridge this gap. It consists of two parts. The first investigates the theories of saints in traditional Islamic studies. I will explore four theories that support the existence of saints and their miracles. The second part examines the theoretical basis of the practices that are observed in saint cults. I would like to demonstrate that these practices are more authentic than we would expect.

Saints in Islamic thought

Although we find many terms for the so-called 'saints' in different areas, for example, *pīr, walī, sharīf, sayyid, sīdī, faqī/fqī* (especially in North Africa and Turkey), and *ishān* (especially in Central Asia), very few words are used to refer to them in traditional Islamic Studies.

In the Qur'an and hadith the only word used to mean 'saint' is *walī*. This word is found 46 times in the Qur'an, and its plural form, *awliyā*, is found 42 times. In the Qur'an, it is not yet established as a technical term for 'saint', but has various meanings, including friend, close relative, God himself, the Prophet; all of which have a connotation of somebody who is near to the

---

1   The theory of the great tradition vs. the little tradition was advocated by Robert Redfield and applied to Islam by von Grunebaum (1976:17–37).

Figure 1 Quranic verses about a saint (walī), Algeria, Saalibi Mosque, 14 August 2006 (photograph: Masatoshi Kisaichi).

speaker. *Walī* is an abbreviation of *walī Allāh*, when it means a 'saint', and was originally used as an antonym to *walī al-shaytān*. People often quote the following passage from the Qur'an: 'Hearken, the friends of Allah, that is those who believe and are ever mindful of their duty to Allah, shall certainly have no fear nor shall they grieve' (Qur'an, 10:62–3). The passage relating to *walī* that is most often cited from the hadith is as follows: 'Indeed My friends from among My servants ... are those who recite (or invocate) by My recitation'.[2]

On the bases of these traditions, *walī* refers to those who have belief (*īmān*) and fear (*taqwā*) of God and always perform invocation (*dhikr*) to Allah. We should pay attention to the fact that this definition does not include any mystical elements. Rather, we should understand this description as an expression of piety, which can be observed in many aspects of Islam. For this reason, we can distinguish between *walī* in a broad sense (*sensu lato*), that is, non-mystical *walī*, and *walī* in a strict sense (*sensu stricto*), that is, Sufi *walī*. The first definition of the word will help us to understand why both direct disciples of the Prophet (*sahāba*) and many scholars have been venerated as *walī*s.

---

2   Ibn Hanbal 1313 (A.H.):430.

Four kinds of theory of saint

Here I would like to draw your attention to the fact that the theory of saints in Islam has historically been understood to be connected almost solely with Sufism. While it is true that Sufism developed the theory of saints (or, more strictly said, that of *walī*), I believe that we should pay more attention to other traditions of the theories of saint. Hereafter, I will explain four kinds of theories in the traditional Islamic studies. They are: 1) the *walī* theory of Sunnite theology; 2) the *walī* theory of Sufism; 3) the imamology (*imām* theory) of Shi'ism; and 4) the sayyid/sharifology. The last word comes from the terms *sayyid/sharīf*, both of which refer to the descendants of the Prophet.

These four types of saint theory can be divided into two categories. The first category discusses those who succeed to their titles according to genealogy, and the second describes those who do not. We can count 1) and 2) in the second category and 3) and 4) in the first category. Out of these types, 2) and 3) have a mystical and inner (*bāṭin*) tendency, whereas 1) and 4) can be understood within the framework of Islam as having an outer (*ẓāhir*) tendency, which is closely related to Islamic jurisprudence and theology.

WALĪ THEORY OF SUNNITE THEOLOGY

In Sunnite theology, *walī* can be defined as those who are authorized by the Qur'an (and hadith) and can do miracles. The existence of *walī* and their ability to do miracles were confirmed early in Sunnite theology. The only exception to the general Sunni belief in their miracles were the Mutazilites. As is well known, the Mutazilites departed from the main stream of Sunnism after their triumph at the Abbasid court in the middle of the ninth century. Therefore, we can safely say that, basically speaking, Sunnite theology in general has the existence of *walī* and their miracles as one of its 'orthodox' creeds. Among the famous theologians who referred to it, we can find Abū Bakr al-Bāqillānī (d. 1013), Abū Bakr Ibn Fūrak (d. 1015), Khatīb al-Baghdādī (d. 1071), 'Abd al-Malik al-Juwaynī (d. 1085), Fakhr al-Dīn al-Rāzī (1209), 'Aḍud al-Dīn al-Ījī (d. 1355) and 'Alī ibn Muhammad al-Jurjānī (d. 1413) among the Asharites; Ahmad al-Tahāwī (d. 933), Abū Hafs al-Nasafī (d. 1142), and Sa'd al-Dīn al-Taftāzānī (d. 1390) among the Maturidites.[3] Wensinck mentions that the first document of this creed appears in *al-Fiqh al-akbar al-thānī*, which seems to have been written between the fourth and tenth centuries by an anonymous author (Wensinck 1979:224). The sixteenth creed of that book begins as follows: 'In this article the reality of the signs of the Prophets as well as that of the miracles of the saints is confessed, the latter in opposition

---

[3] Although some people argue that al-Tahāwī and al-Taftāzānī did not belong to the Maturidites, they can still be seen as representative Sunnite theologians.

Figure 2   Portrait of an 'ulamā', left (private collection Kyoto).

to the Mutazilites.' The theological discussions about *walī* concentrate on the difference between the miracles of saints (*karāma*) and those of prophets (*mu'jiza*). For example, Taftāzānī, commenting on Nasafī's creed, states as follows:

> [The *karāma* of *walī* is truth.] And the *walī* are those who are devoted to loyalty (to Allah), those who avoid revolt (against Allah), and those who know the exalted Allah and His attributes by being people who abandon themselves and his devotion to their own desires. The *karāma* of *walī* is an appearance of something that is against custom, which does not coexist with the claim to be a prophet. That is why anything that is not combined

with belief (*īmān*) and pious deeds is a temptation that leads in the wrong direction. When something is combined with the claim of prophetship, it is (not *karāma* but) *mu'jiza*.[4]

These writers claimed that people must believe that *walī*s do miracles because that is what is recorded in tradition. At the same time, however, they also claimed that people must not disparage the prophets because of their belief in the existence of *walī*s and their miracles. For example, al-Tahāwī states as follows: 'We do not give priority to any *walī*s over any prophets. And we say that (even) one prophet goes before all the *walī*s.'[5] On the same point, Nasafī states: 'It is impossible for any *walī*s to reach the status of a prophet. The slaves of Allah do not reach a level where neither orders nor proscriptions of Allah are required.'[6]

From these passages, we can imagine that their true intentions in writing these creeds relate to strengthening belief in the prophets rather than eulogizing the *walī*s. However, it is more important in the context of this chapter that Sunnite theologians have postulated the existence of *walī*s and their miracles.

THE *WALĪ* THEORY OF SUFISM

The second theory of the saints in Islamic studies is the *walī* theory of Sufism. There has been a considerable amount of research on this topic. We can say that, if a Sufi is an elite Muslim, a *walī* is an elite Sufi, who reaches the experience of mystical union. The *walī* theory of Sufism goes along the same basic track as that of Sunnite theology. The main topic here is also their miracles and the relationship between *walī*s and prophets. First let us observe their opinion about miracles. Sufism claims that *walī*s do miracles by the blessing of Allah and they should still be strictly distinguished from the miracles of prophets. For example, Abū al-Qāsim al-Qushayrī (d. 1072), who had a profound knowledge of Asharite theology, quoting the names of Asharite theologians, stated as follows.

> It is possible for God's friends to perform miracles... When someone performs miracles, this is a sign of his being truthful in his spiritual states. [Conversely,] miracles cannot be performed by someone who is insincere... Miracles must be a matter that breaks the habitual order [of events] (*'āda*)

---

4   Taftāzānī 1987:92. Matter between the square brackets are texts by Nasafī, those in parentheses are my own clarifications.
5   Tahāwī 1993:25.
6   Nasafī 1993:29.

during the period when the [divinely ordained] religious obligation (*taklīf*) is in force. They are performed by an individual who is characterized by saintliness in order to ascertain the truthfulness of his spiritual state. Those who have attained [divine] truth (*ahl al-Haqq*) have talked in great detail regarding the difference between prophetic and saintly miracles. The imam Abu Ishāq al-Isfarā'īnī – may God have mercy on him – argued that prophetic miracles (*muʿjizāt*) [serve as] demonstrations of the truthfulness of the prophets and a proof of [their] prophetic mission, which is unique to prophets.[7]

There are two strands within Sufism regarding the miracles of *walī*s. One strand emphasizes the miracle as a special characteristic of *walī*s. The other emphasizes the gnosis (*maʿrifa*) rather than the miracle, because the latter is only the result of a *walī*'s union with Allah and his achievement of divine knowledge. There are also two opinions about the relationship between a *walī* and a prophet. One emphasizes their differences and claims that prophets are predominant over *walī*s. The other, on the contrary, emphasizes the similarity or continuity between prophets and *walī*s, arguing for the predominance of being a *walī* over being a prophet. The former argument is similar to that of the Sunnite theologians, whereas the latter is original to Sufism.

The hierarchy theory of *walī*s is specific to Sufism, and we cannot find it in Sunnite theology. It advocates that the *walī*s are classified in a hierarchy with *qutb* (pole) or *ghawth* (helper) on the top, and with all *walī*s playing a role in the maintenance of this world. Sufism agrees about the existence of the hierarchy, although there are various opinions about each name within the hierarchy. We can trace the description of the hierarchy to the eighth century at the latest, and the first person who systematized it was Hakīm al-Tirmidhī (d. *c*.936). Here I will describe the explanation offered by Abū al-Hasan al-Hujwīrī (d. *c*.1072) as an example of such a systematization. According to him, the highest rank is *qutb* or *ghawth*, of whom there is only one, the second is *nuqabāʾ* (three people), the third is *awtād* (four people), the fourth is *abrār* (seven people), the fifth is *abdāl* (forty people), and the last and sixth is *akhyār* (three hundred people). When a *walī* dies, another *walī* of a lesser rank will take his place and supplement the whole number of *walī*s. Among these ranks, the *awtād* guard the four different directions (north, south, east and west) and fly in the cosmos during the night. When one of them finds anything that is broken within the cosmos, he reports it to the *qutb*. Here we can see a mythological cosmology in which *walī*s are expected to maintain the cosmos.

---

7   Qushayrī 1998:378; Knysh 2007:357–8.

Figure 3 Tomb of the Sufi Ibn ʿArabī, Syria, Damascus, November 1, 2008 (photograph: Yasushi Tonaga).

IMAMOLOGY OF SHIʿITES

This and the sayyid/sharifology that follows both affirm that one can become a saint through having the correct genealogy. This is contrary to the two previous theories, because Sunnite theology does not clearly distinguish who saints are, and sometimes even affirms that every Muslim can be a *walī*, while Sufism advocates that people can become *walī*s only through their training (or sometimes only if they are chosen by Allah without training). Although both the Shiʿite imamology and sayyid/sharifology agree that only the descendants of the Prophet can be saints, they differ in their definitions of 'who the descendants are'. The narrowest definition is given by Shiʿite imamology, and it admits only the descendants of the ʿAlī and Fāṭima couple.[8] Sayyid/sharifology had a broader definition than this, although its demarcation line has varied over time.

In a sense, we can take Shiʿite imamology as part of sayyid/sharifology and analyze both together. Here, however, I will investigate them separately for the following three reasons. First, the theory of an imam as a divine man is peculiar to Shiʿism, although we can find sayyid/sharifology both in

---

8   Some Shiʿite sects include the descendants of ʿAlī and other wives. But they are in the minority among Shiʿites.

Figure 4   Portraits of the Imam 'Alī bought in May 2002 in Iran (private archives of Yasushi Tonaga).

Sunnism and Shi'ism. Second, imamology has developed a much more refined logic than sayyid/sharifology. Third, imamology can be safely counted as an academic genre in the tradition of Islamic studies, whereas sayyid/sharifology is rather marginal. We may even say that the latter was reconstructed by modern researchers, because it is based on their investigation of genealogy (*nasab*), and is more practical than theoretical. However, we can find an academic tradition within this investigation of genealogy (*nasab*), which has been accumulated during the ages.

Before describing Shi'ite imamology in detail, I will explain the different meanings of the word '*imām*' in the Islamic context. This is used both in Sunnism and Shi'ism. The most basic meaning is a leader of prayer (*salāt*, *namāz*). It also means a leader of the Muslim community after the death of the Prophet. Therefore, if we say '*imāma*' (*imām*-ness, *imām*-ship or imamology) within the Sunnite jurisprudence it refers to the theory of Caliphs. Although we can imagine that originally in Shi'ism the word '*imām*' also implied a leader of the actual community, they inclined toward understanding this word as referring to an inner or spiritual leader. Therefore, *imām* in Shi'ism means an infallible (*ma'sūm*) theanthropic (divine-human) leader. The existence of an *imām* is based on the authority of the Shi'ite hadith, which is different from that of Sunnism.

'*Imāma*' (*imām*-ness, *imām*-ship) in Shi'ism is interwined with '*walāya*' (*walī*-ness, *walī*-ship), as is clear from the fact that the first imam, 'Ali, is called '*walī* Allāh'. This is why Abū Ja'far al-Kulaynī (d. c.939–40), one of the most famous *ithnā-'asharī* theologians, discussed *walāya*. In the meantime, Sunnite theology developed its own *walī* theory and sometimes took the founders of the four jurisprudential schools (*a'imma arba'a*) to be *walī*s. Of course, Shi'ism severely attacked such an opinion, because for them a true *walī* is precisely an *imām* who only can comprehend both the exterior and interior meanings of the Qur'an, and the founders, who only have exterior knowledge, do not deserve to be called *walī*.

We can point out four characteristics of the Shi'ite *imām*. First, he is a vicegerent of Allah on earth. Second, he is an indispensable person, through whom Allah knows human beings. Third, he is the only source of justice. All humankind other than *imām*s makes mistakes. Fourth, he has divine characteristics that originate from Allah.

In relation to miracles, Shi'ite imamology stands on the same track as the *walī* theories of Sunnite theology and Sufism. It starts by admitting that an *imām* can do miracles. Then it moves to the topic of the difference between miracles of *imām*s and those of prophets. In doing so, it adopts the words *karāma* (for miracles performed by *imām*s) and *mu'jiza* (for miracles performed by prophets). We can say that these three theories are parallel on this point.

SAYYID/SHARIFOLOGY[9]

Both *sayyid* and *sharīf* refer to the descendants of the Prophet, although the former originally means a 'master', whereas the latter means a 'noble person'.

---

9   For this rather new notion, please see Kazuo Morimoto, "Toward the Formation of Sayyido-Sharifology: Questioning Accepted Fact", *The Journal of Sophia Asian Studies* 22 (2004), pp. 87-103 and Kazuo Morimoto (ed.), *Sayyids and Sharifs in Muslim Societies: The Living Links to the Prophet*, London and New York: Routledge, 2012.

Figure 5 A *sayyid-sharīf* (heir of the Prophet) with a black turban and a green scarf, Iran (photograph: Kazuo Morimoto).

There is also another, similar, expression, *ahl al-bayt*. These three notions are almost interchangeable, even if we can differentiate between them in some cases. Both groups, as well as Shi'ite imams, belonged to a noble family of the Prophet. The majority of Shi'ites idealized the *imām*s, the last of whom people believe will come back to save Shi'ite people (*raj'a* or *rujū'*) after the *imām*'s occultation from this world (*ghayba*). On the contrary, *sayyid/sharīf* have been part of daily life up to the present day. That is why beggars of *sayyid/sharīf* origin are sometimes reported. Theoretically speaking, however, these people are worshiped as semblances (images) of the Prophet and his cousin 'Ali. Their existence has its own bases in the Qur'an and the hadith. The words 'members of Household' and 'kindred' in the quotations below are thought to refer to *sayyid/sharīf*.

'Ambiguity in context' according to Islamic thought

Figure 6 An example of a certificate of a sayyid-sharīf, Egypt (photograph: Kazuo Morimoto).

Allah desires to remove from you all uncleanness, *members of Household*, and to purify you completely.

(Qur'an 33:33)

Tell them: I ask of you no recompense in return for it, except love as between *kindred*.

(Qur'an 42:23)

I will leave two important things to you (believers). One is the Book of God which was passed from heaven to earth (Qur'an), and another is my 'next of kin' and the 'people of the house'. If you follow these (two), you will not stray in any way.[10]

The 'people of my house' are like Noah's Ark to you. Those who ride in it will be saved, and those who have their back to it will be drowned.[11]

They not only became an object of veneration in society, but also had a prerogative in Islamic jurisprudence. For example, they were given pensions or exempted from taxes. The *waqf*s whose receivers were *sayyid/sharīf* were admitted and there were law courts especially for them. *Sayyid/sharīf* also had explicit outward signs, including green turbans and braided hair.

---

10 Samhūdī 1984:72–3.
11 Samhūdī 1984:31.

We have given overviews of four different kinds of saint theory. We should now pay attention to the fact that various other kinds of saint theories have also been formed and circulated around the Islamic world.

Between the theory of saints and the actual practices of saint cults

Now I would like to move to the second question on the relationship between the practices of saint cults actually observed in the field and saint theory in Islamic studies. Many piles of research have been accumulated on saint cults, both in historical studies and anthropology. Hereafter is my humble attempt to try to bridge the gap between these researches on saint cults and those on theory. First, let us think who are the objects of saint cults. We can say that every person who can do miracles for the common people has been venerated as a saint, without asking his/her origin. Here I will categorize these saints into five types.

1. The founders of *tarīqa*s (Sufi orders) and Sufis.
2. The descendants of the Prophet.
3. Those who are considered as great men/women, in senses such as being disciples of the Prophet, great scholars or historical heroes like conquerors.
4. The prophets prior to Islam.
5. Those who deviate from the normal Islamic morals, such as madmen (*majnūn*), pagan as well as Islamic or Jewish saints, and ancient heroes like pharaohs.

Then, which of the aforementioned four theories of saints can be the foundation for authorizing each of these types? The *walī* theory of Sufism supports the first type. The second type is supported by sayyid/sharifology and Shi'ite imamology. The third and fourth type can be supported by the *walī* theory of Sunni theology. Only the fifth type has no evidence in Islamic studies, although when it is recorded in the hagiographies it is often related to a person or a thing that has some kind of Islamic value.

I believe it already becomes clear that the marginalization of saints in Islam is erroneous. This way of thinking originates from the dichotomy of Sufi saint theory and the actual practice of saint cults, which often includes indigenous non-Islamic elements which have been intermingled with Islam by Sufism. We should underline the fact that saints actually observed in the field have been supported by some theory in the Islamic tradition. Now I will move on to the investigation of some notions about saint cults from the standpoint of Islamic studies.

First comes a *karāma* (miracle). As was shown, this has been a central theme for saint theory in Islam. It is within the 'orthodox' creed for the saints to do miracles. The theological documents not only mention miracles

'Ambiguity in context' according to Islamic thought 81

Figure 7 Man praying at the tomb of a saint in Delhi (Dargah Hazrat Khwaja Muhammad Qutbuddin Bakhtiyar Kaki, 19 March 2008). Photograph: Yasushi Tonaga.

abstractly, but also support concrete miracles as 'orthodox'. Al-Nasafī writes as follows:

> The *karāma* (miracle) of *walī* is truth. Allah shows His blessings for *walī* through the destroying of His customs. For example, space warps in an instant, the appearance of food, drink or clothes, when they are needed, and walking on the water...[12]

Al-Taftāzānī describes miracles more vividly when he comments this main text.

> And then (al-Nasafī) raises his opinion referring to the (general) explanation of *karāma* and the details of some miracles which seem almost impossible to happen as follows. [The *karāma* (miracle) of *walī* is truth. Allah shows His blessings for *walī* through the destroying His customs. For example, space warp in an instant.] This is something like that the fellows of Sulaymān (Solomon) brought the throne of Bilkīs (the queen of Sheba) in

---

12   Nasafī 1993:26.

an instant. [Appearance of food, drink or clothes when they are needed] is something like what (happened) to Maryam (Mary, the mother of Jesus). Because the exalted God mentioned as follows. 'Everytime he enters the sanctuary visiting her, he found some food in front of her. He said, Oh Maryām, why (did) it (come) to you? She said, This was (given) from Allah.' (Qur'an 3:37) [Walking on the water] is like what has been mentioned about many *walīs*...[13]

In Sufism also, we can find descriptions of such concrete miracles.[14]

About *baraka*, which means blessings, I do not think that Islamic studies pick it up as a special topic. Its existence, however, has been taken for granted. Mediation by saints is *shafā'a* and it appears in the Qur'an:

> No one will have the capacity to intercede, save he who has received a promise from the Gracious One. (Nobody has the power of mediation (*shafā'a*) except those who are permitted by the Merciful (Allah).
>
> (Qur'an 19:87[15])

To seek mediation is expressed by such words as *tawassul, istighātha, tashaffu'* and *tawajjuh*. I have not yet investigated the usage of these words in Islamic studies in general. But I have some evidences in the documents of the *'ulamā'*. When they rebutted the Wahhābī's attack on seeking mediations, they took their existence for granted (Tonaga 1995).

Pilgrimage to the shrines is called *ziyāra*. In Sunnism, it is generally considered as a custom of the Prophet (*sunna*) and hadith has documents on it, although some are against this opinion. In Twelver Shi'ism scholars have theorized and promoted it (Yoshida 2004). I have not enough evidence about customs such as votive offering (*nadhr*) which are often performed during the pilgrimage. Nor have I yet investigated the notion of festival (*mawlid*), which I can only imagine is not a topic in Islamic studies at the moment.

After such a brief overview I would like to draw your attention to the fact that even when Islamic studies do not talk about a topic, we cannot easily conclude that the topic was denied or was not discussed because opinion was acquiesced. The case of '*baraka*' is a good example of something not discussed simply because it was taken for granted. We should also underline that the arguments in Islamic scholarly discourse have not addressed pilgrimage or the festival themselves, but rather the practices on such occasions.

---

13 Taftāzānī 1987:92.
14 For the case of al-Tirmidhî, see Radtke 2002:110.
15 We can find similar expressions also in Qur'an 20:109, 34:23 etc.

figure 8 The veneration of a sacred tree at the Mausoleum of the Sufi saint Bahā' al-Dīn Naqshband, Bukhara, Uzbekistan, 7 September 2013 (photograph: Yasushi Tonaga).

Conclusion

What I have argued in this chapter is summarized in the following three points. First, basically speaking, the existence of saints and their miracles belong to the great tradition. Second, related to the first, many saints have their own authentic bases in Islamic studies. Third, the practices are often supported by Islamic studies, although in some other cases they are not. I believe it is now clear that there are dichotomous understandings of theory and actuality about saints and saint cults, and exclusively ascribing the former to Sufism and the latter to indigenous customs is erroneous. I would like to underline the three points. First, there are several types of theories of saints in Islamic studies. Second, actual practices of saint cult have not always been disconnected from the theory. Third, and last, we should scrutinize the gradation between theory and actuality.

References

von Grunebaum, G. E. 1976. 'The Problem: Unity in Diversity'. In *Unity and Variety in Muslim Civilization*, (ed.) G.E. von Grunebaum, pp. 17-37. Chicago, The University of Chicago Press.

Ibn Hanbal, Ahmad. 1313 (A.H.) *Musnad*. Misr (Cairo), al-Matbaʻa al-Maymanīya, vol. 3.

Knysh, A. 2007. *al-Qushayri's Epistle on Sufism: al-Risala al-Qushayriyya fī 'Ilm al-Tasawwuf*. Reading, Garnet Publishing.

Nasafī. Najīm al-Dīn Abū Hafs 'Umar al-. 1993. *al-'Aqīda al-Nasafīya*, Bayrūt (Beyrut), Dār al-Bashā'ir al-Islāmīya.

Qushayrī, Abū al-Qāsim 'Abd al-Karīm b. Hawāzin al-. 1998. *al-Risāla al-Qushayrīya*. Bayrūt (Beyrut), Dār al-Kutub al-'Ilmīya. (Trans. by A. Knysh, 2007, *al-Qushayri's Epistle on Sufism: al-Risala al-Qushayriyya fī 'Ilm al-Tasawwuf*. Reading, Garnet Publishing.)

Radtke, B. 2002. 'Walī: general survey'. *Encyclopaedia of Islam* (new ed., vol. 11), 109–112. Leiden, Brill,.

Samhūdī, 'Alī b. 'Abd Allāh al-. 1984. *Jawāhir al-'Iqdayn fī Fadl al-Sharafayn*. Al-Bunāy al-'Alīlī (ed.), vol. 2., Baghdad, Wizāra al-Awqāf wa al-Shu'ūn al-Dīnīya.

Taftāzānī, Sa'd al-Dīn Mas'ūd b. 'Umar al-. 1987. *Sharh al-'Aqāid al-Nasafīya*, al-Qāhira (Cairo), Maktaba al-Kullīyāt al-Azharīya,

Tahāwī. Abū Ja'far Ahmad b. Mhammad al-. 1993. *al-'Aqīda al-Tahāwīya*, Bayrūt (Beyrut), Dār al-Bashā'ir al-Islāmīya.

Tonaga, Y. 1995. 'Sunnism and Sufism: on the rebutter to the Wahhabis'. In T. Masataka (ed.). *Circulation of Islamic Thought*, 211–236. Tokyo, Eiko Publishers. (東長靖「スンナ派とスーフィズム－ワッハーブ派への反批判をめぐって」竹下政孝編『イスラームの思考回路』（講座イスラーム世界第4巻），栄光教育文化研究所，1995年3月， 211–36頁).

Wensinck, A.J. 1979 [1932]. *The Muslim Creed: Its Genesis and Historical Development*. Cambridge. Reprinted New Delhi, Oriental Books Reprint Corporation.

Yoshida, Kyoko (2004). 'Theoretical aspect of the pilgrimage in Ithna-'Ashariya'. *Religious Studies*. 341:207–28 (吉田京子「12イマーム・シーア派参詣の理論的側面」『宗教研究』341号、2004年、207–28頁).

II

Pilgrimages and sacred places in the Indo-Persian world and China

CHAPTER 4

Chinese, Tibetan and Mongol Buddhists on Wutaishan (China) from the eighteenth to the twenty-first century

Isabelle Charleux

The Wutaishan 五臺山 Mountain in North China, one of the most important Buddhist pilgrimage destinations of East Asia, attracted pilgrims from the entire Buddhist world during the first millennium. It was believed to be the abode of Mañjuśrī, the embodiment of the buddhas' wisdom. From the eighteenth to the twenty-first century, this holy site mostly attracted Mongol and Tibetan followers of Tibetan Gélukpa Buddhism and Chinese[1] followers of Chinese Buddhism, as well as a small number of other ethnicities such as Manchus, Nepalese and Japanese. Two different clergies live on the mountain: monks of Tibetan Gélukpa Buddhism or lamas (called the yellow monks because they dress in yellow), and monks and nuns of Chinese Buddhism or *heshang* 和尚 (called the blue monks because they dress in blue).[2] In addition, local popular Chinese cults are flourishing. Wutaishan remains one of the most active Buddhist centres in modern and contemporary China.

The phenomenon of a shared place of pilgrimage is commonplace in China, where Daoism, Confucianism and Buddhism have cohabited, competed and influenced each other for centuries on the same sites, due to less centralized control and less emphasis on exclusivity than in some other cultures (Naquin and Yü 1992b; Robson 2009). But Wutaishan stood out

---

1   Here 'Chinese' must be understood as denoting the Han 'ethnicity'. I will mostly consider here the two main categories of pilgrims, the Chinese and Mongols – but further studies on this topic should include Tibetans.
2   I will use the terms of yellow and blue monasteries and clergy in this article to avoid any reference to ethnicity.

in inner (Han) China, as the Mongol and Tibetan presence has made it the China's main international pilgrimage site, where various ethnicities viewed as 'Barbarians' interacted with Han Chinese. Wutaishan thus became the main place in China where the Chinese and Tibeto-Mongol Buddhist traditions met in the modern period, entered into competition and eventually dialogued, when in the 1930s Chinese masters studied with Tibetan masters and created a Chinese Gélukpa form of Buddhism (Tuttle 2006). On Wutaishan, questions of competition between religious traditions are superimposed upon questions of ethnicity. It may be interesting to compare this situation with pilgrimages of Uyghur and Chinese Hui to the same holy Muslim sites in Xinjiang.

When Buddhists of different traditions and different ethnicities worshipped at the same site, did they make the same pilgrimage, or should the Wutaishan pilgrimage be viewed as the sum of a number of multi-vocal ethnic pilgrimages? In my book *Nomads on Pilgrimage* (2015),[3] I evidence the contribution of the Mongol pilgrims to the general economic and religious development of Wutaishan in the late nineteenth and early twentieth century. The pilgrimage to Wutaishan was an opportunity for major economic exchanges between Mongol herders (who sold cattle and flocks at the Chinese market), Wutaishan monks and Chinese merchants. Taihuai 臺懷, the central village of Wutaishan, was a busy trade centre that allowed a population of traders and shopkeepers, and also peasants and beggars, to live off the success of the pilgrimage. But were interactions limited to commercial issues, and how far could they go in other fields, for instance of religion, intellectual exchange or personal friendship? Did these different peoples cohabit without conflicts? Could they share a feeling of *communitas* and share common goals, expectations and experiences, or did they behave as individuals with distinct ethnicities and religious traditions? Theories in pilgrimage studies can help us make sense of the very rich Wutaishan material. I will discuss two hypotheses made by Elverskog (2011) about Wutaishan as a central place of *communitas*,

---

3 In my book on the Mongols' pilgrimages to Wutaishan, I used both written and visual historical sources combined with modern anthropological observation. The Mongols left more than 340 stone inscriptions that give clues about why they came to Wutaishan and where they came from. I photographed or copied all the legible stelae and created a database (some of these stelae are listed in Ürinkiyaya 1999:2141–7, nos. 12610–47 and pp. 2178–211, nos. 12786–996). I also used a travel account written by Miyvacir (2008 [1942]), a Mongol duke of the Alasha banner (Western Inner Mongolia) about a pilgrimage he made to Wutaishan in 1938, guidebooks written by Mongol and Tibetan clerics, and travel accounts and gazetteers written by Chinese pilgrims and literati, as well as Western travel literature.

first among Mongols, and second between Mongols, Manchus, Tibetans and Chinese in the Qing empire.

Is Wutaishan Chinese, Mongol or Tibetan?

The geographical configuration of Wutaishan is rather original. It does not look like other Chinese pilgrimage sites – which typically are steep mountains with staircases leading from one monastery to the other, up to the summit, and can be climbed in one or two days; neither does it look like a holy Tibetan mountain which must be circumambulated in a clockwise direction. Wutaishan literally means 'Five-terraced mountain(s)', referring to its five summits with flat tops (all of them about 3,000 metres above sea level), one at each of the cardinal points and the fifth in the middle, surrounding a high valley. The main monasteries are grouped around a gigantic white stupa enshrining a relic of buddha Shakyamuni, but all told, in the early twentieth century there were no less than 99 blue and 26 yellow monasteries, plus hundreds of sacred springs, stones, grottoes and trees ('numinous sites') to visit. There was great freedom about the number and order of places to visit: depending on one's financial means and the aim of the visit, one could make a short (3- or 4-day) journey to worship the dozen must-see places (called the 'small pilgrimage'), a one-week journey including a pilgrimage to the peaks, weather permitting (the 'great pilgrimage'),[4] or a one-month stay to worship most of the holy sites and walk in the mountains, hoping to receive a vision of the Bodhisattva.[5]

Wutaishan is located at the crossroads between Tibet, China and Mongolia. Its landscape, vistas and flora are close to that of the Eastern Tibetan plateau, and Tibetan devotees sometimes consider it as a Tibetan area. For Chinese visitors, Wutaishan has a strong Tibetan flavour, with its population of yellow-clad lamas, its many Tibetan-style stupas, prayer-wheels and Tantric iconography. In the Manchu Qing dynasty (1644–1911), Wutaishan was called 'the Tibet of China' on an imperial stone inscription, and was seen as a Tibetan enclave on the edge of Chinese territory. The head lama of Wutaishan was the representative of the Dalai Lama in China. However, in the nineteenth century, the crowds of Mongols with their yurts

---

4   The pilgrimage of Duke Miyvacir in 1938 is quite representative of the minimum tour for a Mongol (2008 [1942]:403–7). For Chinese pilgrims, see the accounts of the lay Buddhist Gao Henian 2000 [1949] who visited Wutaishan in 1903 and 1912, and of the renowned Chan master Xuyun (1840?–1959) who visited Wutaishan in 1882–3 (Xuyun 1988).
5   Nowadays, due to modern means of transport and the high cost of travel, modern pilgrims generally spend no more than two or three days on Wutaishan.

and flocks who came to worship and trade considerably outnumbered other ethnicities, so Wutaishan also appeared to be an extension of the Mongol plateau. Wutaishan was therefore a perfect meeting place for Buddhists of Tibet, China and Mongolia.

Yet the temples' architecture was kept purely Chinese, except for the Tibetan white bottle-shaped stupas and prayer-wheels.[6] From the thirteenth century on, Tibetan Buddhist communities settled in eighteen ancient, damaged Chinese monasteries, restored them, and adapted their practices and way of life to these Chinese buildings. The eight yellow monasteries that were founded anew in the eighteenth and nineteenth centuries also adopted Chinese architecture, as if Wutaishan was a sanctuary that respected older architectural styles. However, the statues inside and decoration of the yellow monasteries were purely Tibetan. Conversely, the blue monasteries borrowed Tibetan elements such as stupas, prayer-wheels and Tibetan forms of deities. In addition, some monasteries often hired monks of another tradition (and ethnicity) to attract more donors. Wutaishan monasteries therefore seem to have more common features than differences, to such an extent that it is not always obvious for a pilgrim whether he/she is visiting a yellow or a blue monastery.

A layered history

Wutaishan was a holy place for Daoists in the first centuries AD, then from the fourth century onwards Chinese Buddhists of different schools appropriated the mountain. In the thirteenth century, the Mongol emperors of the Yuan dynasty established Tibetan Buddhist monasteries. In addition, the Chinese lay population practised rites of the Chinese popular religion, and the cults of the God of Wealth, Emperor Guan 關帝 and the Jade Emperor, along with processions, opera and communal rituals are still very much alive.

Wutaishan was strongly linked to imperial power, because it was a key sacred site for the ritual protection of the empires that ruled China. Tantric rituals for the protection of the state were practised in the Tang dynasty by Chinese and Central Asian masters; later, the Ming and Qing emperors entrusted lamas to perform similar rituals. The eighteenth-century Changkya Khutugtu Rölpé Dorjé (1717–86) threw bolts of fire from Wutaishan over a distance of hundreds of kilometres to crush a southern rebellion, thus protecting the Qing armies. The Qing emperors presented themselves to Tibetans and Mongols as emanations of the Bodhisattva Manjushri and were patrons of the Gélukpa School, making Wutaishan a key political place for

---

6   Only one monastery, the Cifusi, presents minor architectural Tibetan characteristics.

figure 1   Pilgrims from Central Tibet examining a Xerox copy of the xylograph map of Wutaishan made in 1846. © Isabelle Charleux.

establishing their multi-ethnic empire. Three of them visited Wutaishan in person.

Tibetan Buddhists superimposed their imprint upon the layered past of Wutaishan. Besides building Chinese-style monasteries and Tibetan-style stupas, they established new rituals and festivals, introduced new narratives (apparitions of Tibetan Buddhist deities, legends of Tsongkhapa's visit) and 'discovered' new 'numinous sites' where deities and saints such as Padmasambhava and Avalokiteshvara revealed themselves to devotees or left footprints on a rock. The xylograph map of Wutaishan made in 1846 by a Mongol lama at the Cifusi Monastery (Figure 1), along with Tibetan and Mongolian guidebooks to Wutaishan, shows the superimposition of these different narratives (Chou 2007). The Tibetan Buddhists viewed Wutaishan as populated by a greater number of buddhas, saints and deities than the Chinese: besides Manjushri (who is one of the most important Bodhisattvas in both traditions) and the dragons he tamed (who were turned into one of his manifestations), Yamantaka (Manjushri's fierce manifestation) is a main protector of the place, and Tsongkhapa or his reincarnation, Padmasambhava, Avalokiteshvara and the White Old Man are said to have appeared or resided there, thus diluting the importance of Manjushri.

In the early twentieth century, the yellow monasteries lost their influence because of economic and political difficulties, and survived thanks to

Figure 2 'Han lamas' of the syncretic Tibeto-Chinese tradition of Buddhism, Guangzongsi Monastery. © Isabelle Charleux.

Mongols' donations. But the Chinese tradition of Master Li Xiangshan 李向善, known as Puji Heshang 普濟和尚, who collected large amounts of donations in North China, invigorated the Wutaishan monastic economy. He propagated teachings of the 'Way of Nine Palaces', a northern Chinese religious movement that emphasized the syncretism between Buddhism, Daoism and Confucianism. From 1877 to 1937, he and his disciples appropriated more than twenty monasteries on Wutaishan that were integrated into a national Chinese network, and spent seven million silver dollars to restore or rebuild them. These monasteries were furnished with Buddhist, Daoist and popular Chinese icons (Laozi, Confucius, the Jade Emperor etc.).

While the Way of Nine Palaces declined in the 1940s, the syncretic Tibeto-Chinese tradition of Buddhism flourished on Wutaishan, when the three Chinese masters Nenghai (1886–1967), Fazun (1886–1980, a pioneer in the translation of major Gélukpa doctrinal texts into Chinese) and Qinghai (1922–

90) were active on the mountain. The 'Han lamas' re-appropriated seven old yellow and blue monasteries. Their tradition radiated out from Wutaishan to the whole of China, and their second- and third-generation Han and Mongol disciples continue to practise Chinese Gélukpa Buddhism there (Figure 2).

Cohabitation and cultural mixing of blue and yellow monk communities

The Chinese and Tibetan (Tibeto-Mongol) traditions of Buddhism both stem from the same tradition, the Great Vehicle of Buddhism (Mahayana), but differ in their liturgies, rituals, organization of the canon, way of life, practices and pantheon. Esotericism forms an important component of the Tibetan tradition, while it was almost completely removed from the Chinese tradition in the ninth century. Chinese, Tibetan and Mongol monks wear different garments and are visually distinct (with the exception of modern Chinese Gélukpa lamas).

Chinese fantasies concerning Tibetan monks were and are still composed of a mixture of fascination and repulsion, and have produced long-lasting stereotypes. The Tibetan tradition gained influence in China from the thirteenth century onwards but suffered strong criticism from Confucian officials, who were horrified by Tantric deities in sexual union and performances of magic feats (Charleux 2002). Many Chinese perceived Tibetan Buddhism as a corrupted form of religion practised by 'Barbarians': lamas looked like monks but were not – they ate meat and (some of them) could marry. Of course racism against Barbarians added to the accusations of heterodoxy. But some Chinese who were fascinated by esoteric teachings and magic powers took a Tibetan master and became lamas themselves.

Although the Qing state tried to segregate ethnicities and considered the 'teaching of the lamas' as distinct from (Chinese) Buddhism, and reserved for Tibetans and Mongols only, Wutaishan appeared to be an exception in China. A priori, *heshang* were Chinese and lamas were Tibetans and Mongols, but the clergy of the yellow and blue monasteries was not completely homogeneous ethnically. In the early Qing, Wutaishan's mixed Buddhist communities reflected the multi-ethnicity of the empire. A few Chinese and Manchu lamas lived in the yellow monasteries along with Tibetan and Mongol lamas, and Chinese *heshang* and lamas performed imperially sponsored rituals together for the protection of the state.

Besides, in the early twentieth century, a Mongol monk educated both in Mongolian and in Chinese could, (and still can) be trained in a Chinese monastery, and later relatively easily change affiliation. The Chinese Gélukpa community, which was initially ethnically Han, now accepts Inner Mongols and even Tibetans from Amdo into their ranks (the language spoken in these

Figure 3   Crowds of pilgrims attending the great festival and Chinese opera of the Wanfoge/Wuyemiao (Dragon King Temple). © Isabelle Charleux.

monasteries is Mandarin). Inner Mongol and Tibetan nuns also enrol in Chinese Buddhist nunneries because they can obtain a higher ordination than in Tibetan Buddhism.

The second reason for this religious and cultural mixing was economic: unlike local temples, which were supported by the community, the main source of income for many pilgrimage centres was anonymous donors. Before the nineteenth century, all great and historically important monasteries received subsidies and donations from the imperial court. But after the decline of the Manchu patronage followed by the economic crisis of the mid-nineteenth century, the competition became stiffer: all monasteries had to turn towards pilgrims' donations to survive, especially those of the Mongols, who came by the thousands. In the early twentieth century, in order to welcome and receive donations from Mongol pilgrims, three large blue monasteries (Tayuansi, Xiantongsi, Shuxiangsi) invited a few Mongol lamas to be in residence, and conducted regular offices both in Chinese and in Tibetan. This practice has survived into the twenty-first century: in 2007, at the great festival of the Five Dragon Kings Temple, while Chinese opera was performed on the stage of the first courtyard (Figure 3), a Mongol lama was invited to read Tibetan texts in the back courtyard. However, nowadays the situation is generally reversed, as donations now mostly come from the Chinese: so the Tibetan monasteries have rooms for Chinese ancestors' tablets and a greater number of Chinese icons. The Wutaishan monasteries also used to send their more persuasive monks to China, Tibet, Mongolia and as far as Buryatia to collect funds: these monks went from place to place to gather donations in money, gold or cattle.

Competition therefore existed between blue and yellow monasteries, which both borrowed from each other and tried to attract the same pilgrims. As explained above, yellow monasteries first appropriated ancient blue temples; then the disciples of Monk Puji and the Chinese Gélukpa gained influence and appropriated ancient Tibetan monasteries. During the nineteenth century, antagonism appeared between the Han lamas of the Luohousi Monastery and the Tibetan and Mongol lamas of its monastic hostelry, the Shifangtang, and the latter founded a new monastery. But generally speaking the monasteries competed peacefully with each other to attract visitors and their donations, offering the same services while at the same time distinguishing themselves by having a particular statue, stupa, relic or famous living saint.

This porous ethnic and religious frontier between Chinese and Tibeto-Mongol Buddhist communities exists in other Chinese places such as Beijing, Chengdu or Amdo, but the cultural mixing appears to be much more extensive on Wutaishan.

Did Chinese, Mongols and Tibetans undertake the same or different pilgrimages?

The Wutaishan pilgrimage had a different meaning for Chinese and Mongol pilgrims, but Wutaishan is first and foremost the residence of the Bodhisattva Manjushri, and all pilgrims wished to encounter one of the various guises of the Bodhisattva or witness one of his luminous manifestations. Many of them made the vow to go on pilgrimage once in their life, or to thank Manjushri when a prayer was fulfilled. For Chinese pilgrims, Wutaishan was one of the four sacred mountains to visit (along with Putuoshan in Zhejiang province, Jiuhuashan in Anhui province and Emeishan in Sichuan province), each being the abode of a particular Bodhisattva. Mongol pilgrims said that any good Buddhist had to do the pilgrimage at least once in their lifetime, and they found it highly desirable to be buried there in order to be reborn in paradise.

Pilgrims were monks and laypersons, both men and women, and belonged to all social classes, from literati and nobles to commoners. Pilgrims' records and stone inscriptions show that Chinese and Mongols had similar reasons to undertake the pilgrimage: to accumulate merit and gain a better reincarnation (the official Buddhist aim), gain blessings, fortune, health, longevity, reputation, and sometimes to ask for a particular wish (curing a disease, asking for an heir) or to do a penance. Other non-religious reasons to visit Wutaishan often added to the motivation of making a pilgrimage: trade (many Mongols sold cattle and horses to the Chinese at the great fair of the sixth lunar month), leisure/tourism (literati enjoying the scenery and writing

Figure 4 Lama-pilgrim from Amdo (Eastern Tibet) in great prostration towards the Great White Stupa of the Tayuansi Monastery. © Isabelle Charleux.

Figure 5 Groups of monk- and lay pilgrims praying in the shadow towards the Great White Stupa of the Tayuansi Monastery. © Isabelle Charleux.

Figure 6   Mongol lamas perform a ritual requested by pilgrims and bless Mongol and Han Chinese pilgrims, Luohousi Monastery. © Isabelle Charleux.

poems), political motivations (travelling with the emperor), research (on the history of Buddhism on Wutaishan) and so forth.

Gestures and practices at monasteries

All pilgrims share basic Buddhist gestures and practices. Pilgrims preferably made the pilgrimage on foot (except for the old and infirm), and while walking, prayed and counted the beads of their rosaries. They all made prostrations, ranging from simple bows to full-length prostrations (Figures 4 and 5). Some penitent Mongols and Chinese made and still make full-length prostrations every third step, all the way from their homes, generally begging for their food on the way. Foreign travellers have described their pitiful appearance with ragged clothes and bleeding wounds in spite of protection on their hands and knees. In all Buddhist cultures, religious merit is gained through penitence, but also through giving to the clergy. Major donations were recorded in stone, and smaller ones on paper certificates. Pilgrims also asked for specific rituals (for a long life, to consecrate statues, or to pray for their dead parents), attended monks' assemblies and mass teachings and festivals (Figure 6).

The main difference between Mongol and Tibetan, and Chinese practices was the importance of circumambulation for the former two. One of the terms for pilgrimage in Tibetan is *nékor*, lit. 'circuiting, going around a place',

Figure 7 Han Chinese pilgrims turning a prayer wheel while circumambulating it, Tayuansi Monastery. © Isabelle Charleux.

and in Mongolian, *ergil mörgül*, lit. 'circumambulation while praying/bowing'. In their respective countries, Mongols and Tibetans used to circumambulate the precincts of monasteries – usually following a path punctuated by small shrines, prayer-wheels and stupas – as well as stupas, statues, individual and groups of temples, shrines, cairns, holy trees and whole mountains. This practice, which goes back to Indian Buddhism, was followed by Central Asians and Chinese during the first millennium, but was later abandoned by the Chinese. On Wutaishan, the Chinese architecture of monasteries did not facilitate or even allow for circumambulation, but Mongols and Tibetans practised it wherever it was possible: around stupas, the central Lingjiu 靈鷲 Peak and around the monasteries that were not located right next to a cliff or a precipice.

The other differences in practices and behaviour amongst Chinese, Tibetan and Mongol pilgrims appear to be rather minor. Tibetan and Mongol pilgrims prayed while turning a hand-held prayer-wheel, burnt juniper instead of incense (when available), wrote prayers and ex-votos on 'wind-horse' flags, threw 'wind-horse' papers to be scattered by the wind, asked to be blessed by reincarnated lamas and received from them protective objects (knots, amulets, pills). The Chinese pilgrims always burnt incense when kowtowing in front of icons, set off firecrackers, and practised *fangsheng* 放生 (i.e. releasing animals) and rites to their ancestors (they burnt paper offerings to be transmitted to the dead).

Twenty-first century Chinese pilgrims are also observed performing circumambulations around stupas, turning prayer-wheels (Figure 7), crawling into the womb cave at Fomudong and asking high lamas to bless them; and Mongols and Tibetans also burn paper offerings to the dead and release live squirrels. However, practices may be the same while understandings differ.

Worship of natural numinous sites

When visiting a monastery, the pilgrims enjoyed the mediation of the residing monks and were expected to follow a codified behaviour and to perform normative devotional practices (the basic one, nowadays, being to make three prostrations in front of the statues while a monk hits a gong three times, indicating that the deity has received the homage, and then putting some money in the donation box). But when they visited natural sites endowed with numinous powers, without the mediation of monks, the pilgrims generally adopted an attitude of 'open behavioural code' with emphasis on personal direct experience.[7] With less institutional control, devotional practices and beliefs at the 'numinous traces' (*lingji* 靈蹟) often stemmed from indigenous (Mongol, Tibetan or Chinese) practices turned towards this-worldly expectations: they generally aimed at bringing good luck and material benefits to this life. All pilgrims collected products of the mountain: water at one of the many sacred springs that cured a thousand illnesses, miraculous ice that never melted, stones, earth, pine cones etc.; and rubbed their bodies on buddhas' footprints in stone. Everything that grew on Wutaishan was filled with spiritual power, which was believed to be transferable to individual pilgrims. Pilgrims might also spend the night on a peak hoping to see an apparition of the Bodhisattva or to see the 'buddha lights' for which Wutaishan was famous. Thus, the holy site was experienced with the five senses: contact – with holy footprints, with the earth through prostrations; taste – by ingesting products of the mountain; and the sight, smell and sound of numinous apparitions and phenomena.[8] The Mongols also practised rituals of their own popular religion such as crawling into a narrow womb cave, a rite of rebirth and fertility. This ritual was common in various parts of Mongolia but was unknown in China and in Tibet (Tibetans have 'karma testing' rituals between rocks or in narrow tunnel caves, which

---

7   On pilgrimages ranging in structure from the highly formal (stressing social ritual) like the *hajj* to Mecca, to the highly informal (oriented towards personal expression), see Morinis 1992:14–15.
8   For similar practices in Tibetan pilgrimages, see Buffetrille 1996:296–307; Huber 1994:38.

are different from the womb-cave fertility rituals). Nowadays on Wutaishan, Chinese and Tibetan pilgrims also crawl into the womb cave, following the Mongols' practice. It is well known that at pilgrimage sites shared by different religions or religious schools, the pilgrims tend to imitate what others do and to borrow rituals that do not belong to their own tradition.[9]

The monasteries visited by pilgrims of different ethnicities and confessions

Pilgrims to Wutaishan had a tendency to favour worship at and donations to monasteries of their own confession, but also visited some famous and ancient monasteries of the other Buddhist tradition. The pilgrims started at the White Stupa and the monasteries of Lingjiu Peak, kowtowed to the holy icon of Manjushri in the Pusading and to the one in the Shuxiangsi to inform the Bodhisattva that they had come to fulfil a vow, and continued their pilgrimage according to their priorities, their aim and the weather (on Wutaishan, sudden snowstorms, thunderstorms and hailstorms can happen even in mid-summer and prevent pilgrims from visiting the terraces).

Mongols' Interest in Chinese Buddhism

During the late Qing period, the Mongols showed interest in Chinese Buddhism (Atwood 1992–3) and in its Indian heritage (the White Ashoka Stupa, the Sandalwood buddha); they were conscious of belonging to a Qing multi-ethnic empire united by Buddhism (Elverskog 2006). Mongol devotees from Beijing built a pavilion to enshrine a copy of a famous Sino-Indian statue within the Dailuoding (a blue monastery), and even wrote a whole guidebook about the Shuxiangsi (a blue monastery).[10]

The literate Mongols and Tibetans had access to the Mongol and Tibetan guidebooks, as well as the Chinese gazetteers translated in their own language that informed them that they should see particular sites or icons. The guidebooks as well as the 1846 map propagated the mountain's lore, which was continuously enriched with new stories and events.

Chinese and Mongol pilgrims also interpreted some deities and their icons differently. For instance, the icon of the 'Mother of buddha(s)' (Fomu 佛母), an epithet of Prajnaparamita (in the Fomudong and the Yuhuangmiao 玉皇廟/Puhuasi 普化寺) – an archetypal female deity – was commonly identified

---

9   See the chapters in Albera and Couroucli (eds.) 2009. According to them, holy sites that stand outside the control of religious or political authorities are believed to have more efficacy, and at these sites, inter-confessional frontiers become blurred.

10 *Üjesküleng secig-ün erike kemegdekü orušiba*, written around 1813.

Monasteries	Buddhist tradition	Specificity	Stelae in Ch.	Mon.	Tib.
Monasteries visited by all pilgrims					
Tayuansi 塔院寺	blue (+ lamas)	White Stupa enshrining a relic of Shakyamuni, stele with (a reproduction of) the footprints of Shakyamuni, small stupa enshrining a hair of Manjushri	13	61	–
Shuxiangsi 殊像寺	blue (+ lamas)	'True portrait' of Manjushri with the Buckwheat Head	4	1	–
Xiantongsi 顯通寺	blue (+ lamas)	Beamless Hall, Bronze Hall, 5 stupas representing the 5 terraces, famous ancient relics	5	5	1
Pusading 菩薩頂	yellow	Imperial monastery, 'true portrait' of Manjushri, 108 steps representing the 108 passions to crush with the feet, in order to be cleansed from defilement and freed of sufferings	–	1	–
Luohousi 羅睺寺	yellow	Revolving lotus that opens to reveal a buddha statue when activated by a hidden mechanism, Pine Tree Holy Stupa, White Manjushri	1	47	–
Yuanzhaosi 圓照寺	yellow	Stele of the 'Begging Manjushri,' Shariputra's funerary stupa	4	7	–
Dailuoding 黛螺頂	blue	5 statues of Manjushri representing the 5 terraces, Sandalwood buddha	–	2	–
Jin'gangku 金剛窟	yellow	Vajra Cave that closed itself when Monk Buddhapali disappeared with Manjushri in 683 AD, treasure cave, Manjushri's tooth and handprints	–	–	–
Shouningsi 壽寧寺	yellow	Statue of Old Manjushri	1	2	–
Wanfoge 萬佛閣	blue	Dragon King, now the most popular icon on Wutaishan	–	–	–
Fanxianshan 梵仙山	blue	Terrace to throw 'wind-horse' papers	–	–	–
5 monasteries of the 5 terraces	–	Many sacred springs, ponds, rocks, footprints of Manjushri etc.	–	1 per monastery	–
Monasteries especially visited by Mongol and Tibetan pilgrims					
Zhenhaisi 鎮海寺	yellow	Funerary stupa of the Third Changkya Khutugtu	–	5	–
Fomudong 佛母洞	blue	Womb cave	–	2	–
Guanyindong 觀音洞	yellow	Place where the Sixth Dalai Lama, the Thirteenth Dalai Lama and Avalokiteshvara have meditated; sacred spring that gives fertility	–	1	–

Monasteries	Buddhist tradition	Specificity	Stelae in Ch.	Stelae in Mon.	Stelae in Tib.
Shancaidong 善財洞	yellow	Place where the Third Changkya Khutugtu lived and meditated; sacred spring	–	2	–
Baohuasi 寶華寺	yellow	Stupa enshrining a hair of Tsongkhapa	–	1	2
Shifangtang 十方堂	yellow	Lodging centre for lama pilgrims	–	182	3
Cifusi 慈福寺	yellow	Lodging centre for lama pilgrims	–	7	–
Sanquansi 三泉寺	yellow	Three sacred springs	–	9	1
Monasteries especially visited by Chinese pilgrims					
Nanshansi 南山寺	blue	108 stairs, stupa containing the bowl and the robe of Monk Puji	20	2	–
Longquansi 龍泉寺	blue	Puji's funerary stupa	–	–	–
Bishansi 碧山寺	blue	Monastery that organizes monks' ordinations	6	1	–
Qingliangshi 清涼寺石	blue	2.2 m-high stone called Manjushri's bed	–	–	–
Zhulinsi 竹林寺	blue	Famous historical monastery	–	–	–
Jin'gesi 金閣寺	blue	Famous historical monastery	–	–	–

Table 1   Major monasteries on Wutaishan and numbers of non-imperial donation stelae of the Qing and Republican periods

as Tara by the Mongols and the Tibetans, and as Bodhisattva Guanyin by the Chinese. The Indra Palace Temple (Dishigong 帝釋宮, from the name of the deity of Hindu origin) was renamed Yuhuangmiao (Temple of the Jade Emperor) in the Ming dynasty, when Daoists occupied its buildings and identified the Chinese Jade Emperor with Indra. And the Mongol lamas who ran this temple during the late nineteenth century worshipped the same deity under the name of Qormusta Tngri, i.e. the Mongol form of Ahura Mazda (identified with Indra by the Uyghur Buddhists, and transmitted to Mongols during the fourteenth century). As for the Dragon King of the Wanfoge (a local chthonian deity opposed to Buddhism, but tamed by Manjushri and turned into a protector of Wutaishan), he was the major deity of rain and good harvests for the local farmers. His cult developed considerably in the

---

11   The more than 340 stone inscriptions recording major Mongol donations of the late Qing and Republican periods are preserved on the site. This list is not exhaustive, as some inscriptions have disappeared or have been moved, degraded or lost. Comparatively, for that period, Chinese stelae of donations are much less numerous.

early twentieth century, and nowadays all pilgrims, including Tibetans and Mongols, make a vow in front of the Dragon king, who is said to be an emanation of Manjushri, and said to help pilgrims on their journey back home.

To sum up, all pilgrims frequented more or less the same monasteries and worshipped the same icons and relics, although they had their own preferences and different expectations. They shared many common devotional practices, and adapted some of them to the local context (Mongols erected stone inscriptions – which they very rarely did at home– and attended Chinese rituals; Chinese crawled into the womb cave). Although Chinese pilgrims' garments, the practice of burning incense and paper offerings, or Mongols' and Tibetans' prayer-wheels and circumambulations functioned as ethnic and religious markers, Wutaishan could be at the same time pan-Buddhist and multicultural.

Communitas between pilgrims on Wutaishan?

Although Victor Turner's well-known concepts of *communitas* and *liminality*[12] have been seriously challenged by anthropologists,[13] who have emphasized individual experience in pilgrimage,[14] some particular case studies show that the Turnerian model should not be abandoned altogether.[15] Turner's theories come from the study of homogeneous, mono-confessional pilgrimage sites, but they prove even more interesting when applied to shared pilgrimage sites.[16] Due to the long tradition of cohabitation of different schools and religions, most of Chinese pilgrimage sites seem to be shared between Buddhist and Daoists, or between Chinese and Tibetan Buddhists, with more tolerance than, for instance, sacred sites frequented by both Christians and Muslims in the Near East (Naquin and Yü 1992b).

Do the sources I use to study the Wutaishan pilgrimage allow me to speak of a *communitas* according to Turner's meaning, i.e. at the margins or outside society, in a state of *liminality* or *antistructure* characterized by the

---

12 Turner 1978; Turner and Turner 1978. Turner's theory was inspired by the work of Arnold Van Gennep on rites of passage.
13 Notably Morinis 1992:7–8; Eade and Sallnow 1991:4–5; Albera 2009.
14 In the conclusion of the book he edited with M. Couroucli, Albera (2009:351) prefers speaking of pilgrims having common needs (of a supernatural help) and goals, but rarely interacting with each other.
15 See, for instance, Nancy Frey's study of the present-day Santiago pilgrimage, and Holmes-Rodman's study of a healing shrine in New Mexico (in Badone and Roseman 2004).
16 See the different studies on places where Christian and Muslims cohabitate around the Mediterranean Sea in Albera and Couroucli 2009. For an example of a pilgrimage shared by Hindus and Buddhists in Nepal, see Buffetrille 1994.

Figure 8   Photograph of Manjushri Bodhisattva appearing among the clouds, Scripture Hall, Xiantongsi Monastery. © Isabelle Charleux.

spontaneity of relationships and the abolition of social distinctions?[17] I argue that *temporary* forms of *communitas*, where 'persons normally segregated in secular or profane society are, at least symbolically, integrated into a fluid, ecstatic community of common religious purpose'[18] were certainly almost palpable at some precise moments, for instance, during the great festival organized by the main yellow monasteries during the sixth lunar month, with masked dances gathering together two hundred lamas and a great procession of five hundred participants, during mass teachings, and, above all, during collective visions and miracles, such as the 'buddha lights' that were seen by large groups of people without distinction of ethnicity and rank (Figure 8). Rölpé Dorjé's biography records that light phenomena were spotted by

---

17 According to Turner, pilgrimage is fundamentally anti-structural: the rules and constraints of daily life being temporarily suspended, pilgrims experience egalitarian relationships and create a new community.
18 Gimello 1992:136 n43, also 105, 132n. 31.

crowds, especially during and after Tibetan Buddhist empowerment rituals.[19] In the eighteenth century, the crowds of Chinese, Tibetans and Mongols asking for blessings, teachings and initiation from Rölpé Dorjé, and the communities of 'foreign' and Chinese monks performing rituals together under the leadership of the *jasag lama*, evoke forms of *communitas*. In the 1930s, Alley and Lapwood mention

> a huge procession of lamas, Chinese priests and pilgrims, who had been attending an initiation ceremony at a temple up the valley. These were estimated to be about 3,000 persons in all, and their coloured gowns and robes as they filed along the mountain path showed up well against a hillside already bright with flowers.
> (Alley and Lapwood 1935:119)

Pilgrims following the great procession of the sixth-month festival or queuing to enter the womb cave mingled with each other (a Chinese observer noticed that the festival was an opportunity for Chinese to approach pretty Mongol women). Because of the dangers of the roads (from tigers to bandits) and the risk of getting lost in the mountains,[20] pilgrims of different ethnicities occasionally travelled together on the roads leading to Wutaishan, and formed groups when they climbed to the terraces.[21]

Communitas is naturally present in discourses. Since Manjushri can appear on the mountain in many guises such as an old woman, a beggar in rags or a fox, to test people's level of compassion, people say that one has to be kind to everybody because anybody could be Manjushri in a disguise,[22] and generally consciously adopt an attitude of generosity and friendly behaviour. For instance, Khejok Rinpoché's modern Tibetan guide says that 'in a pilgrimage, the pilgrims would cultivate a mind of faith and devotion on the way there.'[23] Yet the pilgrims' discourses, like official propaganda of the site, tend to over-emphasize harmony and brotherhood over disappointment and tensions, and we must be very cautious about them.[24] Susan Naquin noticed

---

19 Biography of Rölpé Dorjé, transl. Chen Qingying and Ma Lianlong 1988:248–9.
20 Stories abound of pilgrims lost in the dark or in the fog and being saved by an emanation of Manjushri. See, for instance, Gao Henian 2000 [1949]:113–44.
21 Gao Henian 2000 [1949]:117.
22 See, for instance, Tuttle 2006:19. Nowadays many beggars in rags hope that people will give them money in case he/she could be the Bodhisattva.
23 Born in 1936, he is the abbot of Dhétsang Monastery in Eastern Tibet. He now teaches in Australia, and made a pilgrimage to Wutaishan in 1999 (Lim 1999).
24 Many scholars working on pilgrimages point out that this ideal of harmony and solidarity is often absent from the observed practices.

for the Chinese pilgrimage to Miaofengshan 妙峰山 that pilgrims behaved as if they formed one harmonious family. But

> private feelings of discomfort, annoyance, or disappointment were to be suppressed; individuals were subtly pressured into such behaviour by their own and other's expectations.
> (Naquin 1992c:363)

It would be safer to speak of peaceful cohabitation, religious tolerance, and curiosity for 'the other'[25] rather than a durable *communitas* in Turner's terms that levels the gap between ordinary pilgrims, monks, aristocrats and literati, or between different nationalities.[26] Temporary moments of *communitas* certainly happened, but cohabitation and tolerance were probably more common than interactions and cultural exchange. As I will show below, my sources rather describe situations that are closer to Eade and Sallnow's theory, which views pilgrimage as a mosaic in which actors are heterogeneous and viewpoints are diverse.[27] The Wutaishan pilgrimage is 'capable of accommodating diverse

---

25 Comparing the sharing of religious sites in the Balkans and in India, Hayden (2002) argues that competitive sharing is compatible with the passive meaning of tolerance (i.e. non-interference), but incompatible with the active meaning of tolerance (acceptation of the Other, respect and recognition while disagreeing with others' beliefs and practices). Positive, active tolerance would be an illusion in the process of the complete appropriation of a holy site by a group. Albera (2009:356) criticizes Hayden and prefers to highlight the plurality of situations and the difficulty of building theories. See also Hayden's reviews in *Current Anthropology* 43(2) and especially Bowman's comments.

26 Similar observations for a mono-confessional pilgrimage site are made by Buffetrille (1997:88 and 2003): in present-day Tibet, 'pilgrimage groups as a rule do not mix with one another'; 'there is not necessarily good fellowship, brotherhood and equality among all the pilgrims [...] which does not exclude mutual aid in case of difficulty'; 'the quality of *communitas* that Turner (1969, 1974, 1978) observes in all the pilgrimages he studied, is in general not present in the Tibetan world, except during very short periods [...] contrary to what one might think, differences of social status persist during the pilgrimage.' See also Huber 1999:18. But Kapstein (1998:112), who insists on the festive dimension of a pilgrimage, does not reject the Turnerian model.

27 Eade and Sallnow (1991) deconstructed both the first trend of pilgrimage studies, of Durkhemian inspiration, that considers pilgrimage as an element of social cohesion that participates in the construction and the maintenance of larger collective identities such as territorial, political or religious communities, and Turner's theory. Both are still valid in pilgrimage studies though. See, for instance, in the Tibetan context Huber's study of a peripheral, popular pilgrimage where

meanings and practices', though it cannot be considered as being 'void' of beliefs and symbols.[28]

A *communitas* between Mongols?

The stone inscriptions of Wutaishan offer us a glimpse of the Mongol donors as they wanted to appear: they do not talk about impoverished herders and indebted nobles (which they actually were); on the contrary, they showcase the extreme generosity of all patrons towards the Wutaishan monasteries. These Mongols travelling in groups mixing men and women, nobles, lamas and commoners, and pooling their money to pay for rituals and offerings to monasteries would seem to offer an image of community.

Elverskog (2011), who argued that a distinct pan-Mongol identity emerged at the end of the Qing dynasty, cemented by Buddhism and by the heritage of Chinggis Khan, while also being a local identity attached to the banner,[29] proposed that the Wutaishan pilgrimage played a prominent role in the creation of a 'Mongol identity'. The pilgrimage may have fostered 'bonds between the stratified social hierarchies institutionalized by the Qing state':

> it is possible to imagine that Mongols of all social ranks came to share a new 'Mongol' *communitas*. [...] at Wutai Shan the boundaries and nature of what it meant to be Mongol, must have been both challenged and reconceptualized.
>
> (Elverskog 2011:254)

As Elverskog acknowledges, this is a deduction 'based on an awareness of the larger historical context' but not on textual evidence. Mongols'

---

identities and cultural practices were forged anew (1999:3—6, 174); also Albera 2009.

28 In opposition to other theories that emphasize a pilgrimage site that is 'full' of beliefs and symbols, Eade and Sallnow insist on its property of 'void', 'capable of accommodating diverse meanings and practices', of offering 'a variety of clients what each of them desires' (1991:15). They advocate analyzing each specific pilgrimage in terms of its particular social context and its "historically and culturally specific behaviors and meanings' (1991:3—5). Pilgrimage resists analysis and theorization: 'if one can no longer take for granted the meaning of a pilgrimage for its participants, one can no longer take for granted a uniform definition of the phenomenon of "pilgrimage" either' (*ibid.*: 3). Yet Eade's introduction to the second edition of *Contesting the Sacred* (2000) acknowledges that this argument may have been overstated.

29 Elverskog 2006. By 'Qing dynasty Mongols', Elverskog means 'Mongols belonging to the Qing empire', and among them, I assume, mostly Inner Mongol intellectuals.

consciousness of a common identity may of course have been enhanced during the pilgrimage by the simple fact of speaking the same language and travelling together in a foreign territory, but the sources I used do not confirm Elverskog's hypothesis. The stone inscriptions, with their conventional formulas, do not tell us the whole story. Commoners expressed their resentment and anger when they had to pay for their princes' journey to Wutaishan: the horses, cattle, sheep and large amounts of silver offered by nobles to Wutaishan monasteries were actually extorted from the banners' commoners. Following Eade and Sallnow's theory, I would rather say that what actually seemed more distinctive on Wutaishan was not the ethnicity or religious affiliation, but the great variety of pilgrims and pilgrimages: differences between penitents walking in great prostrations to expiate their sins, well-off pilgrims who made a comfortable journey and gave ostentatious offerings, monk-pilgrims seeking for spiritual encounters, and pilgrim-traders who bought and sold cattle at the market, seem to be more salient that differences between Mongol, Chinese or Tibetan pilgrims who shared similar expectations. Nothing allows us to assert Turner's crossing of social frontiers, of *communitas* between rich and poor, high lamas and penitents. Nobles' pilgrimages were certainly very different from commoners' pilgrimages. Similarly, early twentieth-century Chinese cleric accounts show erudite monks that share the Chinese culture of the literati, appreciating calligraphy and writing poems, but do not tell anything of the ordinary pilgrims' practices.

Communitas in a cosmopolitan Qing empire or mutual incomprehension?

Elverskog's second deduction proposes a view of Wutaishan as an ideal place, where all the Buddhist populations of the Qing empire met and exchanged with each other, had the feeling of sharing a 'Qing identity'[30] and experienced a 'Qing *communitas*', where 'Chinese literati, Mongol herders, Tibetan lamas and Manchu bannermen all came together, jostling shoulders at temples and caves in the pursuit of blessings and merit.'

> Coming into contact with the enormous cultural and religious diversity of the Qing empire, in many cases no doubt for the first time, must also have been an amazing experience. [...] pilgrimage to Wutai Shan created the field

---

30 Elverskog had argued in his book *Our Great Qing* (2006, esp. 135–46) that 'Qing dynasty Mongols' acquired a 'pan-Qing identity': thanks to the propaganda orchestrated by the Qing emperors, they viewed themselves as members of a broader community including Chinese, Manchus and Tibetans, in a multicultural empire which entailed a certain 'porousness between Qing culture(s)'.

where such ideas could grow. [...] it was the main, possibly the only place, where all of these new ideas were not only in the air, but also accessible to the widest range of social actors found in the Qing empire. [...] Pilgrimage to Wutai Shan therefore played a fundamental role in familiarizing the Mongols with the new cosmopolitan culture of the Qing since they not only partook of it while at the mountain, but also brought it home. [...] Indeed, how many places in the empire could Mongol nomads, Tibetan lamas, Manchu officials, and Chinese peasants all come together in direct contact and shop for the same commodities, much less partake in the same religious ceremony?

(Elverskog 2011:260–2)

This Qing cosmopolitanism[31] experienced on Wutaishan would have made cultural exchange possible, and in this favourable context Mongols created Sino-Mongol syncretic works in fields as diverse as Buddhist art, literature, theatre and astrology. It is true that some learned Mongols acted as intermediaries in the transmission of Chinese Buddhist history, literature and sciences, and helped bridge Tibeto-Mongol and Chinese Buddhist traditions. Great figures such as Mergen Gegeen or Gombojab had an interest in the Chinese Buddhist tradition and historiography; Chinese-speaking Mongols of Eastern Inner Mongolia, Höhhot, Beijing and Chengde translated the great Chinese novels into Mongolian, and translated, compiled or used as main sources Chinese works about religion, geomancy, astrology and medicine.[32]

Mongols' worship of Wutaishan must not be seen through the lens of Tibetan Buddhism only, but understood as the veneration of an ancient Buddhist holy site connected to India, and of an ancient Chinese Buddhist site.[33] Buddhism provided what was in effect a cultural *lingua franca*.[34] The stone inscriptions and pilgrims' records clearly show that even if every

---

31 Elverskog (2011:255) defines Qing cosmopolitanism as 'the ability of the various peoples within the Manchu state to see, think and act beyond the local, be they Mongol, Tibetan, Manchu, or Chinese'; but 'notions such as being Mongol, Tibetan, or Chinese did not dissipate into a fog of Manchu cosmopolitanism.'
32 Atwood 1992–3:17; Elverskog 2011:257–8.
33 According to Elverskog (2006), Mongols have been convinced that they belonged to a single Buddhist continuum extending from India to Mongolia. Being Mongol (within the Qing empire) had become synonymous with being a Gélukpa Buddhist and a subject of the Qing emperor. Historiographers re-wrote the history of Buddhism in Mongolia, inserting it in the longer history of Buddhism: Chinggis Khan and his descendants were recognized as reincarnations of ancient Indian and Tibetan kings, making the history of Mongolia actually start in India.
34 Kapstein 2009:xvii.

ethnicity had its own preferences, Mongols sponsored monasteries of both traditions, and Chinese laypeople were looking for Tibetan initiations.[35] The Mongolian and Tibetan guidebooks and the 1846 map included old Chinese lore of Wutaishan. In his guidebook, Rölpé Dorjé speaks of 'the pilgrims' without any distinction. As shown in Table 1, the salient feature of a Wutaishan monastery for pilgrims was not its current affiliation to Tibetan or Chinese Buddhism (whether it was staffed by lamas or *heshang*), but its peculiarity that distinguished it in this complex religious landscape: the stupa of a saint, miraculous statues and the 'natural numinous traces'. Sanctity and efficacy (of relics, of sacred icons, of great Buddhist masters) prevailed over sectarian and ethnic differences. The blurred visual frontier between a Gélukpa and a Chinese Buddhist monastery on Wutaishan perhaps enhanced the feeling that Buddhism was one though its traditions were many. Wutaishan was the only place in China where Mongols worshipped Chinese icons on a large scale.

Gray Tuttle also argued that the Tibetan (monastic and lay) elite and the Qing imperial elite (Manchu and Mongol) formed a 'stable, mutually supportive community', from which the Chinese were excluded.[36] On Wutaishan, these elites may have interacted with each other, especially during the emperors' tours, but the sources I used cannot confirm or invalidate this hypothesis for late Qing period commoners. Visiting temples of different Buddhist traditions and worshipping ancient icons does not necessary entail inter-ethnic and inter-religious dialogue. I would say that before being a 'cosmopolitan Qing pilgrimage site' for devotees, Wutaishan was first of all the holy residence of a revered Bodhisattva where one could increase one's vital force and fortune, and ensure happiness in future lives. Following Eade and Sallnow (1991), I propose that the Wutaishan pilgrimage has a plurality of meanings, viewpoints and practices in which egalitarianism and nepotism, fraternity and conflict, unity and divisiveness cohabited. The prejudices, xenophobia or, at best, indifference that are commonly seen nowadays, along with mutual respect, tolerance and some temporary forms of *communitas*, certainly already existed one century ago.[37] Elverskog may have overestimated cultural exchanges and the cosmopolitan culture of the pilgrimage. Mongol commoners may have known stories translated from Chinese that circulated in Mongolia and worshipped Chinese icons, but it does not mean that they were interested in interacting

---

35 Chinese interest in Tibetan Buddhism before the 1930s may have been underestimated, at least for the early Qing period and in some places such as Wutaishan, Beijing and Gansu (see Kapstein 2009).
36 Tuttle 2005:ch. 1.
37 Valtchinova (2009:114) showed that relations between pilgrims of different religions or traditions were in perpetual renegotiation on a Bulgarian pilgrimage.

with Chinese pilgrims or resident monks. Except in case of danger or fear of getting lost and other above-mentioned temporary forms of *communitas*, I found no example of pilgrims of different nationalities mixing with each other. The cultural and linguistic gap has always existed between Tibetan, Mongol and Chinese pilgrims, and even between Kalmyks and Khorchin Mongols, Tibetans from Amdo and from Central Tibet, Han from Shanxi and from Guangdong. Tuttle showed that interactions between Chinese and Tibetan Buddhism at the level of monastic teaching and practice were, before the 1930s, dampened by language and geographical barriers (2005:ch. 1). Except for Chinese shopkeepers and traders[38] who learned to speak some Mongolian, Mongolian-speaking Chinese monks, and some learned Mongols fluent in Tibetan or Chinese, the main cause of mutual incomprehension between the communities was language.[39] In 1912 the Chinese lay Buddhist Gao Henian who enquired about history and stories on Wutaishan complained that he could not discuss with Tibetan lamas.

Early twentieth-century Chinese sources give some insights on Chinese judgements of Mongol and Tibetan monks and pilgrims on Wutaishan. Chinese pilgrims and travellers completely ignored the Tibetan Buddhist tradition. In Chinese scholars' eyes, the Mongols and Tibetans looked exotic because of their costumes and, above all, their ostentatious religious fervour, which was labelled as superstition in modern anti-religious China. Zhang Dungu, a geographer and Buddhist layman who visited Wutaishan in 1911, criticized Mongol lamas for whom monkhood was a lucrative job, but recognized that some pious and ascetic Mongols did not fear sufferings in their search for nirvana. Yet on the next page, he described the repulsive filthiness of the Mongols' faces and clothing, and was shocked by men and women who mixed in monks' rooms and sat together around the *kang* 炕 (heated sleeping platforms).[40] Describing an image of a woman under a bull and having sexual intercourse with it (probably an image of Yama), he explained that when the Xiongnu 'barbarians' were exterminated by the Han dynasty, only one woman was left and she had a son with a bull, who is the ancestor of the all Mongols. His depiction of the monks, who all drank alcohol and ate meat (which did not respect their precepts, as he understood them),

---

38 Zhang Dungu 1911; Bai Meichu 2010 [1925]:*juan* 2, 92.
39 This was also true in the case of medieval European pilgrimages, where language barriers and the absence of promotion of cultural exchange lead to mutual incomprehension, contempt and the swindling of others (Sumption 1975:192).
40 Zhang Dungu 1911:24–5. He quotes a local saying: '[At Wutaishan] houses built from piled rocks do not fall, monks at the gate are nor bitten by dogs, lamas in the bedchamber do not trouble people.' (1911:17).

did illegal things and possessed everything from land and shops to women, is part of the general anticlerical discourse of the time, especially that targeting the lamas (Charleux 2002). I have no comparable sources from a Mongol perspective, and I can only extrapolate from contemporary observations. But there is no doubt that the different ethnic communities observed each other with curiosity and interest, even if it was to discover the other's faults and vices.

Revival of the pilgrimage, 1980s–2010s

Because of the rise of nationalisms, secularization, anticlericalism, ethnic tensions and tourism during the Republican, early communist and contemporary periods, we must be very careful in our attempts to compare the pilgrimages in the twenty-first century with those of the nineteenth century. Wutaishan is no longer an ecumenical Buddhist site in a multi-ethnic empire. But we have no other tools than comparison and extrapolation, as our sources do not tell us what pilgrims thought, felt or experienced.

Wutaishan is now one of the wealthiest Buddhist centres of China. In June 2009, it was named a World Heritage Site by UNESCO, and it received more than four million pilgrims and tourists that year, of which 20,000 were foreigners.[41] On this occasion, the provincial authorities decided to carry out major investments to improve infrastructure and attract tourists from China and abroad. In 2008, the 2.8 million paying visitors had brought 1.4 billion *yuan* (206 million US$) in tourist revenues, according to government figures.[42] Since their land was confiscated, the Wutaishan monasteries have been economically dependent on pilgrims and compete between each other in attracting donations; they run hostelries, ask for an entrance fee, organize a variety of rituals,[43] and take subscriptions to support the building and restoration of temples.

Through the Han Gélukpa School (which represents 11 per cent of the monastic community and has appropriated old Chinese Buddhist and Gélukpa monasteries), but also through visiting Tibetan masters, Tibetan Buddhism played a major part in the Buddhist revival in the late 1980s. In 1987, the Tibetan Nyingmapa master Jikmé Püntsok (also known as Khenpo

---

41 whc.unesco.org/en/news/523 (accessed 18 November 2011).
42 Saiget 2009 Tibetans from Tibet and Chinese from Shanxi Province who have a Buddhist registration (*jushiji* 居士記) do not pay the entrance fees.
43 In 2012, the Shuxiangsi organized at least one ritual a day for pilgrims in summer and up to eight rituals per morning. A short ritual costs 3,000 *yuan*, a bigger one, 7,000 *yuan*. In 2006, two pilgrims from Inner Mongolia donated 6,000 *yuan* for a Chinese ritual.

Jikpün, 1933–2004), who had established the Larung Buddhist Institute near Serthar in Sichuan Province, led three thousand disciples (most of them being Chinese) to Wutaishan (that then counted less than 800 monks). There, he performed rituals of the Great Perfection tradition, gave mass teachings, empowerments, and revealed and concealed Buddhist texts and statues. He offered Tibetan statues to Wutaishan monasteries and re-consecrated icons (Chou 2011:ch. 3). Some of his Chinese disciples perpetuated his teachings at the Shancaidong. Jikmé Püntsok contributed to a revitalization of the Tibetan Buddhist tradition on Wutaishan and created a common ground for Chinese and Tibetans, but his Nyingmapa followers encountered some opposition from the local Gélukpa clergy. Other Tibetan masters of Gélukpa, Nyingmapa or Rimé traditions, living in China or abroad, such as Dilgo Khyentsé (1910–91), Akya (Ajia) Rinpoché (b. 1951), Khejok Rinpoché, Dzongsar Khyentsé Rinpoché (b. 1961) and Sakyong Mipham Rinpoché (b. 1962), contributed to re-empowering Wutaishan through initiations and treasure-discovery, and to reviving the pilgrimage. Funerary stupas of Tibetan masters built on Wutaishan create new 'power places'. Miraculous apparitions of Manjushri in the sky, along with coloured haloes and rainbow lights were spotted by crowds, especially during rituals and initiations performed by Jikmé Püntsok (Germano 1998:84–7). New 'numinous traces' continue to be discovered.

Those who report miracles and discover new numinous sites, write new guidebooks and propagate new stories are Chinese Buddhist monks and Tibetan and Han Chinese lamas writing in Chinese or Tibetan; Mongols are no longer authors of pilgrimage lore. Due to the difficult survival of the Buddhist institutions of Inner Mongolia (owing to many factors, including state control, absence of reincarnations and leading figures, being cut off from Tibet, lack of monastic vocations, Sinicization and a rural exodus), Inner Mongols monks presently do not play an important role in the global revival of Tibeto-Mongol Buddhism in China. On Wutaishan, they are now much less numerous than Tibetan monks from Amdo (Tibetan and Mongol lamas represent 15 per cent of the resident clergy; in addition, about 2,000 Tibetan lamas from Labrang Monastery in Amdo go on pilgrimage to Wutaishan every year).[44]

According to my field observations (2007, 2009, 2010 and 2012), despite of the growing influence of Han Gélukpa lamas, the fact that Inner Mongols can communicate in Chinese, and the general interest of the Chinese in the Tibetan Buddhist tradition, Tibetan, Mongol and Chinese pilgrims generally do not mix with each other and do not share food on Wutaishan.[45] Veiled

---

44 Figures between 2000 and 2007.
45 While I have seen Chinese sharing their picnics with each other, I have never seen Chinese, Mongol and Tibetan pilgrims sharing food and eating together.

tensions and jealousy between ethnicities caused by religious and racial prejudices can be observed behind the apparent *communitas* that stems from the pilgrims' discourse and behaviour. Blue monasteries claim that they offer free meals and cheap lodging to every pilgrim, but in practice they do not accept Tibetans and Mongols in their refectory. Chinese Buddhist monks typically consider the lamas as 'impure' because they eat meat and have a freer life than their own: 'they are not true monks'. Chinese pilgrims also feel they are discriminated against because Tibetans are exempted from the expensive entrance tickets, while they are not. They criticize Tibetans and Mongols for being ignorant, filthy and superstitious. But they show curiosity towards Tibetan customs and sometimes approach Tibetan groups to examine their hand-held prayer-wheels and clothes. Most of the Han Chinese examine the non-Chinese stelae and cannot identify whether the script is Tibetan, Mongol or Manchu. But when a Mongol or a Tibetan reads an inscription aloud, Han Chinese group around him, manifest some surprise and ask him questions about the text.

On the other hand, the Mongol and Tibetan lamas complain that the Chinese are racist and do not try to understand their tradition. Mongols and Tibetans criticize the Chinese for being first and foremost interested in making money: they believe that the Chinese circumambulate stupas to obtain good luck in making money. A Tibetan told me that the Chinese love to wear amulets with the prayer '*Om mani padme hum!*', which they understand as the words 'all money in my home' in English.[46]

However, communication is now facilitated by the fact that many Tibetans and Inner Mongols can speak Chinese, and the monks' communities are less and less segregated, partly thanks to the rise of Han Gélukpa Buddhism and to general interest by Chinese in Tibetan Buddhism. The gap is actually broadening between the Inner Mongols, who have become Chinese citizens, many of whom speak Chinese or have even become Sinicized, and Mongols from Mongolia, for whom the pilgrimage is a very expensive journey in a foreign country they consider as 'hostile'.

But generally speaking these tensions are played down, and Mongol pilgrims continue to journey to Wutaishan hoping to experience *communitas* in an international Pure Land where all ethnicities are equal, and where one can occasionally meet Nepalese, Japanese, Koreans and even Westerners.

In conclusion, Wutaishan is a unique place in China, where the lamas and *heshang* cohabited, but without real dialogue until the twentieth century. In the end, Wutaishan was the place in China where the two traditions

---

46 For mutual criticisms of Tibetan Buddhists and Chinese Buddhists in the Republican period, see Tuttle 2005:70–2.

merged, and we observe what Franck Frégosi calls a 'dynamic of religious hybridization', characterized by 'a transgression of the boundaries between the dominant confessions that shakes up their respective orthodoxies', and 'the creation of spaces of porosity between religious worlds' (2011:104). In order to attract pilgrims from different ethnicities, the monasteries adapted their offers to the pilgrims' needs, borrowed from each other and adopted a syncretic architecture, accumulating icons and rituals from both traditions. Although there was very little communication between the two clergies, monasteries adopted similar strategies, including the appropriation of other monasteries; but Mongol pilgrims also appropriated space through large cemeteries. Wutaishan will certainly never belong to one ethnicity or one religious order. But not all pilgrims are equal and their status is changeable. In the Qing dynasty, Mongols may have viewed Wutaishan as an ecumenical Buddhist site within a multi-ethnic empire. In the twenty-first century, Mongols from Mongolia are foreigners in Chinese territory, while Inner Mongols re-appropriate Wutaishan by their presence, their donations and their cemeteries. By their donations of specific statues and temple decorations, the Mongols contribute to the Tibetanization of blue monasteries, and the Chinese, to the Sinicization of yellow monasteries.

References

Albera, D. 2009. 'Conclusion. Pour une anthropologie de la traversée des frontières entre les religions monothéistes'. In Albera and Couroucli (eds.) 2009:321–59.

Albera, D. and M. Couroucli (eds.), 2009, *Religions traversées. Lieux saints partagés entre chrétiens, musulmans et juifs en Méditerranée*. Arles: Actes Sud/ MMSH.

Alley, R. and R. Lapwood 1935. 'The sacred mountains of China: a trip to Wu T'ai Shan'. *The China Journal* 22(3):114–21.

Atwood, C.P. 1992–3, 'The marvellous lama in Mongolia: the phenomenology of a cultural borrowing'. *Acta Orientalia Academiae Scientiarum Hung* 46(1):3–30.

Badone, E. and S.R. Roseman (eds.) 2004. *Intersecting Journeys: The Anthropology of Pilgrimage and Tourism*. Urbana: University of Illinois Press.

Bai Meichu 白眉初 2010[1925]. *Lu Yu Jin sansheng zhi* 鲁豫晋三省志 [Annals of three provinces: Shandong, Henan and Shanxi]. Reedn Beijing: Zhongyang dixueshe, vol. 4.

Biography of Rölpé Dorjé: Thu'u-bkwan blo-bzang chos-kyi nyi-ma (1737–1802), *Khyab bdag rdo rje sems dpa'i ngo bo dpal ldan bla ma dam pa ye shes bstan pa'i sgron me dpal bzang po'i rnam par thar pa mdo tsam brjod pa dge ldan bstan pa'i mdzes rgyan* [A beautiful ornament of the virtuous teachings: A brief exposition of the complete liberation story of the embodiment of the master Vajrasattva, the glorious holy lama, Yeshe Tenpai Tonme Palzanpo], 1792–94. In 'Collected Works of Thu'u-bkwan blo-bzang chos-kyi nyi-ma vol. 1.' (trans. Chen Qingying 陳慶英 and Ma Lianlong 馬連龍), *Zhangjia guoshi Ruo-bi-duo-ji zhuan* 章嘉國師若必多吉傳. 1988. Beijing: Minzu chubanshe.

Buffetrille, K. 1994. 'The Halase-Maratika caves (Eastern Nepal): a sacred place claimed by both Hindus and Buddhists'. *Pondy Papers in Social Sciences* 16 :70.

——— 1996. Montagnes sacrées, lacs et grottes. Lieux de pèlerinage dans le monde tibétain. Traditions écrites, réalités vivantes. Unpublished Ph.D. dissertation. Université Paris X Nanterre.

——— 1997. 'The great pilgrimage of A-myes rma-chen: written traditions, living realities'. In A.W. Macdonald (ed.) *Mandala and Landscape*, 75–132. New Delhi: D.K. Printworld.

——— 2003. 'The evolution of a Tibetan pilgrimage: the pilgrimage to A myes rMa chen mountain in the 21st century'. In *21st Century Tibet Issue. Symposium on Contemporary Tibetan Studies*, 325–63. Taipei: The Mongolian and Tibetan Affairs Commission.

Charleux, I. 2002. 'Les "lamas" vus de Chine: fascination et répulsion'. *Extrême-Orient Extrême-Occident* 24 (October):133–51.

——— 2015. *Nomads on Pilgrimage: Mongols on Wutaishan (China), 1800–1940*. Leiden and Boston: Brill.

Chou, W.-S. 2007. 'Ineffable paths: mapping Wutaishan in Qing dynasty China'. *The Art Bulletin* 89(1):108–29.

——— 2011. Where our journeys end: visions, exchanges, and encounters in early modern representation of Wutaishan. Unpublished Ph.D. dissertation, University of California, Berkeley.

Eade, J. 2000. 'Introduction'. In J. Eade and M.J. Sallnow (eds.) *Contesting the Sacred. The Anthropology of Christian Pilgrimages* (2nd edn.), ix–xxvii. Urbana: University of Illinois Press.

Eade, J. and M.J. Sallnow 1991. 'Introduction'. In J. Eade and M.J. Sallnow (eds.) *Contesting the Sacred. The Anthropology of Christian Pilgrimage*, 1–29. New York and London: Routledge.

Elverskog, J. 2006. *Our Great Qing: The Mongols, Buddhism, and the State in Late Imperial China*. Honolulu: University of Hawai'i Press.

――― 2011. 'Wutai Shan, Qing cosmopolitanism and the Mongols'. *Journal of the International Association of Tibetan Studies* 6 (December):243–74.

Frégosi, F. 2011. 'Introduction'. *Archives des sciences sociales des religions* 155(3) (special issue, 'Inattendus pèlerinages'):103–8

Gao Henian 高鶴年, 2000[1949]. *Ming shan youfang ji* 名山游訪記 [Record of visits to famous mountains]. Beijing: Zongjiao wenhua chubanshe.

Germano, D. 1998. 'Re-membering the dismembered body of Tibet: contemporary Tibetan visionary movements in the People's Republic of China'. In M.C. Goldstein and M.T. Kapstein (eds.) *Buddhism in Contemporary Tibet*, 53–94. Berkeley: University of California Press.

Gimello, R. 1992. 'Chang Shang-ying on Wu-t'ai Shan'. In Naquin and Yü 1992:89–149.

Hayden, R.M. 2002. 'Antagonistic tolerance: competitive sharing of religious sites in South Asia and the Balkans'. *Current Anthropology* 42(2):205–31; G. Bowman 'Commentary'. *Current Anthropology* 43(2):219–20.

Huber, T. 1994. 'Putting the *gnas* back into *gnas-skor*: rethinking Tibetan Buddhist pilgrimage practice'. *The Tibet Journal* 19(2):23–60.

――― 1999. *The Cult of Pure Crystal Mountain. Popular Pilgrimage and Visionary Landscape in Southeast Tibet*. Oxford: Oxford University Press.

Kapstein, M.T. 1998. 'A pilgrimage of rebirth reborn. The 1992 celebration of the Drigung Powa Chenmo'. In M.C. Goldstein and M.T. Kapstein (eds.) *Buddhism in Contemporary Tibet*, 95–119. Berkeley: University of California Press.

――― 2009. 'Preface' and 'Introduction: mediations and margins'. In M.T. Kapstein (ed.) *Buddhism between Tibet and China*, xv–xviii, 1–18. Boston: Wisdom Publications.

Lim, T. 1999. 'Pilgrimage to Wutaisan, the sacred mountain of Manjushri', www.b-i-a.net/Wutaisan.htm, accessed 24 December 2010.

Miyvacir, 2008 [1942]. *Mergen-i bayasqayci cayan teüke: Alaša qosiyun-u barayun güng-ün iledkel šastir* [White history that rejoices the sages: Report of the Western Duke of Alashan Banner]. Höhhot: Öbür Mongyul-un arad-un keblel-ün qoriya.

Morinis, A. 1992. 'Introduction: the territory of the anthropology of pilgrimage'. In A. Morinis (ed.) *Sacred Journeys: The Anthropology of Pilgrimage*, 1–27. Westport CT: Greenwood.

Naquin, S. and Yü C.-F. (ed.) 1992a. *Pilgrims and Sacred Sites in China*. Berkeley: University of California Press.

――― 1992b. 'Introduction'. In Naquin and Yü (ed.) 1992:1–38.

――― 1992c. 'The Peking pilgrimage to Miao-feng Shan: religious organizations and sacred site'. In Naquin and Yü (ed.) 1992a:333–377.

Robson, J. 2009. *Power of Place: The Religious Landscape of the Southern Sacred Peak (Nanyue* 南嶽*) in Medieval China*. Cambridge: Harvard University Press.

Saiget, R.J., 2009. 'Buddhism thrives as China relaxes religious policy' *AFP*, July 7 www.buddhistchannel.tv/index.php/calendar_central/index. php?id=46,8342,0,0,1,0, accessed 14 April 2011.

Sumption, J. 1975. *Pilgrimage: An Image of Medieval Religion*. London: Faber and Faber.

Turner, V. 1978. 'Pilgrimages as social processes'. *Dramas, Fields, and Metaphors: Symbolic Action in Human Society*. Ithaca: Cornell University Press.

Turner, V. and E. Turner 1978. *Image and Pilgrimage in Christian Culture: Anthropological Perspectives*. New York: Columbia University Press.

Tuttle, G. 2005. *Tibetan Buddhists in the Making of Modern China*. New York: Columbia University Press.

——— 2006. 'Tibetan Buddhism at Ri bo rtse lnga/Wutai shan in modern times'. *Journal of the International Association of Tibetan Studies* 2:1–35.

Üjesküleng secig-ün erike kemegdekü orušiba [The Beautiful Flower Chaplet]. Full title: *Serigün tungyalay ayulan-tu manjusiri lakšan-tu süm-e-yin [/süsüg-ün] yayiqamsiy: jibqulangtu gegen düri-yin cedig ergil-ün kemjiy-e-lüge selte süsügten arad-un durašil-i egüskegci üjesküleng secig-ün erike kemegdekü orušiba* [The Marvels of the Mañjuśrī Body Monastery of the Cool, Clear Mountain. Together with the Story of the Miraculous Bright Image and the Measure of its Circumambulation, that Engenders the Desire of the Believing People, which is Called the Beautiful Flower Chaplet], by *gelöng* Yéshé Döndrup of the Tümed, ca. 1813, printed in Beijing, 29 fol. (also exists in a contemporary Tibetan version). Archives of Inner Mongolia, Höhhot.

Ürinkiyaya (ed.) 1999. *Zhongguo Menggu wen guji zongmu* 中国蒙古文古籍总目—*Dumdadu ulus-un erten-ü mongyul nom bicig-ün yerüngkei yarcay* [Catalogue of Ancient Mongolian Books and Documents of China, 3 vols.]. Beijing: Beijing tushuguan chubanshe.

Valtchinova, G. 2009. 'Le mont de la Croix: partage et construction de frontières dans un lieu de pèlerinage bulgare'. In Albera and Couroucli (eds) 2009:113–40.

Xuyun 1988. *Empty Cloud: The Autobiography of the Chinese Zen Master Xu Yun* (rev. and ed. C. Luk and R. Hunn). Longmead: Element Books.

Zhang Dungu 張沌谷, 1911. *Wutaishan can fo riji* 五臺山參佛日記 [Pilgrimage diary to Wutaishan]. *Dixue zazhi* 地學雜誌 3(1):17–28; 3(2):1a–5b.

CHAPTER 5

Betwixt and between
Figures of ambiguity in the Sufi cult of Lāl Shāhbāz Qalandar (Pakistan)

JÜRGEN WASIM FREMBGEN

Introduction

While scriptural, exclusive and rigid-reformist forms of Sunni Islam seem to turn Pakistan increasingly into a monochromatic society eliminating diversity and pluralism, there is an inclusive and still vivid dimension of everyday religious practice that allows otherness and the grey shades of ambiguity in the sense of unresolved meaning. Thus, the popular Sufi traditions of the Punjab and Sindh in general, and the ecstatic cult of the antinomian saint Lāl Shāhbāz Qalandar in particular, are known for their tolerance of ambiguity. This holds especially true for the ritual context of the pilgrimage to the saint's shrine in Sehwan Sharif (Sindh) and above all for his annual *'urs* (lit. 'holy marriage', the festival marking the saint's death and mystic union with God), which opens a space of tolerance for transgressive performances in the presence of the Qalandar (Figure 1). Liminal figures of 'popular religion', such as peripatetic dervishes (known as *malangs* and *malangnī*s in South Asia), enraptured mad men and women, as well as fringe individuals of the 'third gender', take on important roles as actors throughout the cult and perform in public alongside musicians, trance dancers and Shi'a flagellants (Frembgen 2008a:25, 66–101; 2008b). The event is celebrative and spectacular, and marked by a high emotional intensity of Dionysian character in which the divine is experienced day and night with all the senses.

Following the theories of Arnold van Gennep and Victor Turner, the ritual of pilgrimage includes the phase of liminality with its experiences of *communitas* and temporary abolition of hierarchies among devotees. This is why the *'urs* of the great Qalandar saint, which is the largest in the country,

Figure 1   View of Sehwan Sharif with the golden dome of the shrine of Lāl Shāhbāz Qalandar.

including its preparatory *shām-e Qalandar* rites in Lahore and other cities of the Punjab, represents a unique arena for 'figures of ambiguity' to step out from the margins of society and to indulge in transgressive performances. It allows 'holy fools' to show their antics and eccentricities in the ambiguous, liminal period of the '*urs*, to appear in very strange outfits. Like, for instance, a dancing dervish in Sehwan whose jute-made sleeveless smock had been embroidered with shiny fabrics and stitched all over with a variety of colourful beads, buttons, tassels and *objets trouvés*, and who, in addition, was wearing a large number of necklaces. Another pilgrim had his black hair back-combed in the towering shape of a crown. Thus, the playful comical and carnivalesque, with its characteristic inversions, are an integral part of this performance-oriented event. Ambiguity is also articulated on another level in Sehwan and at other Sufi shrines, namely in the domain of mystic music (as well as in the genre of classical vocal music), when, for instance, a male singer like Nusrat Fateh Ali Khan, the great voice of *qawwālī* Sufi music, praises God in a female voice; and vice versa, when female singers, such as Abida Parveen, Jyoti Nooran or Masuma Anwar, sing *sufiyāna kalām* in a deep, male vocal timbre. In fact, the model for such temporary forms of gender transformation had been the famous mystic poet Amīr Khusraw (d. 1325 CE), who sung for his Sufi master, the saint Nizām al-dīn Awliyā (1236–1325 CE) from Delhi, in a woman's voice like a bride longing for her bridegroom (Kugle 2010:252–3). This mode of 'vocal masquerade', which points beyond male and female, seems to indicate an ideal of complementary perfection achieved through the merging of opposites (Petievich 2008).

Through focusing in the following on the threshold status of three ritual agents, this short chapter interrogates aspects of otherness, gender and inversion. In addition, it also addresses the debate about 'orthodoxy' and 'heterodoxy', as the eccentric deeds of these individuals seriously challenge the behavioural norms of formalized scriptural Islam as promulgated by

Figures of ambiguity in the Sufi cult of Lāl Shāhbāz Qalandar (Pakistan) 121

figure 2   Ecstatic dhamāl dance in Sehwan Sharif.

theologians. I met these three 'figures of ambiguity' – Sain Mūmtaz 'Alī, Sayyid Amjad Husayn Shāh and Rabi'a Gul – on different occasions in Sehwan and the two first-named in addition in Lahore between 2003 and 2009 in the course of field research on the cult of Lāl Shāhbāz Qalandar.

Sain Mūmtaz 'Alī, the 'bangle-wearing *malang*'

Rejecting the conventions and formalism of mainstream society, dervishes and fakirs affiliated to 'free' *bī-shar'* Sufi orders or associated to certain enraptured saints, such as Lāl Shāhbāz Qalandar, Shāh Husayn or Barrī Imām, often transgress boundaries of expected norms. Some ascetics are chained following the model of the Shi'a Imam Zayn al-Abidīn, others cover themselves with ash, wear the 'dress of nakedness' or put on the gay-coloured patched frock of ritual clowns, attracting scorn and derision in line with the ideal of the Malamati 'who try to conceal their spiritual achievements' (Frembgen 2008a:71–97, 133). Some of these 'unruly friends of God' have matted hair with long, braided locks, others shave their body hair, from the hair on their head to beard and eyebrows, and many of them wear fancy jewellery, such as finger rings, bracelets and anklets, necklaces, earrings etc. The latter attributes indicate that a particular *malang*-type, marked 'effeminate' in terms of costume and hair-do, adopts a feminine role and thus plays the role of the female lover in her attachment to a Sufi saint or to God (Frembgen 2008a:99). This corresponds to the transcending of gender divisions by male '*homines*

Figure 3   Sain Mūmtaz 'Alī.

religiosi on their way to sainthood, described by Scott Kugle (2007:121) as 'men become saints by tapping "feminine" qualities that are normally hidden or repressed in men'. In an essay on gender ambiguities he further explains:

> gender crossing signifies that a man takes up the social markers of woman: to wear women's clothing; to adopt women's speech, song, and gesture; to take on a woman's role in erotic interactions or even in sexual interactions. In a complementary but distinct way, male Sufis may shed many of the signs of social status, including the patriarchal status of masculinity, as a sign of surrender without performing these signs of surrender in the outer form of feminine gender. They might do this by wearing outlandishly coloured clothes, wearing no clothes, shaving the beard and moustache, leaving family and ascribed status, or inviting condemnation and blame.
> (Kugle 2010:251).

One of these free-thinking, often peripatetic holy men is Sain Mūmtaz 'Alī, whom I first met in October 2004 in a makeshift tent opposite Data Darbar in Lahore and subsequently during the '*urs* of the Qalandar saint in Sehwan Sharif (Figure 3). He was in his forties, wearing sun glasses, a dark-brown Chitrali cap and a long, brown and flowing garment with a yellowish shawl, his grey hair shoulder-length and his full beard well trimmed. In addition to finger rings on his right hand, a necklace of rose petals, a necklace with a pendant showing an iconic image of the Qalandar and a string of beads on his right upper arm, he was wearing a large number of glass bangles on both wrists. Because of these latter accessories he came to be known by his dervish nickname (*lāqab*) *wangāñ-wālā* which in Punjabi means someone wearing bangles. He confessed that he had been mesmerized by the Punjabi folk singer Arif Lohar's song '*Wangāñ*' which talks about selling bangles at the shrine of the Sufi saint Dātā Ganj Bakhsh in Lahore. The bangle-wearing *malang*'s own speciality was the theatrical and highly emotional performance of singing *qalandrī* songs, as well as folk songs, focused on love until he was so moved that he wept long, passionately and loudly – an aspect of behaviour clearly associated with women, but of course also with the ritual mourning of Shi'a in the month of Muharram.

*Malang*s such as Sain Mūmtaz 'Alī hold an ambiguous position in a double sense: on the social level they are men living in the male-dominated 'public' sphere; yet as celibate ascetics they exist outside the 'normal' social world, which means diametrically opposed to the world of families and women. Nevertheless, as mentioned above, male dervishes often adorn themselves with typically female accessories and social markers, such as glass bangles in case of the Sain, or otherwise they dress like married women. Thus, on the spiritual level, they are male seekers of God who cross-dress as 'true brides' (*sāda suhāgan*) of Allah (Frembgen 2008a:100–1; cf. Kugle 2007:208–9). Within the South Asian concept of 'bride mysticism' male dervishes try to 'approximate' the female gender in order to fulfil this inverted role as a 'bride of God' who yearns to be united with her beloved.

The most famous examples of Sufis who transgressed gender boundaries and danced in abandonment wearing women's clothes and bangles are Mūsa Sāda Sohāg (d. 1449 CE), who danced in this way before the tomb of Nizām al-dīn Awliyā (Frembgen 2008a:100–1; Kugle 2010:254–5), and Bullhe Shāh (1680–1752 CE), who appeared like a transvestite in front of his spiritual master and exclaimed: 'If I would become a dancing girl [of the Kanjar caste], my honour would not diminish, let me appease you through dancing.' (Frembgen 2006:105–207). Another, lesser known case in Sufi hagiography is the saint Sain Sahelī Sarkār (nineteenth century), whose shrine is situated near Muzaffarabad (Azad Kashmir). It is said that his whole attire was very feminine and that he used to wear a lot of flower garlands. His nickname Sahelī means female friend, an equivalent of *suhāgan* (bride).

Sayyid Amjad Husayn Shāh, the 'king of the rattling dancing bell'

A peculiarity of the cult of Lāl Shāhbāz Qalandar is to attract people who are otherwise positioned on the fringes of mainstream society such as *khusre* or *hijre* (plural of *khusra* or *hijra*), that is to say cross-dressing effeminate

Figure 4   Sayyid Amjad Husayn Shāh.

people of the so-called 'third gender', including transsexuals, hermaphrodites, eunuchs and transvestites. Dressed as females they play important auspicious roles during rituals of transition and regeneration (birth, circumcision, marriage), where they dance and ensure virility through gestures using a vulgar language and thereby stimulating the sexual energy of the vital life force. Dancing in abandonment himself, Qalandar is obviously the Sufi saint loved most by *khusre* as well as professional dancing girls and prostitutes. Thus, the community of *khusre* maintains – allegedly since the time of their patron saint Lāl Shāhbāz Qalandar himself – its own *faqīroñ kā derah* or 'camp of fakirs' in Sehwan Sharif, which is known as *Khadran ji marhī*. This large compound serves as a meeting place for all the *khusre* of Pakistan who visit the saint's shrine during the annual pilgrimage. As Amira, a 70- to 75-year-old resident *khusre* in this *marhī* told me in October 2009, the elders of their community would point out that *khusre* had even been the guardians of the saint's tomb in earlier days. *Khusre*, who are usually born as males and are only in rare cases of uncertain gender, consider themselves as fakirs or ascetics 'who have sacrificed their own sexual fulfilment and regenerative powers for the others' (Pfeffer 1995:35). As I frequently observed in Sindh and the Punjab, those *khusre* who for some reason are forced to live outside a *derah* often turn into wandering dervishes or resident fakirs, displaying female attire and demeanour, at a shrine. The ambiguity of their gender and physical appearance sometimes becomes strikingly obvious, for instance in the combination of a long grey beard with the wearing of a golden ladies' handbag.[1]

---

1   The case of Ibrāhīm Faqir at Bhit Shah or the late Bībī Sāhib (Baba Siraj) who lived in Miani graveyard in Lahore.

Figures of ambiguity in the Sufi cult of Lāl Shāhbāz Qalandar (Pakistan) 125

At Qalandar's *'urs* in October 2003 I met a group of *khusre* at the shrine who came from the Punjab and had assembled around their young pir, Sayyid Amjad Husayn Shāh Tohranwalī Sarkār (b. 1978), whom they reverentially and affectionately called *badshāh* ('king') (Figure 4).[2] With henna-dyed long hair, dark moustache, a fancy embroidered cap, bangles and necklaces, the coquettishly smiling, soft-spoken Amjad Husayn appeared to fit well with his *khusre* companions, who coquettishly laughed about their gender-role reversals. Years later, during the *shām-e Qalandar* celebrated on 1 August 2009 at the Moon Market in Allama Iqbal Town/Lahore, I saw Amjad Husayn again, who was joyfully called on the stage upon his arrival and then garlanded and honoured to join in singing a *qasīda* for Imam Husayn. People in the crowd exchanged smiling glances, some boisterously celebrating his appearance. When I asked a couple of bystanders, they derogatorily called him the 'pir of the *khusre* and prostitutes', but added that they would respect him because of his being a Sayyid. Keeping this ambiguous remark in mind, I continued observing this mysterious figure, reflecting on his role within the cult of Lāl Shāhbāz Qalandar and later sharing my thoughts with Pakistani friends. In our opinion he represents the qualities of being soft, gentle and meek, no doubt having a female soul, thus perfectly fitting to the liminal character of the Qalandar cult, in which boundaries are blurred and transcended. He resembled Hermes, the winged messenger of Zeus, who, in the words of Durre Ahmed, 'was considered a mediator, peacemaker, and stood for conciliation, tolerance, peace' (1994: 97). In addition, Amjad Husayn seems to incorporate the ease, fun and joy of life which permeates this vibrant, colourful cult. His dress and transgender behaviour are also strongly reminiscent of the playfulness of the ecstatic saint Shah Husayn from Lahore, who used the dimension of play as an alternative to the asceticism of other Sufis and to the rigour of theologians, thereby challenging ritual formality (Kugle 2007:200, 204). Amjad's *laqab Chayhañ Shāh* – 'King of the rattling dancing bell' – specifically refers to the sound of the *gungru*s (rattling dancing bells) which are bound around his calves. *Gungru*s are also a marker for long-haired, male trance dancers who slip into the role of female devotees venerating God.

On YouTube one finds several slide-shows uploaded in spring 2012 with pictures of Amjad Husayn, who belongs to a saintly family from Phularwan near Sargodha in Central Punjab. These pictures show the young, mildly smiling saint honoured by devotees at shrines or processions. He is depicted in Arab or red Qalandar dress riding a camel, but also in private settings. In some cases it is obvious that his skin is bleached, lips are reddened with a little rouge

---

2   Sayyid Amjad Badshāh comes from Mandi Phularwan, a small town in District Sargodha.

Figure 5   Rabiʿa Gul.

on his cheeks, long hair is coloured with henna, moustache is well trimmed and that he is wearing jewellery, bracelets and rings.

Rabiʿa Gul, the enraptured conductor of trance dance

Mastī is a polyvalent term in South Asia mainly denoting an emotional passion of divine rapture and bewilderment between rationality and holy folly.[3] Thus a person who is 'intoxicated' and 'mad' with love of God is called *mastāna* in the case of a male and *mastānī* in the case of a female. They are per se transgressors and flouters of boundaries. The dancing Lāl Shāhbāz Qalandar himself is considered a model of embodying ecstasy, for one of his Persian poems opens with the line *haydāriam qalandaram mastam* – 'I am a Haydar (dervish), a Qalandar, I am intoxicated'. Often the imprint of rapture is a permanent one, rendering the person in question into an ecstatic mode of life, continuously in a state of liminality.

The eastern courtyard of the Qalandar's shrine in Sehwan Sharif is the main ritual arena for the daily performance of the devotional trance dance known as *dhamāl*. It is a sacred space for dervishes, experienced *dhamāl* dancers and devotees, who all join in this dance as a celebrative form of interaction with their beloved saint, as well as for the pilgrims who watch this spectacular performance (Figure 2). Unconventional mystics, men and women, regularly

---

3   On *mastī* see Frembgen 2008b:156–8.

Figures of ambiguity in the Sufi cult of Lāl Shāhbāz Qalandar (Pakistan) 127

Figure 6   Rabiʿa Gul.

make their appearance in this ritual context, wearing fantastic costumes and equipped with unusual accessories demonstrating remarkable creativity and otherness, thereby attracting the eyes of the onlookers. Among these strange individuals I also happen to observe in October 2009 and again in December 2011 Rabiʿa Gul Mastānī, an 'enraptured' lady and conductor of trance dance (Figures 5 and 6).

Compared to previous years, the organisers of the daily *dhamāl* segregated the dancing men, the seated male spectators and the large group of dancing and possessed women with their families more strictly from each other, using long ropes stretched through the courtyard. But, marking their special status, the few dervishes positioned themselves as usual in front of the male dancers segregated from them by the rope. They performed as 'artists' and 'attractors'. The straight aisle in the middle of the courtyard allowed access from the eastern gate to the saint's mausoleum. The flow of visitors through this aisle should ideally be constant and smooth, but because of the spectacular dancing on both sides, this flow was often blocked by curious onlookers. During four consecutive days in October 2009 I observed a *mastānī* who always positioned herself within the aisle, but very close to the spectacular dancing dervishes. When I later talked to Rabiʿa Gul at a tea stall, I came to know that she was in her early thirties and originally came from Kotri, near Hyderabad/Sindh. Every day this self-confidant, but somewhat hyper and restless woman would wear a new sober dress, either in black, blue or some other colour and design, always

in combination with a baseball cap. Standing ambiguously in the aisle between
the men's and the women's compartments, but closer to the dervishes and
often holding the rope with one hand, she ecstatically waved with one arm or
with both, conducting the dancers and directing them to the saint's tomb. At
times she went into trance herself, moving her body and her wild open hair to
the rhythm of the drums, surrounded by male spectators in the aisle. Then she
went back to her waving, thereby spurring on and conducting the dancers; her
movements accompanied by ecstatic exclamations such as *Allāh to hāl*, *'Alī
wāris, mast – mast* or *'Alī, 'Alī, yā 'Alī haidrī*. From time to time she scared
people off from the aisle, trying to keep it free from onlookers, thus fulfilling
the function of a steward. Likewise, she emptied dustbins at the shrine. Later
on I watched her gripping men by their arm, slapping them on their back
and talking to them, thus transgressing the moral boundaries of patriarchal
norms concerning female modesty and domesticity. While her behaviour was
straightforward and male-like, her appearance was that of a female beauty. In
December 2011 her behaviour was somewhat restrained and less spectacular
than a year before, although continuing her waving movements with her hair
open, she now covered her breasts with a glittering shawl that she at times
pulled up to her eyes.

Conclusion

The above-portrayed figures of ambiguity question and challenge the existing
patriarchal-rational order, counter restrictive and purist behaviour, and
cross boundaries of the socially defined gender divide in order to get closer
to a sacred power. Through their inversion of customary gender roles they
display surrender and devotion (Kugle 2010:251–3). Their unusual behaviour
also creates subjective reflexivity among others, who are confronted with
otherness and in-betweenness. Living outside of conformity, 'figures of
ambiguity' frequently appear at liminal spaces such as Sufi shrines. In the
Foucault terms, the latter are 'something like counter-sites, a kind of effectively
enacted utopia in which the real sites, all the other real sites that can be found
within the culture, are simultaneously represented, contested, and inverted'
(Foucault 1986:24). The permanent placement of these persons in a state
of liminality and their extraordinary transgressive performances at ritually
framed events taking place at these shrines demonstrate the enormous
potential of the Dionysian cult of Lāl Shāhbāz Qalandar to accommodate
difference, otherness and paradox, to include the feminine and thus to deal
with complexity and plurality. Within the context of this cult, figures such
as the bangle-wearing *malang*, the 'king of the rattling dancing bell' and the
enraptured female conductor of trance dance prove the potential for revolt
and experiment embedded in the very ambiguity they live and express.

Transforming their gender they almost seem to personify ambiguity. It has to be emphasized that ambiguity is generally suppressed and even eliminated in 'civilized society' and in Pakistani in particular, where the dominant absolutist mindset is impregnated by 'literalized monotheistic ideals of morality' and 'modern heroic consciousness' with its inherent exclusivist notions (Ahmed 1994:29–31; cf. Diamond 1976: 109, 158). This is the reason why figures of ambiguity such as those portrayed here are increasingly threatened by Islamic reformism and radicalism. Nevertheless, the Qalandar cult seems to reflect an age-old local tradition of ambiguity which enshrines the idea of uncertainty about the divine.

References

Ahmed, D.S. 1994. *Masculinity, Rationality and Religion: A Feminist Perspective.* Lahore: ASR Publications.

Diamond, S. 1976. *Kritik der Zivilisation. Anthropologie und die Wiederentdeckung des Primitiven.* Frankfurt/New York, Campus.

Frembgen, J.W. 2006. *The Friends of God – Sufi Saints in Islam. Popular Poster Art in Pakistan.* Karachi: Oxford University Press.

――― 2008a. *Journey to God. Sufis and Dervishes in Islam.* Karachi, Oxford University Press.

――― 2008b. 'Charisma and the holy fool: Gul Mastān Bābā, the enraptured, saint of Udaipur'. In S.C. Lassen and H. van Skyhawk (eds.) *Sufi Traditions and New Departures. Recent Scholarship on Continuity and Change in South Asian Sufism*, 151–180. Islamabad: Taxila Institute of Asian Civilizations.

Foucault, M. 1986. 'Of other spaces, heterotopias'. *Diacritics* 16(1):22–7.

Kugle, S. 2007. *Sufis and Saints' Bodies. Mysticism, Corporeality, and Sacred Power in Islam.* Chapel Hill: The University of North Carolina Press.

――― 2010. 'Dancing with khusro: gender ambiguities and poetic performance in a Delhi Dargah'. In C.W. Ernst and R.C. Martin (eds.) *Rethinking Islamic Studies. From Orientalism to Cosmopolitanism*, 245–65. Columbia: The University of South Carolina Press.

Petievich, C. 2008. *When Men Speak as Women. Vocal Masquerade in Indo-Muslim Poetry.* Delhi: Oxford University Press.

Pfeffer, G. 1995. 'Manliness in the Punjab: male sexuality and the *khusra*'. *Sociologus* 45:26–39.

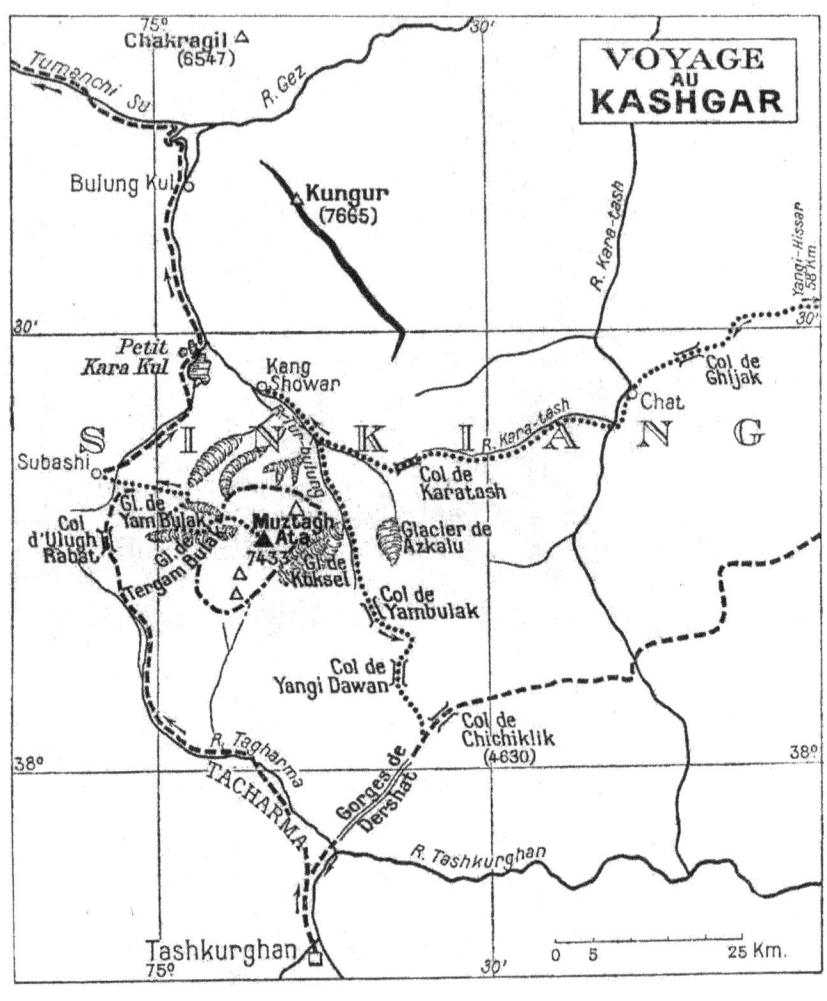

Map 1   'Voyage au Kashgar', in Tilman 1953:146.

CHAPTER 6

Syncretism and the superimposition of Islam on Buddhism in the Pamir

Mountain cults and saint veneration

THIERRY ZARCONE

Ethnic and religious diversity are central characteristics of the part of Asia that was called 'High Asia' (*Haute Asie*) by the French explorers of the nineteenth and twentieth centuries, an area that included Central Asia, Eastern Turkistan, Mongolia and Tibet. High Asia is actually the place where the Chinese, Turko-Mongol and Persian civilizations met. It was at Talas, in what is today Kyrgyzstan, in 751, that the Chinese expansion to the West was stopped by the Arabs. The populations established in this area are in majority Turkic, Mongol and Tibetan, with a Persian-speaking group living in the Pamir ranges, near Afghanistan. The religions of this area are numerous: shamanism, Manicheism, Nestorian Christianity, Zoroastrianism and Buddhism dominated the region until the coming of Islam in eighth century. Thereafter, Islam gradually imposed itself as the main religion in Central Asia and Eastern Turkistan. Shamanism has continued to exist, though in the form of a hybrid movement (Islamized shamanism) that combines Muslim and shamanic ideas and rituals. Buddhism resisted Islam in Tibet and Mongolia, due to the protection of the Himalayas in the former area and of the desert in the latter. The numerous conflicts between Islam and Buddhism in the area have, however, permitted many cultural exchanges between the two religions, including the transfer of knowledge and religious practices, legends and beliefs. This explains why ancient cults and, particularly, Buddhist legends have survived to this day inside some currents of Central Asian Islam, especially in popular Islam, e.g. in saint veneration, Islamized shamanism and tomb veneration.

Figure 1 The Muztagh Ata Mountain as seen from the lake Little Qarakul in Tajikistan, 2012 (© T. Zarcone).

Our subject here is a mountain called the Muztagh Ata ('father of ice-mountains'), one of the most impressive in the Pamir range.[1] This mountain stretches over the autonomous Kyrgyz district (*oblast*) of Kizil-su and the autonomous Tajik county (*nahiye*) of Tashkurgan, both in Xinjiang, not far from the Baltistan district in Pakistan, or from Laddakh or Little Tibet in India. The Muztagh Ata range is composed of twenty-one glaciers, among which, according to the Swedish explorer Sven Hedin, the Tagarma peak (Taghning Bash according to Forsyth, or Taghdumbash – 'head of the mountain') is the highest (Hedin 1895:353) (Figure 1).

The Muztagh Ata range is worthy of our interest for at least three reasons: first, more than elsewhere in High Asia, this place may be judged a religious melting pot, traversing the border between Buddhism and Islam, with the former having there many notables cities in the area up to the eighth century. The major Buddhist city, Kustana (Khotan), situated at the foot of the range, had several large monastic convents and numerous mausoleums (*stupa*) (Bailey 1971; Puri 1987). Furthermore, the mountainous parts of this area are populated nowadays by a Turkish speaking population, the Kyrgyz, whose

---

1 *Muz* = ice; *tagh* = mountain; *ata* = father. I use the form Muztagh (Mūztāgh) mentioned in two Persian manuscripts of sixteenth and seventeenth century: 'Mudhtāgh' in Mir Khāl al-Dīn Kātib ibn-i Mawlānā Qādī Shāh Kūchak al-Yarkandī 1778: fol. 128v.; and 'Mūztāgh' in Akimushkin 2001:102. Also, the popular spellings 'Mous-tagh' and 'Mustagh' are found in several travelogues in nineteenth century.

Islam is impregnated with animistic and shamanic elements. In seventeenth and eighteenth centuries, the situation was considered unacceptable by the Muslim sovereigns in the neighbouring oases at Yarkand and Khotan, and several campaigns of Islamization, though unsuccessful, were launched against the Kyrgyz (Fletcher 1995; Papas 2005). Second, in the Muztagh Ata range exists an unusual religious syncretism, as seen in some legends, which mixes the Turko-Mongol cult of divinized mountains, the Hindu, Buddhist and Mazdean belief in a hidden idyllic kingdom, and the Muslim cult of the saint tombs (*mazār*). Third, the major characteristic of the Muztagh Ata is that the whole mountain was regarded as a Buddhist sanctuary, before becoming in the course of time a Muslim shrine. The rare legends about the place, collected by a Chinese Buddhist pilgrim in sixth or seventh century, and then, by Western travellers and explorers at the end of the nineteenth century and by local folklorists in the beginning of the twentieth, provide us with some information I would like to analyse here.

The Muztagh Ata in Buddhist legends

In sixth or seventh century the Chinese Buddhist monk Xuanzhang, on his way to India, collected an ancient and interesting legend concerning the Muztagh Ata. The mountain was situated, according to this traveller, west of the city of Wu-sha, which corresponds with the oases of Yarkand and Karghalik, west of Khotan (Stein 1907, vol. 1:44–6).

> Two hundred li or so to the west of the city [of Wu-sha] we come to a great mountain. This mountain is covered with brooding vapours, which hang like clouds above the rocks. The crags rise one above another, and seem as if about to fall where they are suspended. On the mountain top is erected a *stupa* of a wonderful and mysterious character. This is the old story: – Many centuries ago this mountain suddenly opened; in the middle was seen a Bhikshu [Buddhist monk], with closed eyes, sitting; his body was of gigantic stature and his form was dried up; his hair descended low on his shoulders and enshrouded his face. A hunter having caught sight of him told the king. The king in person vent to see him and to pay him homage. All the men of the town came spontaneously to burn incense and offer flowers as religions tribute to him. Then the king said, 'What man is this of such great stature?' Then there was a Bhikshu who said in reply, 'This man with his hair descending over his shoulders and clad in a *kashâya* garment [monk coat] is an Arhat who has entered the *samâdhi* [contemplation] which produces extinction of mind. Those who enter this kind of *samâdhi* have to await a certain signal [or period]; some way that if they hear the sound of the *ghantâ* [bell] they awake; others, if they see the shining of the

son, then this is a signal for them to arouse themselves from their ecstasy; in the absence of such signal, they rest unmoved and quiet, whilst the power of their ecstasy keeps their bodies from destruction. When they come from their trance after their long fast, the body ought to be well rubbed with oil and the limbs made supple with soft application after this the *ghantâ* may be sounded to restore the mind plunged in *samâdhi*.' The king said, 'Let it be done,' and then he sounded the gong.

Scarcely had the sound died away, but the Ârhat, recognising the signal, looking down on them from on high for a long time, at length said, 'What creatures are you with forms so small and mean, clothed with brown robes?' They answered, 'We are Bhikshus!' He said, 'And where now dwells my master, Kâśyapa Tathâgata?' They replied, 'He has entered the great *nirvâna* for a long time past.' Having heard this, he shut his eyes, as a man disappointed and ready to die. Then suddenly he asked again, 'Has Śâkya Tathâgata come into the world?' 'He has been born, and having guided the world spiritually, he has also entered *nirvâna*.' Hearing this, he bowed his head, and so remained for a long time. Then rising up into the air, he exhibited spiritual transformations, and at last he was consumed by fire and his bones fell to the ground. The king having collected them, raised over them this *stupa*.

(Si-yu-ki 1884, vol. II:305–6)[2]

This legend is clearly inspired by a well-known set of Buddhist stories with the theme of the 'sage sleeping in the mountain', according to the formulation of Maurice Pinguet ('sage-au-mont-dormant'), who enters meditation in a grotto or mountain, waiting for the coming of the Buddha. There are many equivalent of this story in India, China and Japan (Pinguet 1984:120–1). Briefly, in the legend quoted above, the Muztagh Ata is depicted as a hollow mountain inhabited by a huge Buddhist ascetic (*arhat*) absorbed in meditation (*samadhi*). After the resurrection and the death of this ascetic, a mausoleum (*stupa*) was erected upon his bones, and the mountain became sacred. Aurel Stein writes that 'the remarkable shape of the huge dome of ice rising above all other mountains must have vividly suggested to Buddhist eyes the idea of a gigantic stupa' (Stein 1907, vol. 1:46). Actually, the whole of the Pamir has impressed the travellers since the sixth century. Another Chinese pilgrim, Song Yun, wrote centuries later, that the 'mountains of the onions' (Chinese: *cong ling*), i.e. the southern range which divide the Pamirs, indicates the 'centre of the sky and of the earth'. F. Chavannes, the French translator of Song Yun's

---

2   See also Lévi 1905:255.

text, adds in a footnote that 'here, the idea is that this country is the centre of the universe' (Chavannes 1903, vol. 3:400–1).[3]

According to a Chinese source, there was another 'sleeping sage in mountain' in the Khotan district, in the middle of the sixth century. A 'craggy mountain' in the kingdom of Khotan was regarded as a holy place because twelve Buddhist holy books were conserved there, under the surveillance of the Khotanese. In a grotto situated in this holy mountain were three *arhats* absorbed in meditation (Lévi 1905:255). Although it is not easy to know exactly where this mountain is situated, there is no doubt that it must be either in the Muztagh Ata range or in the Kunlun range, to the east.

Since the end of the nineteenth century, to today, new legends about the Muztagh Ata have been collected among the local Kyrgyz population by Western explorers (Sven Hedin, Aurel Stein, Ella C. Sykes) and local folklorists. It is to be regretted, however, that the cultural history of this mountain has never drawn the attention of any Uyghur anthropologist or historian of religion. Two Uyghur historians nevertheless mention that Muztagh Ata, called 'Muztaghlar Bovisi' – 'father of ice-mountains', was at the centre of a 'cult of the nature' (*täbii choqunush*) (Haji Nur and Guoguang 1995:411). In addition, a manual in Uyghur language dedicated to the preparation of exams in Xinjiang depicts the Muztagh Ata as a 'sacred mountain' (*muqäddäs taghlar*) (Savüt 2002:168).

The 'tomb-mountain' and the mystery of the white camel

The first Western traveller drawn to the Muztagh Ata was the Swedish explorer Sven Hedin, who explored the range in 1894–5 and attempted many times, though unsuccessfully, to reach its peak. The place was considered inaccessible by Hedin's superstitious and frightened Kyrgyz guides (Hedin 1993, vol. 1:217–21). Some legends collected by Hedin demonstrate that the Muslims who became the masters and inhabitants of the range around the ninth century had accepted the sacredness of the mountain, and adapted the Buddhist legend to the new Muslim context, and, thereby, enhanced it with new stories. To this day, the mountain has continued to be a holy and high respected place, and many travellers have noticed that the Kyrgyz kneel and pray when passing nearby the range. The French traveller Guillaume Capus reports in 1890:

> While [the Kyrgyz] were sitting in circle around the fire, talking about the price of the mutton or the selling of a koutass (yak), the wind has chased away the clouds and suddenly, the rounded dome of the Tagarma emerged

3   About the mountains of the onion, see also Stein 1907, vol. 1:28; 1928, vol. 2:764.

in the distance. Djouma-bi stopped talking and streching his arms, said respectfully 'Mousstag-ata' as a subject towards his king.

(Capus 1890:212)[4]

These practices are still performed by the Pamiri peoples of the Tashqurghan district in China. They bow in the morning when looking at the mountain, or recite peculiar prayers to call for his help and for healing, as if it was a saint tomb (Rähman 2009:933).

Furthermore, there is still a mausoleum on the mountain, though the Buddhist *stupa* has been replaced by the tomb of a Muslim saint, and the Buddhist saint (*arhat*) by the prophets of the Bible and of the Quran. Actually, reports Hedin, according to the Kyrgyz, the mountain is 'a gigantic masar [mazar] or burial-mound of saints. Within its interior dwell amongst others the souls of Moses and Imam Ali.' And that the Kyrgyz 'sometimes call it "Hazrett-i-Musa" or the Holy Moses' (Hedin 1993, vol. 1:218). The alleged presence of the Imam ʿAli at this place is probably linked to the existence of an Ismaili community in the southern Pamir, and is reminiscent of the Islamization wars conducted by Shiʿis (which are confirmed by chronicles). Besides, there are many other alleged tomb and 'stepping-place' (*qadam-jā*) of the Imam ʿAli in the Pamirs and in the neighbouring Ferghana Valley (Uzbekistan)[5].

One of the legends collected by Hedin mentions a mysterious white camel:

When Ali lay at the point of death, he prophesied to those about him, that as soon as the breath was gone out of his body, a white camel would come down from heaven and carry him away. As he said, so it comes to pass. When he was dead, the white camel appeared, took the holy man on its back, and hastened with him to Mus-tagh-ata.

(Hedin 1993, vol. 1:218)

This white camel is mentioned in another Pamiri legend, collected in 1924, according to which the Muztagh Ata was haunted by 'camels of a supernatural whiteness' (Sykes 1924:260). In addition, from the hagiography of the famous Naqshbandi saint Badīʿ al-Dīn Nūrī or Shaykh Muslih al-Dīn of Khujand (West of Ferghana Valley, in Tajikistan), we learn that the Prophet Muhammad send one of his companions riding a white camel to this city of Central Asia (Dudoignon 2004:238–9). There also exists a mausoleum near the city of Ferghana (Uzbekistan) which commemorates the coming of ʿAli at this place, riding a white camel (Abdulahatov 2005). Another shrine called

---

4 See also Hedin 1993, vol. 1:218.
5 See Abdulahatov 2005; Olufsen 1904:157–64; Reich 2003.

Syncretism and the superimposition of Islam on Buddhism in the Pamir   137

Figure 2   Calligraphy of the white camel with Imam Ali, paint on glass, 1912–13, private collection, Istanbul.

qadam-jā (stepping-place), near the city of Marghilon, still in the Ferghana district, is known as the '*qadam-jā* of the white camel'. The narrative attached to this shrine refers to a camel which appeared (*paydo bulib*) miraculously, in great secrecy, coming from nowhere, and then disappeared mysteriously (*ghoyib*). This animal was able to travel from the invisible world to the earth (Abdulahatov and Eshonboboev 2007:175).

Beliefs about a camel taking the corpse of 'Alī, as mentioned by Hedin above, or of another Muslim saint, are well known in the Shi'i and Sufi traditions. There are several pictures and calligraphies depicting it, especially in Turkey (Aksel 1967:99–102). The presence of the white camel at the Muztagh Ata is obviously a sign that the mountain has welcomed Shi'i and Sufi ideas and legends (Figure 2).

Aurel Stein (1907, vol. 1:45) collected another legend that may indicate the appropriation of the sanctity of the Muztagh Ata by the Pamiri Ismaili. He was told by a Kyrgyz that a 'hoary Pir resides on the glacier-crowned and wholly inaccessible summit'. This clearly shows that one aspect of the Buddhist legend, the existence of a holy man (*arhat*) living in the mountain, has been

Figure 3 An unknown female Muslim saint mausoleum in South of Xinjiang, 1930, photograph of John Törnquists, in Samuel Fränne Östturkestan Samling, Riksarkivet, Stockholm.

preserved; however, this *arhat* was Islamized and replaced by a *pīr*, a title given to the priest of the Ismaili cult, and also to the Sufi shaykhs.[6]

The eradication of one religion by another is a well-known phenomenon; e.g. Christianity has succeeded paganism in Europe, and Islam succeeded in turn Mazdeism, Christianity and other Asiatic religions in Central Asia. However, in the case of the Muztagh Ata there is a superimposition of Muslim saint veneration on a Buddhist saint cult. A mausoleum has succeeded another mausoleum. It is well known also that saint veneration is a major Muslim trends in Central Asia,[7] and, consequently, it comes as no surprise that many Buddhist sacred places in this region, i.e. *stupa*, monasteries, shrines, ascetics grottoes etc. were succeeded by Muslim tombs, *mazār* (tomb), *qadam-jā* (stepping-place) and *qumbaz* (domed tomb). There are many examples of this. The processes of superimposition of one cult on another are manifold: let me mention the most notable:

- reuse of the ancient sacred perimeter after the Buddhist edifice was destroyed;

---

6 See Daftary 1990:468–9.
7 On the numerous saints tombs on the Pamirian routes, see Zarcone 1996. On mausoleums in Chinese Qaraqorum, see Hüsäyin 1986:58; Qurban 2001:59.

Syncretism and the superimposition of Islam on Buddhism in the Pamir

Figure 4 The mausoleum of Muḥammad Sharīf at Yarkand, 2008 (© T. Zarcone).

- reuse of certain architectural parts of the former edifice for the building of the new one;
- reinterpretation and Islamization of the foundation legend of the Buddhist sacred edifice.

All these phenomena are attested throughout the oases of Khotan where Muslims and Buddhists have fought each others; and the surperimposition of Muslim shrines upon Buddhist *stupa*s is also a widespread phenomenon in India.[8]

---

8   See Chandra 1887; Hamada 2004:1029–30; Servan-Schreiber 1997; Stein 1907, vol. 1:95, 225, 140; vol. 2:460, 463.

Figure 5   Representation of a demon (dīv) in Central Asia, fourteenth century, 'Siyah Qalem', manuscript 2153, Library of the Museum of Topkapi, Istanbul.

Kingdom of the spirits, deity-mountain and tomb-mountain

According to many orally transmitted legends, the Muztagh Ata is a home for both evil and good spirits, as is the case with many of other mountains.[9] The types of spirits are well known and have been inspired by the ancient

---

9   The most complete version of this legend was collected by Sherin Qurban in the Tashkurgan district of Xinjiang (Qurban 2005:93–100). See also Rähman 2009:931–6.

Zoroastrian and Turkic demonology transmitted to the shamans: *div-alvasti* (*div* is close to the Indian *deva* and the Latin *div*) and *pärizat* (from *parī*, the fairy).[10] Two of them are terrible and protect the peak of the mountains against the humans: the 'skeleton-spirit' (*söngäk diva*) or 'skinless-skeleton' (*qaqshal söngäk*) and the 'ferocius tiger' (*yirtquch yolvas*), both probably of Turkic origin (Qurban 2005:95).

Some legends reported by Uyghur ethnologists are about a female spirit, fairy (*pärizat*), who fall in love with a young hunter she met in the mountain. According to these legends, a valorous hunter called Batur didn't fear any trouble from *div-alvasti* (spirits), as he knew that the fairy who protected the mountain could take the shape of many demons, such as the *alvast*, and was able to transform (thanks to her magical incantations, *äpsun*) any intruders into inanimate things. Batur climbed to the summit of the Muztagh, and finally entered a wonderful garden with many flowers and springs, and with a diversity of birds and animals, all living together without hate or animosity. He picked some of the beautiful flowers, which were actually divine flowers (*ilahi gül*) with the power to bring happiness (*bäkht-saadät*) to mankind. The flower was guarded by a female spirit/fairy (*pärizat*) called Gülshän, who ordered the 'skinless-skeleton' and the 'ferocious-tiger' to kill Batur. But the young hunter fought successfully, putting to flight, and then killing them. Impressed by the valour of Batur, Gülshän falls in love with him and, against the will of God (*Tängri*), offers him the flower. As a punishment, God places Gülshän in eternal imprisonment at the summit of the Muztagh. Her tears form the snow and ice-cap of the mountain (*Tashqurghan Tajik Aptonom Nahiyisining Umumi Ähvali* 1988:69; Qurban 2005:93–100).

The image of the mountain, in general, as a sojourn and a kingdom of the spirits is not unknown to Muslim and Central Asian tradition. Sven Hedin has suggested that the Muztagh Ata is reminiscent of the Demavend, the sacred mountain of the Persians, which lies in the Alburz range (Hedin 1898:243; 1993:221). His intuition is right, as the Demavend is also a sojourn of the spirits. There is a great likelihood that the legends about this Persian mountain were influential for the Muztagh Ata, especially through another mountain legend, that of the Mount Qāf, which is in Islam a perfect copy of the Demavend (Aga-Oglu 1946:247–8). The Qāf Mountain is well known in Sunni Islam, as in Shiism, the Sufi traditions and even Islamized shamanism.

---

10 The expression *div-alvasti* is attested in the Pamirs: see Shakarmadov 2005:255–76. See also Sykes 1924: 260, who mentions the existence of fairies (*pari*) in the mountain, along with camels. About the Central Asian pantheon of spirits, see Garrone 2000:156–74 and Sukhareva 1975. On shamanism among the Kyrgyz in contemporary Xinjiang see Hujiexi 2009 and Somfai Kara 2004, 2007.

Figure 6   A Kirghiz Falcon hunter, photograph of Gottfrid Palmbergs, around 1930, in Samuel Fränne Östturkestan Samling, Riksarkivet, Stockholm.

It is called Köykap among the Kyrgyz, which is a deformation of the Persian expression *Kūh-i Qāf* – the Mountain of Qāf (Ögel 1993, vol. 2:437).[11] The names of the spirits who lived in the Qāf Mountain are with few exceptions similar to those who inhabit the Muztagh Ata: *jinn, dīv, ifrīt* and *parī* (Demirci 2001:144–5; Donaldson 1938:35, 44, 89–94; Streck and Miquel 1978:418–9; Sykes 1901:274). In addition, during a healing ceremony by a Muslim shaman

---

11   On the mountain in general for the Turco-Mongols populations, see Roux 1984:149–54.

Syncretism and the superimposition of Islam on Buddhism in the Pamir 143

in the Kazakh-Kyrgyz region, the Qāf Mountain is evoked, because it is the home of the spirits: 'O! Spirits who dwell in the Moutains of Qāf.' (Divaev 1899:13; Garrone 2000:68). Moreover, this mountain is not only the home of the spirits, it is also their kingdom and the place where hidden cities and secret palaces exist. According to an Indo-Persian legend, a 'golden city' (*shahristān Zarrīn*) ruled by Ifrit, another Persian name for the spirits, was built on the *Kūh-i Qāf* (Temple 1886:293). Other legends tell that the fabulous bird Simurgh (Anka for the Arabs) lived as a recluse in a palace situated at the summit of the Mountain, though advising the rulers of the world.[12] All this is confirmed by an Anatolian legend telling that a 'palace made of diamonds and ruby' exists on the Qāf Mountain (Boratav 1991:233).

It is clear that Mustagh Ata is a mixture of many different mountain cults that have followed one another in the Pamir: Buddhist first, then Turco-Mongol, Tibetan and finally Muslim, especially Shi'i-Ismaili and Sufi. In addition to the Buddhist legend of the 'sleeping sage in mountain', there is a belief in underground and hidden kingdoms and, by extension, the cave that plays a major role in the Turco-Mongol mythology (Ogudin 2003a). The Kyrgyz, as a mountain people, are very respectful of these beliefs and regard the mountain in general as their ancestor-deity, and the Mustagh Ata as a god. The personification of the mountain among the Kyrgyz – be reminded that Mustagh Ata means 'Father of ice-mountains' – is far from a rare phenomenon among the other Turkic peoples, where many deity-mountains are venerated and some mountains are regarded as the graves of mythical ancestors (İnan 2000:52–3). There are some other ranges in the Kyrgyz area which bear the names of ancestors with the name '*ata* (father): Kochkor-Ata (Kochkorskoj doline in the Tianshan range) and Markan Ata (Abramzon 1990: 318). We find also a mountain called Mustag (Snow mountain) among the Shor people in the Altaï (Potapov 1946:145–60; Ögel 1993, vol. 2;:437–8). In addition, Turks and Tibetans, especially those who are living nowadays in the Baltistan province (Pakistan and India), close to the Pamir range, share the belief in deity-mountains.[13]

Thus, as a 'mountain-tomb', the Muztagh Ata may be classified between the cults of deity-mountains and those of saints and grave veneration. But we must not confuse the cult of the Muztagh Ata with the veneration of 'tombs of the mountain',[14] the later usually situated at the foot, on the side or at the

---

12 See Attar 1991; Demirci 2001:144–5; Streck and Miquel 1978:418–19.
13 On the deity-mountains among the Tibetans, see Blondeau 1998. On the same belief in Baltistan, see Stein 1959:8, 135, 274, 525–6.
14 An expression coined by Abashin 2013.

summit of a mountain (two are well known, the Throne of Solomon at Ush, in Kyrgyzstan, and the Boboi-ob, in the valley of Ferghana).[15]

Heavenly and hidden kingdoms

There is a second reading of the Muslim legend of the Muztagh Ata I would like to investigate. It is based on the shift from the Buddhist myth of the hollow mountain to the myth of the hidden city, as told by two texts collected by Hedin in a Kyrgyz village (Su-Bashi) in Pamir:

> The Kirghiz of Su-Bashi told me this story about the holy mountain. Many hundred years ago an aged *ishan* (holy man) [rather Sufi shaykh] went up the mountain by himself. And when he came a certain way up it, he found a lake and a little stream, with a white camel grazing on the shore. There was also a large garden planted with plum-trees, and under the plum-trees there walked to and from a number of venerable old men dressed in white garment. The holy man plucked some of the fruit and ate it. Then came one of the venerable inhabitants of the garden, and said to him, that it was well he has done so; for if he had despised the fruit, as all those aged men had done, he would have been condemned like them to stay on the mountain, walking up and down the garden, to the end of time. Then came a rider on a white horse, and caught up the holy man, and galloped with him down the steep mountain-side. And when the ishan came to himself, he found that he was down in the valley, and could only remember dimly all the marvellous things he had seen.
>
> (Hedin 1993, vol. 1:218.)

The myth of the hidden and heavenly kingdom appears in another legend, in which the hidden city is given a precise name, though one that is quite mysterious: 'Janaidar'. According to a Russian study of some Pamirian legends, Janaidar is rewritten 'Jal-Hay-Dar' without any explanation (Gornenskij 2000:36–8). The author of this study states that Janaidar comes from Jannat-dar, an Arabo-Persian compound with the meaning of 'heavenly place, heaven', a hypothesis, I find acceptable.[16] The Arabic plural *jannat* indeed refers to gardens or orchards, and also to paradise/heaven, i.e. a garden where Muslims will live after their death. This hypothesis is confirmed by a legend collected few years ago by a Tajik folklorist, according to which the hidden garden in the Muztagh Ata was 'created by God in imitation of the Paradise' ('*Bu Allah taripdin Jännätkä täqlid qilip yasalghan jay*', Qurban 2005:94) (Figure

---

15   See Ogudin 2003b:41–68 and Zarcone 2013.
16   See also Chvyr' 2006:185.

Syncretism and the superimposition of Islam on Buddhism in the Pamir 145

Figure 7   A representation of paradise in Islam, in 'Ahvāl-i qiyāmat', manuscript sixteenth-seventeenth century, And 1998:200.

7). The word 'Janaidar' appears also in the toponym 'Janaidar-sai' that is the name nowadays of the upper side of the Alayi Valley, linked to Tajikistan and Kyrgyzstan in the Pamirs range. The upper side of this green valley, situated at an elevation of 3,500 m and watered by the Kizil-Su River, is surrounded by exceptional mountains which reach more than 7,000 m at their peaks. The Valley has been for many centuries the best way to enter China and one of the main silk roads. It is impossible, however, to say if Janaidar-sai, in the Ferghana Valley, is the origin of the name Janaidar in the myth of the hidden city, or if the upper side of the Alayi Valley was called Janaidar-sai to remind of the legendary city.[17] Actually, both are situated in a wonderful area, peaceful and more or less inaccessible, that is to say a 'little paradise'. The continuation of the Alayi Valley beyond the pass of Taldik in Chinese territory belongs to the Kizil-Su Kyrgyz Autonomous Prefecture. However, there is a valley in this prefecture, in the north of Atush, that bears the name of Jay Ata, a name which is very similar to that of Janaidar. This valley has many trees, rocks and springs that are considered sacred, and seven holy tombs of saints; one of them is dedicated to a camel (Somfai Kara 2007:51–2).

> The Kirghiz tell further, that on the top of Mus-tagh-ata there exists an ancient city named Janaidar, which was built in the days when universal happiness and universal peace reigned throughout the world. But since that time has been no intercourse between the people of Janaidar and the inhabitants of the earth. Consequently the former still enjoy an existence of unblemished happiness. In the city of bliss there are fruit-trees which bear magnificent fruit all the year round, flowers which never wither, women who never grow old and never lose their beauty. The choicest pleasures of life are as common there as bread; death, cold, and darkness are banished from its confines forever.
> (Hedin 1993, vol. 1:221)

> According to the tradition, an intrepid young man, while hunting a wild goat in the Mountain [Mustagh Ata], discovered the amazing Jal-Hay-Dar. Once in his home, he gathered his friends, and all went to the place. But they never find the way to the city and get lost in the Muztagh Ata.
> (Gornenskij 2000:44–6)

About ten years ago, a folklorist collected in the Tajik autonomous county another version of the hidden kingdom, or garden of Muztagh Ata. This version confirms the information given in the texts collected by Hedin and Gornenskij, and gives more details about the hidden kingdom (Qurban 2005:93–100).

In brief, according to the oral tradition of the Kyrgyz, a hidden city named Janaidar was supposed to exist at the summit, or a valley, of the Muztagh Ata. The city had a marvellous garden with trees covered with fruit all year round, and its inhabitants, dressed all in white, lived eternally without pain. The model for this utopian city may be Turco-Mongolian. However, because of some of its characteristics and of the proximity of Tibet (all reinforced by the

---

17 Janaidar-sai is also mentioned in Stein 1928, vol. 2:846.

Syncretism and the superimposition of Islam on Buddhism in the Pamir   147

fact that Eastern Turkistan was occupied by Tibetans in the ninth century and by Buddhist Mongols in seventeenth century), a Tibetan-Buddhist model, that of the city of Shambhala, should be more relevant. Which is not to neglect the possibility of the model of the Mazdean city, influential upon the Muztagh Ata through Ismaelism and the legend of the Qāf Mountain, where a 'golden city' or a palace was also situated.

The legend of the idyllic and utopian city of Shambhala, literally 'source of happiness', which appeared in India in tenth to eleventh century and in Tibet in the thirteenth century, is based on several similar Hindus myths: those of the city of Uttarakuru in the Mahabharata and the Ramayana, and of the city of Uddiyana, country of the Dakinis in Vajrayana Buddhism, linked to the teachings of Padma Sambhava, the introducer of Buddhism in Tibet (Bernbaum 1985:118, 165–6, 171–8). These legendary cities were established, according to the written tradition, in the north of India and Tibet, precisely in the north of the river Sita (Tarim), in Eastern Turkistan, in the country of the Hor (Turcs, Mongols, Uyghurs...) (Bernbaum 1985:39).[18] Actually, the north was regarded by Hinduism and Buddhism as a sacred 'direction' and a sacred 'centre' (Bernbaum 1985:244; R.A. Stein 1959:274).

Moreover, the myth of Shambhala is likely to have been influential on the Kyrgyz legends about the Muztagh Ata because the 'model for the hidden kingdom' and for Shambhala, writes Edwin Marshall Bernbaum, is the neighbouring kingdom of Khotan. Firstly, Vaiśravana, the king-guardian of the North, who is the model for the king of Shambhala, is the mythical ancestor of the sovereigns of Khotan. Secondly, there is an analogy between the destruction of Khotan by the Muslims in the ninth century and the prophecy of Shambhala that announces the collapse of Buddhism.[19] Finally, the myth of Shambhala appeared in India in the tenth to eleventh century after the Buddhism had disappeared from the south of Central Asia (Bernbaum 1985:107). According to Bernbaum, it is clear that Khotan was the origin of the Kalacakra Tantra, which contains the myth of Shambhala and the model of the ideal kingdom (ibid.:107, 174). The legend of Shambhala that emerged in the tenth to eleventh century underwent many developments in the following centuries, and travel guides dedicated to pilgrims going to this mythical country were published in Tibet up to the seventeenth century. We must admit that the Pamir area, neighbouring to Tibet, which was at the end of the seventeenth century under the control of the Buddhist Mongols, cannot

---

18   See the descriptions of Shambhala in Kollmar-Paulenz 1992–3 and Gar-j K'am-trül Rinpoche 1978. On the hidden valleys and cities among the Tibetans, see Ehrhard 1996:37–53; Orofino 1991:239–71.
19   Bernbaum 1985:103; R.A. Stein 1959:282–4; Yamazaki 1990:67–8.

have been immune to this legend.[20] So, there are many analogies between the Tibetan-Buddhist and Hindu myths of the heavenly kingdom and the Pamirian city of Janaidar. Both are heavenly places and the 'venerable old men dressed in white garment' of Janaidar resemble the *arhat* of Shambhala or the magicians of the Hindu hidden kingdom of Svetadvipa in the Ramayana.[21] Similarly, these two places have 'various kinds of woods and groves, and many fruit-bearing trees' and the people do not know sickness.[22] Finally, Karénina Kollmar-Paulenz, who writes on the Shambhala concept, makes the following remark: 'Other elements in the idea of Śambhala remind us of similar oriental conceptions. The outer appearance of Śambhala, its snow-covered mountains, forest, and the miraculous groves are similar to the concept of the paradise in form of a garden which we already find in the Old Testament.' (Kollmar-Paulenz 1992–3:86); that is, the description of Janaidar actually mingles the Buddhist utopic city and the Biblical paradise.

Conclusion

The explorer and archaeologist Aurel Stein reported in 1907 that the legend of the Muztagh Ata 'affords fresh evidence of the tenacity with which popular tradition and worship in Turkistan, as elsewhere in the East, survive all religious and ethnical changes' (Stein 1907, vol. 1: 44). Buddhist legends, in a sense, survived the extinction of Buddhism, and were then Islamized. This is the case not only of the Muztagh Ata but also of several other Muslim shrines in the South of Xinjiang (see footnote 9).

The Muztagh Ata combines the veneration of mountains and of saints since the Buddhist period, and this characteristic has encouraged the criss-crossing of the traditions of the religious currents of the area – Buddhism, Zoroastrism, shamanism and Islam – which all venerate mountains. Some elements and ideas have been entirely accepted from the Buddhist past with onomastic changes only, as the elements were shared by all religions: the mountain, the tomb and the saint. The ascetic is respected in Buddhism (*arhat*) and in Ismaili Islam (*pīr*). Similarly, since, as we know, saint veneration is strongly cultivated in these two religions, the Buddhist mausoleum (*stupa*) became a Muslim mausoleum (*mazār*); so the mountain-*stupa* was then regarded as a mountain-*mazār*. On the other hand, the Hindu and Buddhist underground and hidden kingdom were reinterpreted by Muslims, who replaced them with the paradise of the Quran and its marvellous gardens. So

---

20 About the cultural exchanges between Buddhist, Muslims and Sufis at this time, see Papas 2005 and 2010; Zarcone 1995 and 2010.
21 R.A. Stein 1959:526, 532 n. 56.
22 Kollmar-Paulenz 1992–3:79, 84, 86.

the superimposition of Mazdeism and Islam on a Buddhist legend has been facilitated by religious ideas, almost universally accepted, in all the religions.

The cult of the Muztagh Ata, however, presents a double ambiguity. The first is the fact that there is no shrine, no sanctuary, no tomb in this mountain – although imaginary – because the mountain *is* the sanctuary, the *stupa* and the *mazār* (an idea claimed both by the Buddhist and Muslim legends). As a consequence, there are no specific rituals of devotion executed there, with the exception, nevertheless, of intercession prayers, which are recited everywhere in the mountain by the Kyrgyz and Pamiri population. The second ambiguity comes from the fact that the Muztagh Ata is now venerated by three separate currents of Islam, sometimes strongly opposed to each other, who defend various interpretations of the sanctity of the mountain: Sunni Muslims (usually Uyghurs), who regards the Muztagh Ata as the burial of Biblical or Quranic Prophets (e.g. Moses); the Ismaili-Sh'is, who consider the mountain as the mausoleum of Ali or of an Ismaili priest (*pīr*); and the half-Islamized Kyrgyz population, who venerate the Muztagh Ata as a deity or a spirit. However, these three currents share the mountain and, thanks to this veneration, obviate the apparent religious borders.

References

And, M. 1998. *Minyatürlerle Osmanlı-İslâm Mitologyası* (Muslim and Ottoman Mythology through Miniatures). Istanbul, Yapıkredi Y.

Anon. *Tashqurghan Tajik Aptonom Nahiyisining Umumi Ähvali* 1988. (General Situation in the Tajik Autonomous District of Tashqurghan). Ürümchi: Shinjang Khälq Näshriyati.

Abashin, S. 2013. 'Mazars of Boboi-ob: typical and untypical features of holy places in Central Asia'. In Y. Shinmen; M. Sawada, and E. Waite (eds), *Muslim Saints and Mausoleums in Central Asia and Xinjiang*, 91–105. Paris: Jean Maisonneuve.

Abdulahatov, N. 2005. 'The cult of St. Ali ('Ali ibn Abi Talib) in the Ferghana Valley (c. 600–661)', Conference on 'Mazars in Ferghana and in Xinjiang'. Tokyo University of Foreign Studies, Tokyo, November 2005, mimeographed.

Abdulahatov, N. and Eshonboboev, Ö. 2007. *Köhna Marghilon Ziyaratgahlari* [Pilgrimages of the Old Marghilon]. Farghona: Farghona Nashriyati.

Abramzon, S.M. 1990. *Kirgizi i ikh èthnogenetichskie i istoriko-kul'turnye svjazi*. Frunze, Kyrgystan.

Aga-Oglu, M. 1946. 'The Origin of the term mīnā and its meanings'. *Journal of Near Eastern Studie* 5(4):241–56.

Akimushkin, O.F. (ed.) 2001. *Tārikh-i Kāshgar. Anonimnaja tjurkskaja khronika vladetelej Vostochnogo Turkestana po konets* XVII *veka*. Saint Petersburg: Institut Vostokvedenija Rossijskoj Akademi Nauk Sankt-Peterburgskij filial.

Aksel, M. 1967. *Türklerde Dinî Resimler* [Religious Images among the Turks]. Istanbul: Elif.

Attar. Fakhr al-Dīn 1991. *Le Langage des oiseaux*. Paris: Sindbad.

Bailey, H.W. 1971. 'The culture of the Iranian Kingdom of Ancient Khotan in Chinese Turkestan'. *Memoirs of the Toyo Bunko* 29:17–29.

Bernbaum, E.M. 1985. 'The Mythic Journey and its Symbolism: a Study of the Development of Buddhist Guidebooks to Sambhala in Relation to their Antecedents in Hindu Mythology'. Ph.D. thesis, University of California, Berkeley.

Blondeau, A.-M. (ed.) 1998. *Tibetan Mountains Deities, their Cults and representations*. Wien: Verlag der Österreichischen Akademie der Wissenschaften.

Boratav, P.N. 1991. 'Les légendes de Sari-Kiz et d'Al-kiz'. *Turcica* 21–3:221–33.

Capus, G. 1890. *Le Toit du monde*. Paris: Hachette.

Chandra, B.S. 1887. 'Buddhist and other legend about Khoten'. *Journal of the Asiatic Society of Bengal* LV(I):193–203.

Chavannes, F. 1903. 'Voyage de Song Yun dans l'Udyana et le Gandhara'. *Bulletin de l'Ecole française d'Extrême-Orient* 3:518–22.

Chvyr', L.A. 2006. *Obrjady i verovanija ujgurov v XIX–XX vv.* [Rites and Beliefs of the Uyghurs in the nineteenth and twentieth centuries]. Moscow:Izdatel'skaja Firma Vostochnaja Literatura RAN.

Daftary, F. 1990. *The Ismâ'îlîs: their History and Doctrines*. Cambridge: Cambridge University Press.

Demirci, K. 2001. 'Kafdağı'. In *Türkiye Diyanet Vakfı İslam Ansiklopedisi* 24:144. Istanbul: ISAM.

Divaev, A. 1899. 'Baksy, kak lekar'i koldun' [The shaman as a healer and a witch doctor]. *Iz Izvestija oblasti kirghizskih verovanij*. Kazan'.

Donaldson, B.A. 1938. *The Wild Rue. A Study of Muhammadan Magic and Folklore in Iran*. London: Luzac.

Dudoignon, S.A. 2004. 'Local lore, the transmission of learning, and communal identity in late 20th-century Tajikistan: the Khujand-nāma of 'Ārifān Yahyāzād Khujandī'. In Stéphane A. Dudoignon, ed., *Devout Societies vs. Impious States. Transmitting Islamic Learning in Russia, central Asia and China, through the Twentieth Century*, 215–42. Berlin: Klaus Schwarz.

Ehrhard, F.-K. 1996. 'Political and ritual aspects of the search for Himalayan sacred lands'. *Studies in Central and East Asian Religions* 9:37–53.

Fletcher, J.F. 1995. 'Confrontations between Muslim missionaries and nomad unbelievers in the late sixteenth century. Notes on four passages from the "Diyā' al-Qulūb"'. In W. Heissig, (ed.), *Tractata Altaica*, 167–74. Wiesbaden: Otto Harrassowitz.

Gar-j K'am-trül Rinpoche 1978. 'A geography and history of Shambhala'. *The Tibet Journal* III(3):3–11.

Garrone, P. 2000. *Chamanisme et Islam en Asie centrale*. Paris : Jean Maisonneuve.

Gornenskij, I. 2000. *Legendy Pamira i Gindukusha* [Legends from the Pamir and the Hindukush]. Moscow: Aleteja.

Haji Nur Haji and Chen Guoguang 1995. *Shinjang islam tarikhi* [History of Islam in Xinjiang]. Ürümchi: Millätlär Näshriyati.

Hamada, Masami 2004. 'Le Pouvoir des lieux saints dans le Turkestan oriental'. *Annales* 59(5–6):1019–40.

Hedin, S. 1895. 'Attempts to ascend Mustagh Ata'. *The Geographical Journal* 6(4):350–67.

––– 1898. 'Four years' travel in Central Asia'. *The Geographical Journal* 11(3):240–58.

––– 1993 [1899]. *Through Asia*, 2 vols. Delhi: Book Faith India.

Hujiexi, G. 2009. 'Keerkeze zu samande zhouyu he shenge' [Songs and incantations of the Kirghiz shamans]. In J. Seyin (ed.) *Saman xinyang yu minzi wenhua* [Shamanic Beliefs and National Cultures], pp. 383–413. Beijing: Zhungguo shehui kexue chubanshe.

Hüsäyin, N. 1986. 'Qaraqorum Uyghurlirining Hazirqi zaman Örp-Adätliri' [The present customs of the Uyghurs of the Qaraqorum]. *Shinjang Mädäniyiti* 3:54–65.

İnan, A. 2000 [1954]. *Tarihte ve Bugün Şamanizm* [Shamanism in History and Nowadays]. Ankara: TTK.

Kollmar-Paulenz, K. 1992–3. 'Utopian thought in Tibetan Buddhism'. *Studies in Central and East Asian Religions* 5(6):78–96.

Lévi, S. 1905. 'Notes chinoises sur l'Inde'. *Bulletin de l'Ecole française d'Extrême-Orient* V:1–2.

Mir Khāl al-Dīn Kātib ibn-i Mawlānā Qādī Shāh Kūchak al-Yarkandī 1778. 'Hidāyat-nāma'. Persian manuscript no. 1682, Institut of Orientalism of Tashkent, Uzbekistan (Institut Vostokvedenija Akademii Nauk), copied in 1778 (original dated 1729–30).

Ögel, B. 1993. *Türk Mitolojisi (Kaynakları ve açıklamaları ile destanlar)* [Turkish Mythology (Sources and Epics with Commentary)], 2 vols. Ankara : Türk Tarih Kurumu Y.

Ogudin, V.N. 2003a. 'Kul't peshcher v narodnom islame' [The cult of caves in popular Islam]. *Etnograficheskoe obozrenie* 1:71–88.

––– 2003b. 'Gora Boboi-ob – drevniaia sviatynia narodov severo-zapadnoi Fergany (The Mountain Baba-yi Ab, an ancient sanctuary of the people of north-west Fergana). In S.N. Abashin and V.O. Bobrovnikov (eds) *Podvizhniki islama: kul't sviatykh i sufizm v Srednei Azii i na Kavkaze*, pp. 41–68. Moscow, Vostochnaia literatura.

Olufsen, O. 1904. *Through the Unknown Pamirs. The Second Danish Pamir Expedition 1898–99 (Vakhan and Garan)*. London: W. Heinemann.

Orofino, G. 1991. 'The Tibetan myth of the hidden valley in the visionary geography of Nepal'. *East and West* (Instituto Italiano per il Medio ed Estremo Oriente) 41(1–4):239–71.

Papas, A. 2005. *Soufisme et Politique entre Chine, Tibet et Turkestan*. Paris: Jean Maisonneuve.

––– 2010. 'So close to Samarkand, Lhasa. Sufi hagiographies, founder myths and sacred space in Himalayan Islam'. In A. Akasoy, C. Burnett and R. Roeil-Tlalim (eds), *Islam and Tibet. Interactions along the Musk Routes*, pp. 261–79. London: Ashgate – Warburg Institute.

Pinguet, M. 1984. *La Mort volontaire au Japon*. Paris: Gallimard.

Potapov, L.P. 1946. 'Kult' gor na Altae' [The cult of mountain in the Altaï]. *Sovetskaja Ètnografija* 2:145–60.

Puri, B.N. 1987. *Buddhism in Central Asia*. Delhi: Motilal Banarsidass Publishers.

Qurban, M. 2001. 'Qaraqorum Uygurlirining Örp-Adätliri' [Customs of the Uyghurs of Qaraqorul]. *Shinjang Üniversiti Jurnali* 5:47–60.

Qurban, S. 2005. *Tajik Khalq Eghiz Ädäbiyati Toplimi, Rivayätlär* [A collection of texts of oral and popular Tajik literature]. Ürümchi: Shinjang Universiteti Näshriyati.

Rähman, A. 2009. *Äzizanä Qäshqär* [Beloved Kashgar], vol. 1. Ürümchi: Shinjang Universiteti Näshriyati.

Reich, K. 2003. 'Hero and saint: Islamic elements in Uighur oral epics'. *Journal of the History of Sufism* 3:7–24.

Roux, J.-P. 1984. *La Religion des Turcs et des Mongols*. Paris: Payot.

Savüt, T.M. 2002. *Uyghur Folkloridin konsultatsiyä* (Explanations on Uyghur Folklore). Ürümchi: Shinjang Pän-Tekhnika Sähiyä Näshriyati.

Servan-Schreiber 1997. 'Partage de sites et partage de textes. Un modèle d'acculturation de l'islam au Bihar'. In J. Assayag and G. Tarabout (eds) *Altérité et Identité. Islam et Christianisme en Inde*, pp. 143–69. Paris: EHESS.

Shakarmadov, N. 2005. *Folklori Pomir. Asotir, rivoiat* [sic] *va naqlho* [Folklore of the Pamir. Myths, legends and traditions]. Dushanbe: Imperial-Grupp (Akademiiai ilmhoi Jumhurii Tojikiston, Pazhuhishgohi ulumi insonii Bakhshi Pomiri AI JT).

Si-yu-ki 1884. *Buddhist Records of the Western World* (trans. S. Beal), 2 vols. London: Trübner.

Somfai Kara, D. 2004. 'Kirghiz shamanism'. In M.N. Walter and E.J.N. Fridman (eds) *Shamanism, an Encyclopedia of World Beliefs, Practices and Culture*, vol. II, pp. 579–82. Santa Barbara, California: ABC Clio.

––– 2007. The sacred valley of Jay Ata and a Kirghiz Shaman from Xinjiang, China' (contrib. M. Hoppál, musical anal. J. Sipos). *Shaman* 15:47–68.

Stein, A. 1907. *Ancient Khotan Detailed Report of Archaelogical Explorations in Chinese Turkestan*, 2 vols. Oxford: Clarendon Press.

––– 1928. *Innermost Asia. Detailed Report of Explorations in Central Asia, Kan-su, and Eastern Îrân*, 4 vols. Oxford: Clarendon Press.

Stein, R.A. 1959. *Recherches sur l'épopée et le barde au Tibet*. Paris : Presses universitaires de France.

Streck, M. and Miquel, A. 1978. 'Kāf'. *Encyclopédie de l'islam*, vol. 4, pp. 418–19. Leiden: Brill.

Sukhareva, O.A. 1975. 'Perezhitki demonologii i shamanstva y ravninnykh Tadzhikov'. In *Domusulmanskie verovanija i obrjady ve Srednej Azii*, pp. 5–93. Moscow: Akademija Nauk SSSR.

Sykes, E.C. 1901. 'Persian folklore'. *Folklore* 12(3):261–80.

––– 1924. 'Notes on the folklore of Chinese Turkestan'. *Folklore* 35(3) :249–61.

Temple, R.C. 1886. 'Bibliography of folk-lore. Vernacular publications in the Panjab'. *The Folk-Lore Journal* 4(4):273–307.

Tilman, H.W. 1953. *Deux Montagnes et une rivière*. French translation of *Two Mountains and a River* (1949). Paris: Arthaud.

Vorozhejkin, Z.N. 1961. 'Doislamskie verovanija Kirgizov v XVI v. (po rukopisi 'Zija al-Kulub')' [Pre-Islamic Beliefs of the Kirghizs in 16th Century. About the Manuscript of Diyā al-Qulūb]. In *Vosprosy filologii i istorii stran sovetskogo i zarubezhnogo vostoka*, pp. 182–9. Moscow: Izdatel'stvo Vostchnoj Literatury, 1961.

Yamazaki, G. 1990. 'The legend of the foundation of Khotan'. *Memoirs of the research Department of the Toyo Bunko* 48:55–80.

Zarcone, T. 1995. 'Sufism from Central Asia among the Tibetans in the 16–17th Centuries'. *The Tibet Journal* 20(3):96–114.

––– 1996. 'Une route de sainteté islamique entre l'Asie centrale et l'Inde: la voie Ush-Kashghar-Srinagar'. In T. Zarcone (ed.) *Inde-Asie centrale. Routes du commerce et des idées, Cahiers d'Asie Centrale*, pp. 227–54. Aix-en-Provence, Édisud.

––– 2010. 'Between legend and history: about the 'conversion' to Islam of two Prominent Lamaists in 17th–18th Century'. In A. Akasoy, C. Burnett and R. Roeil-Tlalim (eds) *Islam and Tibet. Interactions along the Musk Routes*, pp. 281–92. London: Ashgate – Warburg Institute.

––– 2013. 'Atypical mausoleum: the case of the Solomon Throne (Kirghizistan), *qadamjāy*, demons-cult and itinerary-pilgrimage '. In Y. Shinmen; M. Sawada and E. Waite (eds) *Saint-Cult in Muslim Saints and Mausoleums in Central Asia and in Xinjiang*, pp. 73–89. Paris: Jean Maisonneuve.

III

Ambiguous sites cross-culturally

Figure 1   View from Ascona overlooking lake Maggore. Photographed by M. Hobart.

CHAPTER 7

Monte Verita, the 'Mountain of Truth' in Ascona

A pilgrimage site of paradoxes and contradictions

ANGELA HOBART

The name Monte Verita, 'Mountain of Truth', evokes the idea of a pilgrimage site, a place that releases humans from their everyday-life routine, permitting them a creative and liberating personal transformation. Victor and Edith Turner (1978:251), in their classic on pilgrimage, commented on the idiosyncratic, quirky, subversive and utopian nature of this genre of travel. These attributes come vividly to the fore in discussing Monte Verita, a verdant plateau, with a magnificent view over the village Ascona and Lake Maggiore (Figure 1), which flows from south Switzerland into Italy. It is a site that since the beginning of the twentieth century has accommodated diverse, at times conflicting, religious and secular meanings and practices. This is epitomized by the regal statue of the multi-breasted Goddess Artemis von Ephesos (Figure 2), who inspired Harald Szeemann in designing the permanent exhibition on the history of Monte Verita in 1978. The Goddess's many breasts suggested to Szeeman (1980:5) that the notion of 'truth' as conjured up by Monte Verita has many perspectives, begging the question whether it is naïve to seek for one universal truth in a social world that, as Morris Bloch (2008:22–30) argued, is the product of dialogue, discourses and diverse cultures. This is borne out by the different small communities that were drawn at the beginning of the twentieth century to Monte Verita and the surrounding environment in search of alternative, more liberated ways of life. These included utopians, anarchists, bohemians, nudists, vegetarians, Rosicrucians, artists, intellectuals, writers, and psychoanalysts, among others.

I want to draw attention to a strand that flows subtly through the entire discussion: that is, the resurgence of the power of nature, of Mother Earth in

Figure 2 Goddess Artemis von Ephesos, second century. Archaeology Museum Naples. Courtesy of the Superintendent for Archaeological Heritage of the provinces of Naples and Caserta.

her many facets, that is experienced by pilgrims, wayfarers and increasingly these days by tourists, who visit in a spirit of mindfulness. After introducing Monte Verita and its surroundings, my chapter is divided into three sections: briefly, the Celtic and early Christian period; the life-reform communities and anarchists around the turn of the twentieth century; and the contemporary period. Because of space restraints I mention only some of the key individuals who left their imprint on this area.[1]

Introduction

Up to the fourteenth century the plateau of Monte Verita was called Monascia, a name that suggests a monastic site. In the local Italian dialect it was designated I Mott (meaning 'unkempt hairy mons Veneris'). The term was used to refer to three forest-covered hills between the villages of Arcegno, Ronco and Ascona in the canton of Ticino (Wackernagel 2005:176). These hills were said to resemble a nude woman asleep, with her prominent mons Veneris displayed, or three fertile breasts of the goddess Artemis (ibid.:17).

Three areas in Switzerland are attributed with great magnetic force – and particular reference has been made to Monte Verita in this context (Szeeman 1980:6; Wackernagel 2005:176). Szeeman (1980:82) describes the magnetic irregularity of the geology, of the subsoil of the mountains between Lake Maggiore and Centrovalli, the region in which Monte Verita is situated. These rock formations originate from deep inside the earth, which accounts for the intense magnetism of the region called the Ivrea zone – a tectonic terrain in the Italian Alps named after the city of Ivrea.[2] Both the climate and the magnetism of the region are deemed responsible for the rich semi-tropic vegetation. Perhaps the magnetic force has affinity with the power, spirit or consciousness that shamans say imbue the world of nature (Vitebsky 1995:22). The physicist Peat (1994:266–7) points out that the significance of a place and the energy or spirit associated with it is intrinsic to indigenous science worldwide. It is evident in megalithic Europe, geomancy in China and the

---

1 I want to express my special gratitude to Giovanni and Laura Simona, Reto Mortasini, Carzzetti and Anna-Maria zur Dohna, who gave me relevant information on Monte Verita. Apart for Maria zur Dohna all are from the Ticino; the last informant lives in the areas since many years. I also thank Caroline Ifeke and Doreen Irwin for their comments.
2 This irregularity was confirmed by Dr Joerg Hansen from the Geological Office in Bellinzona (Szeeman 1980:6). The Swiss geographer Dr Giovanni Simona pointed out to me (pers. comm. 2011) that Monte Verita was located at the boundary between the Eurasian and African plates. This accounts for the rocks of high density (with a high content of a special iron and magnesium) in the region, which in turn produced the magnetic and gravitational anomalies.

Figure 3   Celtic birds of blue glass. Archaeology Museum Locarno. Photographed by A. Hobart.

dream tracks of the Australian Aborigines. Aligning a sacred site with specific times and sunlight or moonlight could also be deemed important. Such power, like magnetic force, has its own impetus and dynamic. Some people are more attuned to this than others.

The Celts and early Christian period

The magnetic force attributed to the environment finds affinity in the worldview evoked by the Celts (the Helvetia) who reached Switzerland around 500 BC. Iron weapons, tools and artefacts were found at the site of La Trene on Lake Neuchatel, demonstrating their development of Iron Age technology (Alcock 2009:4). Although the origin of the Celtic people is obscure, they consisted of groups, identified with a common language, whose territory stretches from the British Isles across central Europe to Asia Minor and southwards to the Mediterranean countries (ibid.:1–18). Evidence of Celtic society is primarily derived from Julius Caesar's accounts of the Gallic wars and myths carried down by oral tradition, especially the colourful Irish tales (ibid.:19).[3] From my conversation with Mr Carazzetti (20 June 2010), the keeper of the local

---

3   The Celtic civilization came to a decline in part through internal warfare between tribes, as well as invasions from northern tribes such as the Vandals and Huns in the fifth century. This paved the way for the Romans, with their disciplined military tactics and organization, to conquer the Celts, whose cultural traditions became Romanized (Alcock 2009:169 – 76).

Monte Verita, the 'Mountain of Truth' in Ascona

Archaeological Museum in Locarno, the script on a megalith in the area testifies to the intermingling of Celtic and Etruscan influences. The remains of a fortress on one of the hills, referred by the Celtic term Baladrum, also points to the presence of the Celtic people (Wackernagel 2005:176). It is noteworthy that one of literal meanings of the name Ascona, is the Lady or the Queen of Ace,[4] which relates to prehistoric times and the importance of maternal deities (ibid.:176); Mr Carazzetti gave an additional possible meaning to 'ascona': in Celtic it may imply large fields where animals graze, and it is known that cattle and grain crops were of special importance for the livelihood of the people (Alcock 2009:81–94). The museum has an earthenware bowl and glass birds (Figure 3) facing one another – a typical Celtic motif – that provide additional evidence of Celtic influence, though the techniques for using glass were introduced by the Romans, who controlled Swiss territory until about 400 AD. Inscriptions, reliefs and sculpture indicate that grottos, trees, stones, fire and water – connected with thunder and lightning - played an important role in Celtic rituals. All natural phenomena were imbued with vital power and associated with deities that helped protect against and pacify malign forces (Alcock 2009:131–4). These privileged natural elements also participated in cosmic fecundity among the Taoists (Eliade 1954:153) who, as will emerge, left a profound impact on twentieth-century movements at Monte Verita .

Good (2008:14–17) draws attention to the prominence of earth deities, with special reference to Mother Earth, an important healing figure in many part of the world still today. This Great Goddess became associated with the Black Earth Goddess, the Black Madonna, who is found in various parts of Europe – Italy, Spain, France and Poland. Thousands of pilgrims annually visit her shrine in Einsiedeln in Bavaria because of her known healing efficacy. In Ascona there is one small shrine with a dignified image of the Black Madonna (Figure 4) situated on a narrow, winding path behind the fifteenth-century church San Michele, erected at the Celtic site Baladrum. She can be identified with the Egyptian Goddess Iris, the Ephesian Diana, Rangda in Bali, Sita or Kali in India. Black is the colour of fertility, like the rich black soil of the Nile. The goddess, as David Napier (2003:282) argues, is associated with the apparently non-rational, which if harnessed and contextualized, can lead to a deeper reality and renewal.[5] During the centuries following the Celts, the Catholic faith became embedded in the Ticino, and it remains the most Catholic canton in the country. Images of the Virgin Mary, who asserts the

---

4   Wackernagel writes 'La Dame ou la Reine des As ou des Ases'.
5   Andrew Harvey (1995:37) describes the Black Madonna as the Queen of Nature, 'the transcendental Kali-Mother, the black womb of light' out of which all worlds arise and fall back to.

Figure 4 Black Madonna by the path behind the fifteenth century church San Michele leading to Monte Verita. Photographed by A. Hobart.

gentler qualities of purity and obedience, sought to displace the dark, hidden qualities of the Black Madonna. The many shrines, medieval chapels and churches in the valleys between the rivers and the sky, such as Madonna del Sasso in Locarno or Madonna della Fontanna, Chapel of the Goddess of the Fountain, built in the seventeenth century, are witnesses to this process.

Madonna dell Fontanna still remains a quiet pilgrimage site near Monte Verita. Its myth of origin (Good 2008:15) acts as a warrant to activities performed there. This myth tells of a deaf girl who would herd her sheep. However, the sheep died because of a drought in the area. But she saw a spring of water in a grotto, and mysteriously was cured of her deafness after drinking some of the water, while at the same time the land became fertile once more. Irrespective that a modern underground tunnel for a road joining Locarno to Bellinzona has recently been cut into the land, polluting the water, pilgrims continue to visit the sacred site. The crutches, rosaries, amulets there show its healing orientation. The grotto also celebrates nature's beauty, as illustrated in a few lines from an anonymous poem hanging on a paper on the wall.

> The Goddess of the Fountain is manifest in nature,
> in a growing tree, the colours of a flower, the fragrance of a rose.
> I am present in the consciousness of everything –
> in the exquisite shape of a stone, in a tiny grain of sand,
> in the majesty of a mountain, in the rhythms of nature.
>   All this surrounds you.
>   I am in your heart-centre.[6]

The Reform Communities at Monte Verita at the turn of the twentieth century

Monte Verita is not a pilgrimage site like Mecca, Jerusalem, Lourdes, Rome or Mount Kailash. However, there are other circumstances when the term pilgrimage has been applied, for instance, in relation to war graves, concentration camps or even an Elvis Presley shrine. At the beginning of the twentieth century anarchists and life-reform communities settled at Monte Verita and its vicinities. These people can be called pilgrims as they are essentially 'archetypical seekers' (Coleman and Eade 2004:6). Prominent figures who inspired them were such writers and philosophers as Jean-Jacques Rousseau (1712–78), Nietzsche (1828–1910) and Leo Tolstoy (1828–1910).

The industrial revolution of the nineteenth century wrought profound changes in the life of the people, that were also impacted by the rise of capitalism, Protestantism and the Enlightenment. This is not the place to discuss the complexities of the industrialization in Europe, except to point out that the effects, while favourable to some, brought squalor and suffering

---

6   This is my translation from the Italian: *Nella natura tu vedi me, nella crescita di un albero, nel colore di un fiore, nel profumo di una rosa. Io sono presente in ogni cosa, si sempre consapvole in questo. Nella bellezza e nella forma di una pietra, in un minuscolo granello di sabbia, nella maestra di una montagna, io sono la. Scorri col ritmo della natura. Fonditi con tutto quanto e intorno a te. Ti troverai circondato dal meglio.*

Figure 5 The pilgrim Gusto Graeser's on his nomadic wanders in Germany. Courtesy Deutsche Monte-Verita Archive, Freudenstein.

in their wake. It is against this backdrop that individuals sought to escape from an encompassing social structure. In Martin Green's words: 'For artists, the anarchists, the theosophists, Ascona was a natural centre, a home of the spirit. It was an unofficial centre, in a sense secret, in many ways scandalous, but a ganglion of the protest system of all Europe.' (cited in Schwab 2003:247).

The history of Monte Verita, as such, began when a small group of predominantly German people came to the Ticino. In 1900 they founded a vegetarian and naturist colony and sanatorium at a site they named Monte Verita, 'Mountain of Truth'. Prominent members of this founding group were the pianist Ida Hofman, a rich industrialist's son, Henri Oedenkoven from Belgian, and Karl and Gusto Graeser (Wackernagel 2005:180–2).

Among these early Montevertani, i.e. migrants to Monte Verita, I want here to draw attention only to the wandering pilgrim Gusto Graeser (1879–1958) (Figure 5). He was born in Rumania and died near Munich. He was a charismatic figure, who loosely participated in the activities at Monte Verita. A tall, imposing man, Gusto Graeser wandered throughout Europe. Scholars have pointed out that walking for hours on foot can be viewed as a form of self-sacrifice, an act of endurance and austerity (Coleman and Eade 2004:11). Graeser lived off his speeches and from selling his poems to passers-by on the streets. Finally he settled in a grotto behind Monte Verita near to a camp for Polish refugees from Nazi Germany (Wackernagel 2005:182). He was a poet, strict pacifist and nature-prophet drawn to the ideals of both Nietzsche and Saint Francis of Assisi. Similar to the Tolstoy, Graeser conjoined non-violence and spiritual anarchy. Some people referred to him as the Gandhi of the West; others considered him 'mad', describing him as having a 'small green sparrow' (*ein Gruenspecht*) in his head (ibid.:182). In fact Gusto Graeser was sent twice to prison and threatened with deportation to the concentration camp Buchenwald for his bizarre, asocial behaviour.

Graeser became deeply interested in Eastern philosophy, specifically Taoism, and even produced a rerendering of the Tao Te Ching of the third century BC by Lao-Tzu, which he passed over to his friend, the poet and novelist Herman Hesse. For Taoists, Tao means 'the way the universe works' and can also be translated as the 'way of the vital spirit'(Waley, 1977:30, 39). The 'way' cannot be grasped by the ordinary senses nor described in words. Hence sages speak in riddles and paradoxes, at times like fools (Okakura 1964:20). This could describe Graeser.

Herman Hesse (1877–1962) lived for several years in the Ticino and was cured from his alcohol dependency during his three weeks sojourn at the Monte Verita sanatorium. He and Graeser studied the Upanishads and the Tao Te Ching together (Wackernagel 2005:181). Graeser's influence on Hesse is evident in such works as *Siddharta, Demian* or *Monte Verita (Der Weltverbesserer)*.

The yearning to reconnect with the processes of nature, the substance of the earth, the wilderness, also propelled the early Monteveritani in the life-reform (*Lebensreform*) programmes at Monte Verita, which was conceived of as a 'temple site' (see Szeemann 1980:62). Their aim was 'to live only from the fruits of the earth in a radical return to nature' (Mautner 2000:6). Jean Jacques Rousseau's philosophy is reflected in this phrase. Rousseau, the eighteenth-century scholar from Geneva, argued that city life, with its inherent economic inequality, led to corrupted morals; he advocated humans return to nature in order to rediscover their natural innate goodness – hence his metaphor 'the noble savage' (see Mautner 2000:490–2). The early twentieth century is a complicated period, when concepts from both the West and the East intermingled, and became intertwined with conflicting images, values and beliefs derived from paganism, spiritualism, natural medicine, the Rosicrucian brotherhood and theosophy, atheism, anarchism and communism or libertarian socialism.

The life-reform programmes (see, for instance, Mros 2009a; Schwab 2003) that unfolded in the vegetarian cooperative at Monte Verita sought to pave the way for a new utopia. Hundreds of Germans, but also visitors

Figure 6   Dancer at Monte Verita, with the title 'Free Love and Anarchy'. Courtesy Verlag/Book and Media GmbH, Munich.

from France, Russia, Italy, even Argentina, apart from Swiss themselves, were drawn to the site, where they in general stayed about six weeks (Mros 2009 a:263). The opening of the Gottard tunnel in 1882 in Switzerland and the advancement in land transformation of course made travel easier. The main programmes run at the sanatorium included:

- Strict vegetarianism and abstinence of alcohol.
- Nudism in order to recapture sensuous feelings and reconnect with nature.
- Freedom of expression in dance, music, poetry and free love. The dancers were nude or wore scanty clothes. The Hungarian Rudolf von Laban (1879–1958) became a key figure in the sphere of dance and music and hence is singled out. His notation, known as Labannotation, has left an impact on numerous systems of dance in Europe. He sought to unite the arts (sound, dance and word). His emphasis on free body expression in combination with communal dance was essentially a vital protest against all institutional artistic forms and social conventions that underpinned bourgeois society of the time (Figure 6). This talented choreographer of dance defined his dancing community as the 'Cathedral of the Future' (Mara Folini 2000:29).
- Women's emancipation – 'women should not act like puppets but like humans' (Schwab 2003:84). Women were seen to have an important role at this time in mediating between sensory experience and rational, disembodied reason.

- Reform of clothing. It should be simple. Women need not wear restrictive clothes, like corsets. Men wore loose shirts, trousers to the calves and sandals, or remained barefoot.
- Reform of writing, for example, no use of capital letters.

The outdoor activities conducted at Monte Verita were interconnected and can be considered holistic, not being dominated by the Cartesian dualism that separates mind from body, spirit from matter. Yet they took on their own individualistic, at times quirky, lurid and subversive colouring. A ritualistic element comes to the fore in the dance performances instigated by the Hungarian aristocrat Rudolf von Laban in an attempted reconciliation by humans with the earth and the elements: for instance, the torchlight processions with dance celebrating hymns to the sun performed during the height of the First World War[7] or the majestic dances by Charlotte Bara, suggestive of Egyptian mythology (Mara Folini 2000:29). These performances were essentially 'liminal' or 'quasi-liminal' events that in Turner and Turner's (1978:253) words are characteristically found in modern industrial societies. Such performances were liberating and potentially healing for those participating.

The anarchists who found their way to Monte Verita deserve special mention. The most remarkable were Michael Bakunin (1814–76) and Prince Peter Kropotkin (1842–1921), who left behind a legacy of original and influential literary works. To cite the Turners (1978:3), their pilgrimage may have been about 'potentiality' as well as 'transition', providing a testing ground for new ideas. These intellectuals refuted all kinds of domination, specifically challenging the legitimacy of state power. Bakunin's viewpoint is vividly illustrated in his fragmented literary study *God and the State*:

> The privileged man, whether politically or economically, is a man depraved in mind and heart. That is a social law which admits of no exception, and is as applicable to entire nations as well as classes, corporations, and individuals. It is the law of equality, the supreme condition of liberty and humanity.
>
> (Bakunin 1970:31)

---

7   Von Laban was an important figure in the history of dance. In 1913 he moved his dance school from Munich to Monte Verita, where it became an integral part of the individualistic Vegetarian Cooperative. He became a member of the O.T.O., the Order of Oriental Templars, led by Theodor Reuss, who frequented Monte Verita, and van Laban's 'Songs to the Sun' drew disparate mystics, Rosicrucians, Templars and Gnostics to the area.

Bakunin further emphasized,

> I recognise no infallible authority... Authority is imposed upon me by no one, neither by men nor God. Otherwise I would repel them with horror, and bid the devil take their counsels.
>
> (ibid.:33)

The historian David Goodway (1988:5) argues that anarchist precursors can be traced back to Chinese Taoism, Lao Tzu and Chunag T'zu, as well as to Greek Antiquity and Zeno of Citium. To quote from the Tao Te Ching:

> The man of highest 'power' does not reveal himself as a possessor of 'power'
> Therefore he keeps his 'power'
> The man of inferior 'power' cannot rid it of the appearance of 'power'
> Therefore he is in truth without 'power'.
> The man of highest 'power' neither acts nor is there
> any who so regard him.
>
> (Waley 1968:189)

It is clear that the Taoist position accords with that of anarchism and libertarianism, which asserts the absence of a master, of a sovereign (Goodway 2006:4). This point is lucidly expressed in Ivan Turgenev's classic, *Father and Son*, where one of the characters says 'A Nihilist is a man who doesn't acknowledge any authorities, who doesn't accept a single principle on faith, no matter how much that principle may be surrounded by respect.' (Turgenev 2008:23).

Like the Taoists, the anarchists, while known for their diverse approaches, all rejected the ruling classes; it must be remembered that the semi-feudal Russian state at the time was oppressive and harsh (Goodway 2006:9). Bakunin and Kropotkin travelled widely. Yet their pilgrimages were in some ways internal ones. In tune with the magic of Taoism, many anarchists assumed the universe was malleable through reflective thought, contemplation, stillness, becoming one with the rhythms of nature, yielding like water against which nothing can prevail (see Waley 1968:238). The small and large waterfalls that gush and flow down cliffs into the river valleys in the Ticino beautifully display this quality.

The fruits of anarchism are still widespread today, especially in terms of discontent with the state. However, the life-reform movements at Monte Verita petered out to an end in the 1920s. A number of reasons can be outlined to explain their decline (see Schwab 2003:259–66). The idealist concepts underpinning the sanatorium lost their momentum as it became ever-more commercial, regressing into a private enterprise. The site remained an attraction for the bourgeois elite from all over the world, while the sanatorium became a healthcare centre like many others, especially in Germany. Two of the original founders went to Brazil, and Karl Graeser left the colony disillusioned with the sanatorium's concessions the early Monteveritani were never integrated into the Ticino community; they remained essentially in a structural void, neither incorporated into their homeland nor Ticino society. Indeed locals referred to them derogatively as *ballabiot*, which in the Ticino dialect means 'those who walk around in the nude and are barmy' (pers. comm. Reto Mortazini 2010). One elderly female inhabitant of the area who recalled the bizarre doings at the site by the standards of the villagers described the reform community thus:

> Monte Verita was a Babel Tower of Sin [*Suenden Babel*], a site that yielded to the temptations of the flesh and desire. People slept with one another indiscriminately. Their total lack of restraint was shocking.
> (anon. Ticinese pers. comm. 2009)

In effect, the site remained a self-enclosed, self-absorbed colony of select foreign visitors, travellers and pilgrims in search of a new paradise. Ascona around the turn of the twentieth century was not a deluxe tourist resort, but a poor fishing village, exacerbating the inhabitants' sense of alienation from Monte Verita.

I want to make brief mention of the artists who came to the Ticino. Names that come to mind are Huga Ball, Hans Arp, Alexej von Jawlensky and other, less well-known, artists of the Bauhaus. The Russian painter Marianne von Werefkin (1860–1938) (Figure 7) deserves singling out. She migrated to Ascona, where she settled, mixing with the villagers, many of whom respected her. Her paintings of lakes, people and mountains in the Ticino are in whirling yellows, reds, deep greens and blues. Their capacity to release matter into a light seems to hint at an element of self-sacrifice. In this they have affinity with Impressionist paintings that depict the continuous play of light and shade in the environment, including the magnetic forces inherent in nature that Jungian analysts associate with female powers and the Dark Goddess (see Woodman and Dickson 1997:192–6).

Ultimately, the life-reform colony at Monte Verita could not sustain itself financially and was sold to Baron Eduard von der Heydt in 1926. Before turning to the contemporary era, I want to mention the Eranos conferences, many of which, in the early years, took place at Monte Verita. The story of Eranos, which means 'Sacred Banquet' in ancient Greek, implying an 'offering meal' (Hakl 2001:96), blends with the history of Monte Verita as a

Figure 7 Painting of the 'Big Moon' by Marienne Werefkin. Courtesy Museum Commuale d'Art Moderna Ascona.

pilgrimage site. Hakl (2001) is the only scholar to have written extensively about Eranos. These conferences drew eminent intellectuals from religious studies, philosophy, art and science to Ascona annually, for about three weeks in the summer, from 1933 for at least seventy years. Outstanding among the scholars who participated fairly regularly are Carl Gustav Jung, Erich Newmann, Mircea Eliade, Martin Buber, Paul Tillich, Henri Corbin, Teitaro Suzuki and Annemarie Schimmel, among many others. Eranos meetings are still continuing, though with less grandeur, at Monte Verita.

Eranos was founded by the notable Swiss, formerly Dutch, art historian Olga Fröbe-Kapteyn. In her inaugurating speech at Eranos, she explained that she sought to stimulate through the meetings interchange between Western psychology and Eastern spirituality (Hakl 2001:88). Fröbe-Kapteyn's vision of Eranos as a pilgrimage site, a meeting centre for intellectuals on a quest, emerges in her appellation of it as 'a Grail [einen Gral] hanging between heaven and earth'. This is an evocative metaphor for the conferences; the discussions were coupled with meals where the scholars sat together – probably in her imagination 'around a table' (ibid.:82) like the knights of King Arthur.

Carl Gustav Jung (1875–1961) had a profound impact on the Eranos conferences for over twenty years (ibid.:87). An influential thinker and clinician, he founded analytical psychology and the Jungian Institute of Psychotherapy at Zurich. Jung stressed the importance of studying Eastern and Western philosophy, alchemy, sociology and the arts, and of remaining separate from political movements at the time.[8] His teachings on the collective unconscious, 'archetypes' and 'individuation' (see Perera 1981:95–6) left an impact on Eranos (Hakl 2001:91). His own spiritual and healing journey largely began after Freud and he disagreed on theoretical issues and parted ways, after which he went through a drawn-out disturbed period. It was during this time that Jung began to self-experiment, trying to understand the images, symbols and myths that surfaced from his unconscious, especially during dreams, and their efficacious power.[9] His concepts of archetypes resonated with pagan prototypes evident in the Ticino. We need merely to consider the Anima, expressed as the Great Mother or Mother Earth, the dark goddess, who epitomizes active, ambivalent energy, and other female archetypes. Other dominant archetypes are the mandala (circle in Sanskrit), the snake or dragon. In 1916 Jung painted his first mandala, which summed up his inner realization of the cosmic passage in which the macrocosmic and microcosmic are integrated (ibid.:75). Jung recounted that the image had emerged in a dream:

---

8 Jung's political stance is nebulous. Although some of his articles have racist and fascist overtones, he also helped some Jews escape from Germany. He emphasized the necessity of Eranos remaining separate from all political movements (Hakl 2001:125–33).

9 Jung's orientation emerges vividly in the *Red Book* (2009), a folio volume which is bound in red leather. It is written in elegant calligraphy and richly illustrated by Jung. He wrote the manuscript between 1914 and 1930 after his relationship with Freud ruptured. The volume (see Jafee 1979:66–75) is a masterpiece in which Jung explores his experiences and insight that inner images are linked to the collective unconscious, archetypes and the spiritual realm.

I found myself in a dirty, sooty city which was Liverpool. I walked through the dark streets with a number of Swiss people. The city seemed to be above a harbour, on cliffs. When we reached the plateau we found that many streets converged into a square. In the centre (of the square) was a round pool, and in the middle of it a small island. While everything round was obscured by rain, fog, smoke, and dimly lit darkness, the little island blazed with sunlight. On it stood a single tree, a magnolia, in a shower of reddish blossoms.

(Jaffe 1979:92)

The magnolia tree represents the axis mundi, or centre of the cosmos, which conjoins the spheres of heaven, earth and underworld. Magnolia trees happen to flourish in the Ticino, where in spring they are covered with deep red, white or pink blossoms that Jung must have seen during his frequent visits to the region.

The mandala expressed to Jung 'wholeness', the "regulating centre of the personality which transcends the ego' (Perera 1981:96). Undoubtedly his own psychological experiences and fantasies drew him to study in depth such manuscripts as the Chinese book *The Secret of the Golden Flower*, which Richard Wilheim (1957) translated and Jung commented on. The text combines Taoist and Buddhist techniques of meditation. A quote from Jung highlights the proximity of his thinking to some ancient Eastern philosophies.

The Golden Flower (or 'heavenly heart') is a mandala symbol... It is drawn either seen from above as a regular geometric ornament, or as a blossom growing from a plant. The plant is frequently a structure in brilliant fiery colours growing out of a bed of darkness, and carrying the blossom of light up top.

(ibid.:101)

The golden mandala in this painting by Jung (see Jaffe 1979:71) is surrounded by a fierce dragon (Figure 8) – an image known in Taoism as evoking 'the spirit of Cosmic Change' (Okakura 1906:20).

Jung's extensive travels led him to India and New Mexico, where he became aware that varied forms of mandalas were used in diverse settings; for instance, in the sand paintings of the Navajo or Pueblo Indians during curing rituals. He also encouraged his patients to draw circular formations in order to revitalize their realities. Many of Jung's ideas continued to be explored at Eranos conferences (at both Monte Verita and Villa Gabriella) by such renowned scholars as the Jewish kabbalah specialist Gershom Scholem (1897–1982), the Islamic philosopher Henri Corbin (1903–78), the historian

Monte Verita, the 'Mountain of Truth' in Ascona 173

Figure 8   Painting of golden mandala surrounded by a dragon evoking 'the spirit of cosmic change' in Taoism by Carl Gustaf Jung. The Red Book (Sonu Shamdasani), 2009. Courtesy Norton and Company, New York, London.

of religion Mircea Eliade (1907–86) and the Jungian psychotherapist James Hillman (1926–2011) (Hakl 2001:249–73, 329– 38).

Were the travellers, intellectuals and interested laypeople who travelled to Eranos pilgrims? Although 'communitas' probably did not arise during Eranos conferences, they undoubtedly encouraged voluntary comradeship between participants, especially if they came regularly, whereby it is worth noting that the participants belonged primarily to the intellectual elite. At this point I want to turn to the contempory era at Monte Verita. It will become apparent that themes and motives of the past are echoed in the present.

Figure 9   Baron von der Heydt standing in front of the old Building of Monte Verita 1926, ymago.net. The symbols of yin and yang are inscribed on the terrace and windows. They represent the two complementary principles in Taoisim – the female, dark one and the male, bright one – that interact and affect all things in the universe.

The contemporary era

Baron von der Heydt, who acquired Monte Verita in 1926 (Figure 9), is primarily important in the context of this chapter due to his encouragement of prominent intellectuals and artists to follow their quests and develop their ideas.[10] After his death in 1964 we enter modern times, when secular society's driving force, money, emerges. In this period self-conscious attempts are made, in part through money, to engage the senses and the imagination in order to reconnect humans to something meaningful outside themselves, the land and the natural elements.

In his will the Baron donated Monte Verita to the canton of Ticino with the explicit wish that it should become a cultural centre. In 1989 the canton took over the debts of the complex and it became a private foundation. The canton, the Municipal Council of Ascona and Stefano Franscini of the Federal Institute of Technology at Zurich now cooperate to put on international conferences and workshops in the sciences and humanities. At the same time, it is a hotel

---

10   Von der Heydt was a complex and ambiguous person. He came from a wealthy German family of bankers and politicians, as well as patrons of the arts. How far he supported the German National Socialist party during World War Two remains unclear (see Mrosb 2000).

providing beds for eighty-eight guests. In 2002, Claudio Rossetti became the Director of the Board of the Foundation till 2011. He was dynamic in this position and put his own stamp on Monte Verita. Lorenzo Sonognini took over from Rossetti and is the present director of the hotel.[11] Can the site in the twenty-first century be conceived of as a modern pilgrimage centre? Claudio Rossetti, as well as Lorenzo Sonognini, clearly wish to honour the best of the site's heritage while concentrating on human rights and peace. International conferences and workshops are organized throughout the year. In the same way as the Eranos conferences, especially in their heyday, they provide, in Coleman and Eade's words in their analysis of pilgrimages, 'a testing ground of new ideas ... that tend be populist, anarchical, and even anticlerical' (2004:2). Three specific projects initiated in recent years by Monte Verita may be seen within the context of pilgrimages.

Firstly, visitors are encouraged to take walks through the woods in the vicinity of the hotel. The paths are winding and sometimes can barely be discerned amongst the plant growth, rocks and stones. When the sky is clear, the sunlight shining through the pine trees reveals the textures, shades and colours of the variegated terrain. An intimate relationship may be experienced between the wayfarer, the experience of walking along, and nature, something the anthropologist Tim Ingold refers to 'as becoming knowledgeable'. In his poetic words, 'knowledge is grown along the myriad paths we take as we make our ways through the (weather-) world' (2010:121). Potentially restorative rituals are performed in the dark forest, at a place called Valle del Silenzio, marked by what appear as Celtic stones.[12]

Secondly, a Japanese tea house (Figure 10) and small tea plantation were created on the Monte Verita premises in 2006. The tea ceremony has Taoist and Zen associations. Zen, which is derived from the Sanskrit term, *dyana*, meaning meditation, reiterates the Taoist principles that underlie the tea ritual performed in the tea house by a host a few participants (Okakura 1964:25). The water in the ritual represents *yin* and fire in the heath *yang*, the 'life-breath of Earth' and the 'life-breath of Heaven' (Waley 1968:110). The ceremony has aesthetic and imaginative dimensions. All items used during the ritual, which lasts for about half an hour, are treated with a deference that requires moving the body mindfully. The fragrant silence of the tea, the incense, the simplicity

---

[11] Lorenzo Sonognini views Monte Verita as a place of peace and regeneration that helps to restore balance between people and nature.
[12] I participated, for example, in a Paraguayan harp-music performance initiated by the Monte Verita management. It took place late in the evening under a starlit sky at the Valle del Silenzio in 2009. Many such events were organized during the time that Rossetti was director and may still be performed these days.

Figure 10   Japanese tea ceremony at Monte Verita. Photographed by A. Hobart.

and organic harmony of the wooden room all evoke ideals of harmony, tranquillity, purity and respect that attune the participants to one another and nature's vibrations. The ceremony is noticeably for the cosmopolitan elite, who subscribe to global and democratic ideals beyond a particular nation-state. It is costly to attend (SF 35 per head in 2010). A Japanese scholar (whom I met in Ascona), who is also a tea master, indicated that the ritual at Monte Verita had become largely a business enterprise for rich international tourists. Hence, money intrudes again as a mediator and valuation of the tea-sipping experience. Yet the specific purposes of tea ceremonies have always changed over time. So are the guests who come to the tea ceremony at Monte Verita pilgrims or rich tourists? Eric Cohen (quoted in Coleman and Eade 2004:9), among other scholars, argues that in modernity the transition between a pilgrim and a tourist is fluid. It depends on the seriousness of their journey and search for local 'authenticity'. Undoubtedly, through the tea ritual and money Monte Verita is contextualized as a global destination for those seeking to reconnect with the woodlands, water and light.

The respect and homage engendered during the tea ritual subtly reiterates an important aim of the directors of Monte Verita – to further human rights that recognize the inherent dignity, equality and rights of all individuals (Rapport and Overing 2007:212). Specific plants in Monte Verita's park are identified with the thirty articles of the Human Rights Declaration. A sign next to the tea plants indicates that tea symbolizes Article Seven: 'equality'. Switzerland is often called the richest and most democratic country in Europe. One of the translations of democracy is of a state in which all have equal rights (Oxford English Dictionary). Certainly the republic of Switzerland has a unique form of administration which to a remarkable degree depends on the will of the people. Decisions on all issues are reached in each canton through a majority vote of the citizens. In linking trees with human rights discourses the previous and present director emphasize their desire to generate comradeship, equalitarianism and openness – key aspects also of a pilgrimage (Turner and Turner 1978:250). Yet is equality an illusion? This is not the place to bring up the complex subject of the corporate or business state, as the nation-state has been referred to. Already globalization processes and the free self-regulating market economy place practical limits on the equal rights of individuals. One local from the Ticino mentioned to me that social difficulties and tensions, exemplified by the high rate of suicide in Switzerland, are 'swept under the carpet'.[13] I have not done sufficient research in the country to corroborate this statement, yet the tea ceremony at Monte Verita, among other things, alludes to the problematic nature of equality in the country.

The third project to which I want to draw attention is the 'Chiara Rainbow' trail leading to a mandala. The trail and the mandala, which are prominently displayed in front of the contemporary main hotel (Figure 11) in the Monte Verita park, are constructed of pieces of variegated and coloured Venetian glass. This artistic configuration was completed in 2003 and is scientifically aligned with the magnetic field of the region. The text on the notice board that underlines the meaning of the design is summarized below:

---

13 This point is dramatically emphasized by the poster produced in 2009 by the Swiss People's Party Union, Democratica di Centro (UDC), the biggest party in Switzerland. In the illustration three white sheep kick the alien black sheep out over the Swiss border. This poster was shown throughout the country, conspicuously at main train stations.

Figure 11 Serpent path leading to a mosaic mandala in front of the contemporary hotel Monte Verita. Photographed by A. Hobart.

The Rainbow is aimed at intertwining physical and mental health with the magnetic forces (telluric) inherent in the Ascona region, and Monte Verita in particular. Visitors strolling down the colourful trail reach their own centre in the mandala, i.e. the point linked to the highest concentration of electromagnetic radiation. The mandala in the East is used as a means of meditation – a dynamic leading to purity of Consciousness...

The archaeologist George Coedes (1966:46) views are of interest in the context. His research indicated that the rainbow expresses the bridge between humans and gods in Hindu cosmology. Moreover, throughout East Asia and India, the rainbow is compared to a multi-coloured serpent, a motif which brings to mind Kundalini (coiled) 'serpent power' (Danielou 1963:254), Mother Earth or the dark goddess. Tadeusz Skorupski (pers. comm. 2010) further pointed out that the rainbow body (in Tibetan: *'ja' lus*) denotes the time of dying of great yogins, who at that moment dissolve their (mental) bodies into rainbow bodies, namely the universal sphere of luminosity.

At this stage I want to turn to the Ticino artist Malu Cortesi,[14] whose vision inspired the design of the trail and mandala. On the notice board is written: the 'trail is dedicated to Chiara who beholds her rainbow from afar as a bridge of light between Earth and Heaven'. Chiara was Malu's daughter, who died in hospital at the age of twelve from bone cancer. Father and daughter were close. To while away the time and banish dismal thoughts during the last two years of her life they drew coloured mandalas together at her hospital bed, each taking turns until the mandala was finished. In the father's words, 'this dynamic was healing and revitalizing for both of them'; both were involved in a cosmic passage, a recreative motion of the macrocosm in the microcosm. Malu's experiences with his daughter just before she died were transmitted (by his friend Dr Hartmann) to Claudio Rossetti, the Director of Monte Verita at the time, who subsequently requested it be realized in the hotel's park.

Malu is a creative artist who has worked throughout his life in the Ticino community with such social and medical issues as drug addiction, juvenile delinquents, the sick and the elderly. He now teaches painting in the Art College in Lugano, as well as in the prison. He often uses the mandala motif when working with prisoners. This brings to mind Jung, who, as previously mentioned, also used mandalas to heal and transform consciousness. Malu's background experiences and creative works echo a quality that all spiritual paths or pilgrimages strive to generate – that of empathy or compassion. In Taoist terms, 'when the great compassion is stirred, its power breaks down all limiting barriers of the ego-self' (Chang Chung-yuan, 1963:180); the self expands beyond itself towards the other, the environment and the cosmos.

Conclusion

In reviewing the history of Monte Verita from its ancient roots, its development in the early twentieth century to contemporary times, a shadowy aura of the past lingers on in the present that hints at the multi-faceted, paradoxical power of nature, Mother Earth, who can protect, destroy, recreate and heal. These transformative capacities are also embodied by humans whose existence is intertwined with others and the environment. Yet our modern world-view has tended to fragment mind and body, the individual and the society, the spirit and the land. In the words of the Jungian psychoanalyst Kübler-Ross, 'Earth has been abused for too long without regard for any serious consequences.'

---

14   Malu Cortesi was born in Locarno in the Ticino in 1958. He is a talented artist and committed social worker. Exhibitions of his work have been held in Switzerland and Italy. His paintings are abstract, sensitive and delicately coloured. They draw attention to his reflective disposition and social concern with the psychologically or physically ill, and generally the suffering humans may encounter.

Figure 12   Rainbow spanning a waterfall in the valley Maggia. Photographed by G. Simona.

(1998:286). Weapons, greed, materialism and destructiveness are rampant. Indeed, humans have in recent years witnessed tremendous earthquakes, floods, volcanic eruptions and other natural disasters on an unprecedented scale.

The rainbow – here spanning a waterfall rushing down cliffs in the valley Maggia (Figure 12) – exemplifies the enticing, elusive nature of the world, *maya*, the essence of which is contradiction. As such, this ephemeral phenomenon composed of waves of colour, light and energy hints at the baffling power of reality that can direct humans towards violence and destruction, but also to beauty and the sublime at the edge of conceptual reason (see Kapferer and Hobart 2005).

To conclude, I suggest that it is irrelevant whether the people who came and continue to come to Monte Verita are called anarchists, nudists, health reformers, bohemians, vagrants, dancers, painters, intellectuals, tourists or pilgrims. As Eade and Sallnow (2000:xvi) say, the emphasis on 'religious' pilgrimage may in any case be too narrow. Being released temporarily from the mundane structure of their particular societies, travellers may reflect on their human existence as 'archetypical seekers' and create a sense of comradeship when together, while, at the same time, striving to extend towards new horizons of potential.

References

Alcock, J. 2009. *Daily Life of the Pagan Celts*. Oxford: Greenwood World Publishing.
Bakunin, M. 1970. *God and the State*. New York: Dover Publications.
Bloch, M. 2008. 'Truth and sight: generalizing without universalizing', *Journal of the Royal Anthropological Institute* 14(s1):S22–S32.
Chang, C. 1963. *Creativity and Taoism: A Study of Chinese Philosophy, Art, and Poetry*.
Danielou, A. 1963. *Hindu Polytheism*, London, Routledge and Kegan Paul.
New York: The Julian Press. Coedes, G. 1966. *Angkor: An Introduction*. London: Oxford University Press.
Eade, J. and Coleman, S. (eds.) 2004. *Reframing Pilgrimage: Cultures in Motion*. London: Routledge.
Eade, J. and Sallnow, M.J. (eds.) 2000. *Contesting the Sacred: The Anthropology of the Christian Pilgrimages*. London: Routledge.
Eliade, M. 1954. *The Myth of the Eternal Return* (Bollingen Series XLVI). Princeton: Princeton University Press.
Good, E. 2008. *Magisches Tessin*. Baden: VT Verlag.
Goodway, D. 2006. *Anarchist Seeds Beneath the Snow*. Liverpool; Liverpool University Press.
Hakl, H.T. 2001. *Der Verborgene Geist von Eranos. Unbekannte Begegnungen von Wissenschaft und Esoterik. Eine Alternative Geistesgeschichte des 20 Jahrhunderts*. Bretten: Scientia Nova Verlag.
Harvey, A. 1995. *The Return of the Mother*. Berkeley: Frog.
Ingold, T. 2010. 'Footprints through the weather-world: walking, breathing, knowing'. *Journal of the Royal Anthropological Institute Special Issue: Making Knowledge*: 121–38.
Jaffe, A. (ed.) 1979 *C. G. Jung: Word and Image* (Bollingen Series XCVII). Princeton: Princeton University Press.
Jung, C.G. 2009. *The Red Book Liber Novus* (ed. and trans S. Shamdasani). New York: Norton and Company.
Kapferer, B. and Hobart, A. (eds.) 2005. *Aesthetics in Performance: Formations of Symbolic Construction and Experience*. New York: Berghahn Books.
Kübler-Ross, E. 1998: *The Wheel of Life: A Memoir of Living and Dying*. London: Bantam Press.
Linse, U. 1983. *Barfuessige Propheten: Erloeser der Zwanziger Jahre*. Berlin: Siedler.
Mara Folini, M. 2000. *Monte Verita: Ascona's Mountain of Truth*. Berne: Society for the History of Swiss Art.

Mautner, T. (ed.) 2000. *The Penguin Dictionary of Philosophy*. London: Penguin Books.

Mros, E. 2007a. *Reformversuche und ihre Protagonisten*. Ascona: Mros.

Mros, E. 2007b. *Phaenomen Monte Verita: Barong Eduard von der Heydt's Widerspruechliches Leben und Die Legende vom Nazi-Gold auf dem 'Berg der Wahrheit*. Ascona: Mros.

Napier, D. 2003. *The Age of Immunology*. Chicago: The University of Chicago Press.

Okakura, K. 1964. *The Book of Tea*. New York: Dover Publications.

Perera, S.B. 1981. *Descent to the Goddess: A Way for Initiation for Women*. Toronto: Inner City Books.

Peat, D. 1994. *Blackfoot Physics; A Journey into the Native American Universe*. London: Fourth Estate.

Rapport, N. and Overing J. (eds.) 2007. *Social and Cultural Anthropology: The Key Concepts*. London: Routledge.

Schwab, A. 2003. *Monte Verita – Sanatorium der Sehnsucht*. Zurich: Orell Fuessli Verlag.

Szeemann, H. 1980. *Monte Verita Ascona*. Milan: Electra Editrice.

Turgenev, I. 2008. *Fathers and Sons* (trans. R. Freeborn). Oxford: Oxford University Press.

Turner, V. 1973. "The center out there: pilgrim's goal". *History of Religions* 12(3):191–230.

Turner, V and Turner, E. 1978. *Image and Pilgrimage in Christian Culture: Anthropological Perspectives*. New York: Columbia University Press.

Vitebsky, P. 1995. *The Shaman: Voyages of the Soul: Trance, Ecstacy and Healing from Siberia to the Amazon*. London: Macmillan.

Wackernagel, W. 2005. 'Mystique, avant-garde et marginale dans le village du Monte Verita'. In A. Dierkena and B. Beyer de Ryke (eds.) *Mystique: La Passion de l'Un de L'Antiquite a Nos Jours*, pp. 175–87. Bruxelles: l'Universite de Bruxelles.

Waley, A. 1977. *The Way and Its Power: The Tao Te Ching and its Place in Chinese Thought*. London: Unwin Paperbacks.

Wilhelm, R. (trans.) 1957. *The Secret of the Golden Flower* (commentary C.G. Jung). London: Routledge and Kegan Paul.

Woodman, M. and Dickson, E. 1997. *Dancing in the Flames: The Dark Goddess in the Transformation of Consciousness*. Boston: Shambhala.

CHAPTER 8

The Seven Sleepers pilgrimage in Brittany
The ambiguity of a Christian-Muslim heterotopia

MANOËL PÉNICAUD[1]

Every year, at the end of July, Christian and Muslim pilgrims meet at the Sept-Saints hamlet near the village of Vieux-Marché in Brittany (Côtes d'Armor), France. As early as 1954, Louis Massignon, an Islamologist and teacher at the College de France, invited immigrant Muslims to a local, Catholic, Breton pilgrimage called a '*pardon*',[2] dedicated to the Seven Sleepers of Ephesus. Because these saints are also known in Islam as *Ahl al-Kahf* ('Those of the Cave', in Arabic), Louis Massignon wished to prepare a spiritual 'reconciliation' between Christians and Muslims. In other words, he 'invented' this Christian-Muslim pilgrimage in Brittany. I use the verb 'to invent' here in the sense of a 'creation' or 'construction'. I consider Massignon as the 'religious entrepreneur' of this unexpected pilgrimage. Furthermore, this singular enterprise is one of the oldest attempts at Christian-Muslim dialogue in France. Indeed, this initiative preceded the promotion of inter-religious dialogue by the Second Vatican Council. Nowadays, the idea of an 'experiment' is emphasized by the expression of 'grafting' used by pilgrims in talking of adding the Christian-Muslim dimension onto the local and Catholic *pardon*, which still continues.

---

1   This chapter was written in the course of research at the laboratory of excellence Labexmed – Human and Social Sciences at the heart of interdisciplinarity for the Mediterranean, with the reference 10-LabX-0090. This chapter concerns the pilgrimage's situation to the end of 2010. For further analysis, see Pénicaud 2016.
2   For an anthropological study of the revival of a local and Catholic *pardon* in Brittany, see Badone 2007.

'Grafting' indicates something is added, artificially, and that the pilgrimage process is not spontaneous.

The pilgrimage of the Seven Sleepers is a matrix of ambiguities, and I go on to focus on three specific aspects. First of all, my aim is to demonstrate that it is a Christian-Muslim heterotopia, i.e. an accomplished and localized utopia, according to Michel Foucault's concept (Foucault 2001). In my opinion, Louis Massignon tried to realize his ideal of religious reconciliation. The second question directly concerns the Christian-Muslim pilgrimage's condition: is it a syncretic or non-syncretic phenomenon? The last point deals with the pilgrimage's heterogeneity: that of spaces, practices and pilgrims. Indeed, many different types of people visit the shrine: Breton Catholics, Muslims and Christian-Muslim pilgrims, but also New Agers, neo-Celts, neo-shamans, tourists, non-believers, etc.

This chapter is divided into two parts: first, the founding of the Christian-Muslim pilgrimage in the 1950s; second, the contemporary situation and the re-creation of the pilgrimage (from the 1990s to the present). But a preliminary section is necessary in order to present the pilgrimage.

The Seven Sleepers and the context of the pilgrimage

Who are these holy sleepers? According to the legend, at the time of Christian persecution in the third century, seven Christian youths fled to a cave near the city of Ephesus (Turkey), and there fell into a miraculous sleep for 198 years. They then awoke in the fifth century when the Empire had become Christian and were discovered by the population. Then, the bishop recognized the miracle before they went to sleep forever.[3] Their reawakening attested to the resurrection of the body. The miracle was very popular and became known all over the Christian world. Afterwards, in the seventh century, it passed into Islam. It appears in the eighteenth sura of the Qur'an, called 'The Cave' after that of the Seven Sleepers, though the sleepers are called *Ashab al-Kahf* ('Companions of the Cave'). It is more or less the same story, but shorter and the style is more elliptic and less detailed than in the Christian version.[4] This sura is very famous for Muslims and, moreover, some hadiths recommend believers to read it every Friday in order to be blessed until the next Friday. For whatever reason, the legend spread to the entire Muslim world, from

---

3   I indicate 198 years, but the sleep duration of the miracle varies depending on the version of the legend.
4   For example, the Koranic version gives an imprecise number of Sleepers (3, 5 or 7) with their dog-called Qaṭmīr; the sleep duration is 309 years and the Ephesus location is not mentioned. This last point can explain why many Muslim Seven Sleepers sites have emerged as the original and miraculous cave.

Figure 1 The Seven Sleepers (Ashāb al-Kahf) by Muhammad Siyāh Qalam (seventeenth century). This copy comes from the private collection of Louis Massignon, Paris.

Andalusia to China, creating local forms of devotion to the *Ahl al-Kahf* (Jourdan 2001; Massignon 1950, 1954–63; Zarcone and Loubes forthcoming) (Figure 1).

Let us return to Brittany. What is the configuration of the contemporary Seven Sleepers pilgrimage? It takes place on the fourth weekend of July and is composed of several sequences. It begins on the Saturday afternoon with an inter-religious dialogue debate in Vieux-Marché village hall, four kilometres from the Sept-Saints hamlet. Most of the audience (around 200 people) are Catholic and retired; the significant point is that there are very few Muslims (less than ten). A local association called 'Springs of the Seven Sleepers' ('Sources des Sept Dormants', in French) organizes this event (Figure 2). After the discussion, cultural activities are proposed to the 'Christian-Muslim

Figure 2   Inter-religious dialogue debate in Vieux-Marché, © Pénicaud, 2009.

pilgrims',[5] such as a lecture on Islamic calligraphy or a concert by a Christian-Muslim couple.

At the end of the day, everybody goes to the Sept-Saints hamlet where the local *pardon* has already started. People visit the chapel, built at the beginning of the eighteenth century (Figure 3). It is a traditional little chapel, except for the crypt. In fact, the church was built over a Neolithic dolmen. This old megalith was considered as the Seven Sleepers' Cave. Nobody knows when their cult arrived in Brittany, but Louis Massignon thought it was at the beginning of the Middle Ages. In any case, this is not our subject of investigation. In the 'dolmen-crypt' are eight old wood statues (the Seven Sleepers and the Virgin Mary) and two Christian-Muslim symbols: an ex-voto offered by Massignon in 1958 (a boat with seven candles, which according to him symbolizes Islam) and a photograph of the Orientalist during his last pilgrimage in July 1962 (Figure 4). The Catholic mass starts at sunset. Many pilgrims remain outside because the chapel is exiguous. The mass is classical, but the main priest – called the '*pardonneur*' in French – always has a personal link with the Arabic Muslim world. In his sermon, he always speaks about the necessity of dialogue with Islam and refers to the Seven Sleepers. At the end of the mass, the traditional procession – with banners, crosses and Mary's statue – leaves the chapel and makes a round of a field before reaching the hamlet's

---

5   I use the expression 'Christian-Muslim pilgrims' to distinguish them from the Breton and Catholic pilgrims of the local *pardon*. In effect, I will show that there are two pilgrims groups, and two different dimensions to the same pilgrimage.

The Seven Sleepers pilgrimage in Brittany

Figure 3   Chapel of the Seven-Saints, © Pénicaud, 2008.

Figure 4   'Dolmen-crypt' of the Seven-Saints' Chapel, © Pénicaud, 2008.

square, named after Louis Massignon in tribute to the pilgrimage's founder. There, the *pardonneur* lights a bonfire (*tantad*, in Breton) (Figure 5). When the celebration is over, the profane part of the pilgrimage (*fest noz*, 'night festival') begins, with Breton music, traditional dances and a great deal of alcohol. Moreover, the refreshment stall becomes the profane epicentre of the night. This more festive sequence is organized by another local association:

Figure 5   Bonfire (tantad, in Breton), © Pénicaud, 2008.

'Tud ar Seiz Sant' ('People of the Seven Saints', in Breton), whose aim consists to promote the local animation and folklore of the hamlet.

On Sunday morning, the Great Mass is at 11 a.m. There are more people than on the Saturday. Most of them are Bretons and Catholics, and the rare Muslims remain outside the chapel, except those who are guests of honour. This is more or less the same celebration as the day before. After the mass, the *pardonneur* invites the congregation to follow another procession, to the Sept-Saints spring. Many people do not and stay around the chapel, but about two hundred people go to this fountain, three hundred metres away. In Brittany, every chapel has its holy water and spring, but the particularity of this one is that it has seven holes (because of the Seven Sleepers). This is the place where the eighteenth sura is recited by an imam (Figure 6). It is the high point of the Christian-Muslim gathering, organized by the 'Springs of the Seven Sleepers' Association. It is also a time for inter-religious speeches and for respects to be paid to Louis Massignon (Figure 7). Afterwards, these pilgrims join the others in a meadow in front of the church to eat a *mechoui* (a North African meal). But, investigation has revealed that the mutton is not halal ('licit', according to the Qur'an), and this is one of the big ambiguities of the Christian-Muslim pilgrimage that I shall explain. When the pilgrims have finished, some of them meet in the chapel for more dialogue organized by the local clergy. This moment is intended for Catholics and only one Muslim, the imam, is present to answer to their questions. At the end of afternoon, most of the pilgrims have left the Sept-Saints hamlet until the following year.

The Seven Sleepers pilgrimage in Brittany 189

Figure 6   The eighteenth sura of Qur`an is recited by an imam. In the centre, the Jesuit Paolo Dall'Oglio, who is one of Massignon's followers, © Pénicaud, 2007.

Figure 7   Tribute to Louis Massignon at the Sept-Saints spring, © Pénicaud, 2009.

Founding by Louis Massignon (1950s)

Louis Massignon (1883–1962) was one of the most famous French Orientalists and an Islamic studies specialist of the twentieth century. As such, he held the Chair of 'Muslim Sociography' at the College de France for almost thirty years, and he dedicated his whole life to understanding Islam. But he was also a Catholic believer. After his death, it was said in Cairo that he was 'the greatest Christian among Muslims and the greatest Muslim among Christians' (Plate 8). In fact, the two sides of his personality were inseparable: the rigour of the scientist and the faith of the mystic believer. Few people know that he was secretly ordained as a Catholic Melkite priest in 1950, in Egypt, by a special derogation (*indult*) from Pope Pius XII. Consequently, he did not found the Christian-Muslim pilgrimage as a layman but as a cleric. This initiative happened when he had just retired from the College de France and his academic career in 1954.

Moreover, Massignon was a French '*intellectuel catholique*'; he was often controversial and sometimes even considered a 'government spy', though this is rather a caricature. In any case, he sat on many committees, and was committed to many causes, such as decolonization, non-violence and, especially, the recognition of Islam. However, even in these situations, he used three forms of action: prayer, fasting and pilgrimages.

In 1952 his daughter Genevieve, an ethnologist, discovered the existence of the little Sept-Saints *pardon* in Brittany. He was immediately interested by analogies and similarities between the Breton song – called a '*gwerz* '– and the eighteenth sura of the Qur'an. As a consequence, he started a legitimation process for this Breton sacred place, using detailed scientific research (Massignon 1954–63, 1992). For example, he attempted to demonstrate the Oriental origin of this western veneration of the Seven Sleepers, when other specialists saw only an avatar of devotion to the seven evangelists and first bishops of Brittany (venerated in another famous Breton summer pilgrimage called *Tro Breizh*).

The first Christian-Muslim pilgrimage was organized in July 1954, for 'serene peace in Algeria', even before the beginning of war in this French colony. The year after, Massignon decided to invite Muslim workers from Paris as there were no many Muslims in Brittany. Together they read the Fātiha (the first sura of the Qur'an) in front of the dolmen, then they joined the Christian procession to the bonfire, with a singular and unique banner on which the beginning of the *Ave Maria* was written in Arabic (from 1959 to the beginning of the 1970s).[6]

Local reception of this 'graft' was very ambiguous: it produced curiosity and pride, but also aloofness. Given that the initiative preceded the Second Vatican Council, the clergy were disoriented and suspicious. As an old Breton who witnessed this remembers today:

---

6   The banner had been blessed by the Bishop of Lourdes during a pilgrimage in 1958. It is a specific innovation of the 'grafting' that produces ambiguity.

It was not very well accepted by the locals. Especially because they fought in the Algerian war. Some of them were angry, but there were no fights or anything. They just did not approve. But we could not disagree with an initiative that wanted to bring people together and make peace, because we are Christians.

Despite the peaceful attitude, the tensions caused by the external transformation of their traditional pilgrimage have not been forgotten. However, Louis Massignon 'grafted' something else new onto the *pardon*: he introduced a Melkite mass before the Latin one on the Sunday morning. This celebration in Arabic was very strange for the local people. Nevertheless, the Orientalist continued to innovate with a new ritual of the eighteenth sura: in 1961, he asked his friend Amadou Hampāte Bā to psalmody the *Ahl al-Kahf* sura at the Sept-Saints Fountain.

In the end, the pilgrimage was more or less successful. Despite the tensions mentioned, and thanks to Louis Massignon, it was supported by different media (press, radio, television) and political personalities (e.g. General De Gaulle and ministers, though secretly), and the Catholic high church in the Vatican. This resulted in the chapel being classified as a national '*monument historique*': this was the beginning of the pilgrimage's heritagization.

All these elements of this experimental pilgrimage lead one to think of it as Louis Massignon's 'heterotopia', in Michel Foucault's terms (Foucault 2001; Pénicaud 2011, 2016). The French philosopher defines these as 'other spaces', i.e. a realized 'utopia' in a localized space. In that sense, the Seven Sleepers pilgrimage is the concretization of Louis Massignon's ideal. First and foremost, he wanted to prepare the reconciliation between Christians and Muslims before the Last Judgement in an eschatological perspective. Therefore, his overall project concerned not only Brittany but all humanity. He wanted to anticipate the final gathering of humanity in Jerusalem. Secondly, he wished to gather together all Abraham's children, including the Jews (but later). This is what I call Massignon's 'Abrahamic ecumenism'. While the pilgrimage was intra-mundane and of this world, his project was primarily eschatological (Pénicaud 2014). Moreover, in parallel with Brittany, he tried to 'invent' other pilgrimages under the Seven Sleepers banner in Germany, Morocco, Algeria and Turkey, as well as in the Comoros Islands[7]. His aim was to create a Seven Sleepers network, but his twinning projects failed, except in Brittany (Pénicaud 2016).

---

7   The Louis Massignon's private archives – in which I could research deeply, thanks to his family – reveal these initiatives.

Figure 8   Louis Massignon during his last pilgrimage with Mohamed Taki, 1962 ©
Louis-Claude Duchesne.

Louis Massignon died in 1962, but some of his followers – called 'Massignonans' – maintained the Christian-Muslim initiative in Brittany. Those most involved were his children and family, but he also had few 'disciples'. Indeed, the founder's charisma was still present. Hence, the Christian-Muslim pilgrimage continued and was substantially facilitated by the post-Vatican II context. For example, in 1967 Massignon's followers introduced a debate between Christians and Muslims on the Saturday evening in the village of Vieux-Marché. This was the beginning of the 'inter-religious dialogue' period. But in the 1980s, the pilgrimage declined. The followers were getting older and after 1983 (the centenary of Massignon's birth), they decided to put an end to the Christian-Muslim organization. Some of them continued to come from Paris, but privately. It was the end of the Christian-Muslim pilgrimage's first life, though it should be mentioned that the Catholic *pardon* continued without the graft.

The Christian-Muslim pilgrimage's 'reawakening'

At the beginning of the 1990s, a new local association, that of the 'Spring of the Seven Sleepers', revived the Christian-Muslim pilgrimage organizing inter-religious dialogue debate on the Saturday afternoon in the village of Vieux-Marché. Christian and Muslim speakers were invited to discuss social themes (Plate 2). The main values proclaimed were peace, coexistence and social cohesion. But this initiative was first developed by non-believers, members of the communist municipal council. They wanted to promote intercultural dialogue thanks to the existence of the pilgrimage, but in a horizontal way without a preponderant transcendental intention (as Louis Massignon had). Though linked to a pilgrimage, the aim is also humanistic and not strictly religious. As a consequence, the phenomenon's specificity in the contemporary French Christian-Muslim network is to be a place of both pilgrimage and dialogue. In fact, it is a dialogue gathering grafted onto a pilgrimage centre. And this leads to ambiguity. Indeed, the project is not successful because of local reactions: local people are not in fact interested in the debates. They think them too intellectual and do not feel concerned by the Christian-Muslim themes. One of the reasons for this is certainly that there are not many Muslims in this rural area, but other factors also explain this lack of interest.

During the pilgrimage, Muslim attendance is very low. Each year, there are only between five and ten Muslims. Though there are Muslims living in the nearest town of Lannion, they boycott the pilgrimage. Why? Because they are not really invited by the promoters and organisers. Some of these Muslims come once, but do not return. For them, it is a Catholic gathering organized to meet Muslims, but it is not for Muslims. The case of the *mechoui* is emblematic: the organizers propose this North African meal in order to include Muslim pilgrims but, in fact, the meat is not halal. Therefore, Muslims are not totally respected; some of them consider this an outrage and will not come the following year. Furthermore, the pilgrimage only lasts two days a year and there is no more collaboration or other contact the rest of the year. After the pilgrimage, everybody goes back to normal life, without continuing the dialogue. This short activity does not produce a significant lasting impact.

The strongest ambiguity is the relationship to Islam. Despite the dialogue's values, such as hospitality, peace and coexistence, many local people have a bad perception of Islam. Some are afraid of Muslims because of terrorism and the geopolitical crisis. For example, one of them fears that the chapel will become a mosque and, in 2009, someone broke the portrait of Louis Massignon in the crypt (Plate 4), burned pages of the book for prayers having a link with Islam and damaged the fountain. In 2010, the same fountain was partially destroyed, and the police are investigating. These acts of vandalism reveal an undeniable problem: the pilgrimage also generates Islamophobia instead of Islamophilia.

The ambiguity begins because of the two juxtaposed events: the *pardon* on the one hand, and the graft on the other. In fact, these two dimensions are independent and not really superimposed. The Christian-Muslim pilgrimage seeks to build bridges, but differences remain strong. We find Bretons attached to the traditional 'pardon' on the one side, and 'Christian-Muslim pilgrims' on the other. In fact, their intentions are very different. Breton people participate for the Catholic celebration, commonality, tradition and the local festival, whereas Christian-Muslim pilgrims do so for the inter-religious gathering, dialogue debates and ritual psalmody. This observation shows the dialectic between local and non-local expectations. In addition, local people do not really accept the 'foreigners'. Some of them have already said: 'Please, do not change our *pardon*!' To them, the graft is an external event that they did not choose. Therefore, some of them feel the Christian-Muslim participation to be an intrusion. Paradoxically, this protectionism is produced by the 'graft' whose aim is to promote dialogue and open-mindedness.

Furthermore, the 'inter-religious pilgrimage' is now organized by Catholics alone, who select the themes for dialogue. Therefore, Muslims are not part of the organization; they have never been so and I do not think they ever will be. For them, it is a Catholic event, to which just a few liberal Muslims are invited. Indeed, this is an invited religion (Islam) in an invented pilgrimage (the Christian-Muslim graft). Consequently, there is a pronounced numeric asymmetry between Catholics and Muslims, as in most of the Christian-Muslim gatherings in France (Lamine 2004, 2005).

Unlike certain contemporary cases in the Mediterranean area (Albera and Couroucli 2012; Barkan and Barkey 2014; Bowman 2012b; Dépret and Dye 2012), inter-religious crossings in Brittany, like in France in general, are neither popular nor spontaneous, but are instead artificial. There, the meetings of the religions are constructed and elaborated by an elite. It is not a spontaneous phenomenon but an intellectual one. For example, Christian-Muslim pilgrims do not have special recourse to the saints (vows, prayers for the sick or the dead etc.). There are more traditional attempts, but by local Breton pilgrims rather than outsiders. The external pilgrims come primarily because of the opportunity for dialogue. But the bridging significance of the Seven Sleepers remains symbolic. The gathering is thus more symbolic than effective.

Another question concerns the syncretism of the Christian-Muslim pilgrimage. Many people, who have never attended it, would like to see it as a syncretic initiative, though this is definitely not the case. Even if Massignon's heterotopia was Abrahamic reconciliation, his aim was not to invent syncretism between Islam and Christianity. Indeed, there never was a third religious entity born from the first two. In fact, the pilgrimage's actors are 'anti-syncretists' according to the Charles Stewart and Rosalind Shaw's terminology (Stewart and Shaw 1994). For the pilgrims, syncretism is a pejorative word. It would concern an alteration, something undefined, impure and illegitimate. To be seen as syncretists would be an accusation, and they categorically adopt an anti-syncretic position. My observations confirm that the pilgrimage is not syncretic. Its aim is the inter-religious gathering and not fusion in a new religious element. Believers keep to their own religion and place. In other words, religious borders are not really transgressed. There is no common prayer said together. In reality, the Muslims attend the Catholics' prayers, and vice versa. At the end of the pilgrimage, everyone goes home keeping his one faith. So the answer to the question asked by Glenn Bowman in his reflection on syncretism, 'Is a shared sanctuary necessarily syncretic?', is no in the case of the Sept-Saints (Bowman 2012a). To see syncretism would be a misinterpretation. In addition, the Christian-Muslim pilgrimage seems to confirm the pilgrim's own faith. There is no room for proselytism. Like syncretism, it is forbidden and it was already the case in the time of Louis Massignon (Pénicaud 2016). Paradoxically, this inter-religious event is an opportunity for the reaffirmation of religious identity and the consolidation of values (differences even).

Another ambiguity of the recent and reawakened gathering is that it is open to non-believers. While this is not specific to this particular dialogue experience (the trend concerns many inter-religious places in our secularized societies), it is paradoxical in a religious pilgrimage. Since 2005, a humanist speaker has taken part in the inter-religious debates at Vieux-Marché, in the name of the open-mindedness and coexistence sought by the Springs of the Seven Sleepers Association. The aim is to share reflections about the quest for civil and social peace all over the world. Then, in 2008, this humanist speaker introduced a 'minute of silence', which is a kind of secularized prayer, just before the Muslim psalmody in the clearing. The humanist position is to claim that intercultural dialogue includes the inter-religious one. To them, belief is just one conviction among others. However, the problem is that believers (Christians and Muslims) and Massignon's followers think that it is necessary to keep the Christian-Muslim base, without enlarging it to include all faiths and ideologies. In fact, they fear a kind of 'intercultural soup', or a 'kaleidoscopic gathering' as one of them said to me during an interview. In any case, this tendency underlines the undeniable process of the pilgrimage's secularization.

Cultural activities (concerts, photography exhibitions, calligraphy workshops, documentaries) have been organized since the creation of the Springs of the Seven Sleepers Association (1990s). They attract a new audience, what is the association's aim. This tendency is linked to the intercultural development. In this case, cultural and intercultural approaches work together. The idea is that the arts contribute to dialogue in a different manner than speeches and conferences. Such development is parallel to the festive expansion of the *pardon*. Today, the local Tud Ar Seiz Sant Association organizes many activities: children's games, traditional dancing and music, and a flea market. While these profane aspects have always existed in the *pardon*, they play a larger role in it than before. This shows that pilgrims and visitors come not only for the religious/inter-religious event, but also for festive and communal features. Another tendency is the growth of tourism and heritagization. The tourism potential is largely untapped, but the organizers are beginning to think that tourists could help to develop the pilgrimage. For example, the Tud Ar Seiz Sant Association is working on the valorisation of the cultural and natural heritage of the hamlet during the pilgrimage, organizing for example guided walks to visit different fountains in the surrounding area.

In fact, the pilgrimage is a place of competition between organizers. They are principally complementary but, on a secondary level, they are more or less competitors. Nowadays, there are three main actors: the Spring of the Seven Sleepers Association, the Catholic clergy and the local and Breton association called 'Tud Ar Seiz Sant'. If we look at their spatial positions, the three organizers interpenetrate the same place, that is the Sept-Saints hamlet. Their competition space thus illustrates their complex relationships. Today, the Christian-Muslim aspects are no longer spatially central but peripheral, whereas the *pardon* dimension is preponderant. In Louis Massignon's time, the Muslims prayed in front of the crypt, but now their most important sequence only occurs around the fountain, three hundred metres away from the shrine. Another example is the spatial interpenetration of the devout Catholics and the Tud Ar Seiz Sant Association: the procession of the banners' route is 'disturbed' by the growing profane features (big tents, dance floor, refreshment stall) developed by this association. The spatial relations show tensions and a kind of competition. That is why the Catholic diocese asks for more organization. In contrast with the malleability of the Christian-Muslim element, the clergy call for more rigour and coordination. On one hand, there is an associative approach, which is modular but fragile and unstable, and, on the other, the Catholic Church needs something stable, strong and established. All these contradictions also lead to ambiguities. The phenomenon thus appears as an arena, according to John Eade and Michael Sallnow's pilgrimage theory (Eade and Sallnow 1991). This not a peaceful and harmonized area under the sign of Victor Turner's *communitas* (Turner and Turner 1978), but a space of competition where social differences are still profoundly at work.

In addition to this observation, I must add a comment about what I call the 'charisma of the place', in echo to James J. Preston who spoke about the 'spiritual magnetism' of pilgrimage centres (Preston 1992). Before the Christian-Muslim graft, the site was a superimposition of many occupants (Neolithic men, Celts, Romans, then Christians). But, after the last graft by Masscignon, the site became a place of juxtaposition. Nowadays, many kinds of pilgrims come to the same site with different intentions, practices, representations and expectancies. For example, many New Agers visit the site: they can be neo-Celts, neo-druids, neo-shamans, dowsers or magnetic healers. They do not come especially during the Christian-Muslim pilgrimage, nor do they come for the dialogue, but for the 'power' of the place. Added to the other pilgrims (Breton and Christian-Muslim ones, but also tourists or curious people), their presence confirms the pilgrimage's heterogeneity and mosaic attendance.

To conclude, the little Breton pilgrimage has undergone many transformations since the 1950s. The most important is the transition from a local *pardon* to an unique Christian-Muslim pilgrimage. I have compared the two different lives of the pilgrimage: on the one hand, the creating 'graft' onto a Breton pardon, its success, then its maintenance and finally its decline; and, on the other, its reawakening when local people took it over with inter-religious debates and the development of 'intercultural' and 'profane' activities, but at which Muslim attendance is very low, and even questioned.

The founder Louis Massignon chose the Seven Sleepers because of their eschatological significance in Islam and Christianity: the resurrection of the body at the Last Judgement. He wanted to prepare for the 'final reconciliation', and this is what I called his heterotopia. But today, the project he began has changed and has become less eschatological. The goal is more worldly and horizontal (coexistence) than extra-mundane and vertical (resurrection). In fact, the Seven Sleepers have now become a symbol and perhaps a kind of pretext for the gathering, and their position is no longer central. This point confirms the pilgrimage's artificiality: the inter-religious interaction is not spontaneous but organized and intellectualized. This is an 'experimental' pilgrimage elaborated by Catholics for dialogue, and Muslims are merely invited. In this sense, the pilgrimage is a new dimension of the shared shrines phenomenon that has been studied in other cultural contexts (Albera and Couroucli 2012; Albera, Pénicaud and Marquette 2015; Barkan and Barkey 2014; Bowman 2012b; Hasluck 2000).

Moreover, the charisma of the site attracts many different kinds of people: not only Breton and Christian-Muslim pilgrims, but also tourists, non-believers, and New Agers. In fact, this heterogeneity is a consequence of Massignon's heterotopia. As if he has 'unlocked' and 'opened' a local tradition to the rest of the world. He did not intend this project to become an arena, though this is the result today. In this sense, it has become an inclusive pilgrimage centre. Different pilgrims come and give their own significance to the shrine, according to John Eade and Michael Sallnow's theory of pilgrimages now considered an 'empty vessel' that pilgrims fill with the meaning of their choice (Eade and Sallnow 1991).

What of the pilgrimage's future? Nobody can be sure, but I think it will continue. The succession of transformations proves its vitality and capacity to adapt. But it is true that one association is declining while the other grows. Of the two, the Catholic Church seems to be the most likely to take it over. Though they were very suspicious for many years, the Catholic clergy seem now ready to be part of the organization the inter-religious gathering and pilgrimage. This is actually what Louis Massignon had wanted from the beginning. Last but not least, there is the concept of 'heterotopia': Louis Massignon constructed his own heterotopia thanks to his scientific and mystic charisma. According to Michel Foucault's concept, the Seven Sleepers pilgrimage is a kind of 'heterotopic mirror' (Foucault 2001) that shows aspects and reflections of the coexisting realities and difficulties that concern the whole society.

References

Albera, D. and M. Couroucli (eds.) 2012. *Sharing Sacred Spaces in the Mediterranean. Christians, Muslims, and Jews at Shrines and Sanctuaries*. Bloomington: Indiana University Press.

Albera, D., M. Pénicaud and I. Marquette (eds.) 2015. *Lieux saints partagés*. Arles: Actes-Sud/MuCEM.

Badone, E. 2007. 'Echoes from Kerizinen: pilgrimage, narrative, and the construction of sacred history at a Marian shrine in northwest France'. *Journal of the Royal Anthropological Institute* (NS) 13:453–70.

Barkan, E. and K. Barkey (eds.) 2014. *Choreographies of Shared Sacred Sites. Religion, Politics, and Conflict Resolution*. New York: Columbia University Press.

Bowman, G. 2012a. 'Identification and Identity Formation around Shared Shrines in West Bank Palestine and Western Macedonia'. In D. Albera and M. Couroucli, *Sharing Sacred Spaces in the Mediterranean*. 27–52. Bloomington: Indiana University Press.

——— (ed.) 2012b. *Sharing the Sacra. The Politics and Pragmatics of Intercommunal Relations around Holy Places*. Oxford: Berghahn.

Dépret, I. and Dye, G. (eds.) 2012. *Partage du sacré. Transferts, dévotions mixtes, rivalités interconfessionnelles*. Fernelmont: EME.

Eade, J. and M. Sallnow (eds.) 1991. *Contesting the Sacred. The Anthropology of Christian Pilgrimage*. London: Routledge.

Foucault, M. 2001. 'Des espaces autres'. In M. Foucault. *Dits et écrits* vol. II, 1571–81. Paris, Gallimard.

Hasluck, F. 2000 [1929]. *Christianity and Islam Under the Sultan*. Istanbul: Isis Press.

Jourdan, F. 2001 [1983]. *La Tradition des Sept Dormants. Une rencontre entre chrétiens et musulmans*. Paris: Maisonneuve et Larose.

Lamine, A.-S. 2004. *La Cohabitation des dieux. Pluralité religieuse et laïcité*. Paris: PUF.

––– 2005. 'Mise en scène de la 'bonne entente' interreligieuse et reconnaissance'. *Archives de sciences sociales des religions* 129:83–96.

Massignon, L. 1950. 'Les Sept Dormants, apocalypse de l'Islam'. *Mélanges Paul Peeters*. Bruxelles: Société des Bollandistes II:245–60.

––– 1954–63. 'Les Sept Dormants d'Éphèse (ahl Al-Kahf) en Islam et en Chrétienté. Recueil documentaire et iconographique'. *Revue des Études Islamiques* (series of seven fascicules published between 1954 and 1963).

––– 1992 [1958]. 'La crypte-dolmen des VII Saints Dormants d'Éphèse au Stiffel'. *Extrait des Mémoires de la Société d'Émulation des Côtes-du-Nord*. Saint-Brieuc: Les Presses bretonnes.

––– 2009. Écrits Mémorables (ed. C. Jambet, F. Angelier, F. L'Yvonnet and S. Ayada). Paris: Robert Laffont.

Morinis, A. (ed.) 1992. *Sacred Journeys. The Anthropology of Pilgrimage*. Westport, CT: Greenwood Press.

Pénicaud, M. 2011. 'L'hétérotopie des Sept Dormants en Bretagne'. *Archives de Sciences Sociales des Religions* 155:131–48.

––– 2014. 'Louis Massignon, entrepreneur et 'prophète' de la réconciliation eschatologique ? In E. Aubin-Boltanski and C. Gauthier (eds.) *Penser la fin du monde* 303–24. Paris, CNRS Éditions.

––– 2016. Le Réveil des Sept Dormants. Un pèlerinage islamo-chrétien en Bretagne. Paris: Cerf.

Preston, J.J. 1992. 'Spiritual magnetism: an organizing principle for the study of pilgrimage'. In A. Morinis (ed.) *Sacred Journeys. The Anthropology of Pilgrimage*, 32–46. Westport, CT: Greenwood Press.

Sallnow, M.J. 1981. 'Communitas reconsidered: the sociology of Andean pilgrimage'. *Man* 16(2):163–82.

Stewart, C. and R. Shaw (eds.) 1994. *Syncretism/Anti-syncretism: the Politics of Religious Synthesis*. London: Routledge.

Turner, V.W. and E. Turner 1978. *Image and Pilgrimage in Christian Culture: Anthropological Perspectives*. Oxford: Basil Blackwell.

Zarcone, T. and J.-P. Loubes forthcoming. *En Islam uyghur. Les Sept Dormants sur la route de la Soie*. Paris: CNRS Editions.

CHAPTER 9

Multi-centric mythscapes

Sanctuaries and pilgrimages in north-west Amazonian Arawakan religious traditions

ROBIN M. WRIGHT, OMAR GONZÁLEZ ÑÁÑEZ AND

CARLOS CÉSAR XAVIER LEAL

Introduction

The region of the north-west Amazon (Map 1) is known for both its social and linguistic heterogeneity and yet, to a high degree, also its cultural homogeneity. The more than 22 ethnic groups who consider themselves as distinct socio-political units are grouped by linguists into three major language families: northern Arawak, eastern Tukano and Maku. Despite their linguistic diversity, all these peoples share a number of cultural patterns and institutions, among them the sacred rites of passage involving a set of ancestral flutes and trumpets that are considered to be the body of the first ancestral being from which are descended the ancestors of all peoples. At the present time, some of the indigenous religious traditions are undergoing a period of revitalization and remembering, after a long period of repression by missionaries and the forgetting of the rituals. In the not-too-distant past, the knowledge of the rituals was guarded mostly by the healer *pajés* (shamans) and the priestly elders.[1]

This study is concerned with the northern Arawak speaking (sometimes called Maipurean) peoples who, today, inhabit the upper Guainia River and its tributaries and the Içana River and its tributaries, in the frontier region of

---

1 Over the last few years, there has been a notable effort on the part of indigenous organizations and government agencies in Colombia and Brazil to support the revitalization of this cultural heritage through recognition by UNESCO. There have also been numerous cultural revitalization projects supported by humanitarian and charitable foundations over the past 20 years.

Map 1   Arawak in the north of South America.

Brazil, Venezuela and Colombia. Specifically, we focus on the Hohodene, a large sib of the Baniwa that inhabits the Aiary River in Brazil; the Kuripako, an ethno-linguistic group consisting of multiple sibs on the upper Içana River in Brazil and Colombia; and the Warekena and Baniva of the upper Guainia and Cassiquiare rivers in Venezuela. Research has been conducted by Wright since the mid-1970s; by Gonzalez-Ñáñez, since the late 1960s/early 1970s; and by Xavier Leal in the first decade of the present century.

The term 'pilgrimage' refers to a journey, especially a long one, made to some sacred place as an act of religious devotion; the term 'sanctuary' is understood as a place where someone or something is protected or given shelter. As these terms apply to the traditions of northern Arawak-speaking peoples, there are numerous interconnected sacred places where events of major importance to the creation of the world are marked, often by petroglyphs or meaningful arrangements of boulders. Sacred narratives recount that in primordial times the creators of the world made long journeys

Multi-centric mythscapes

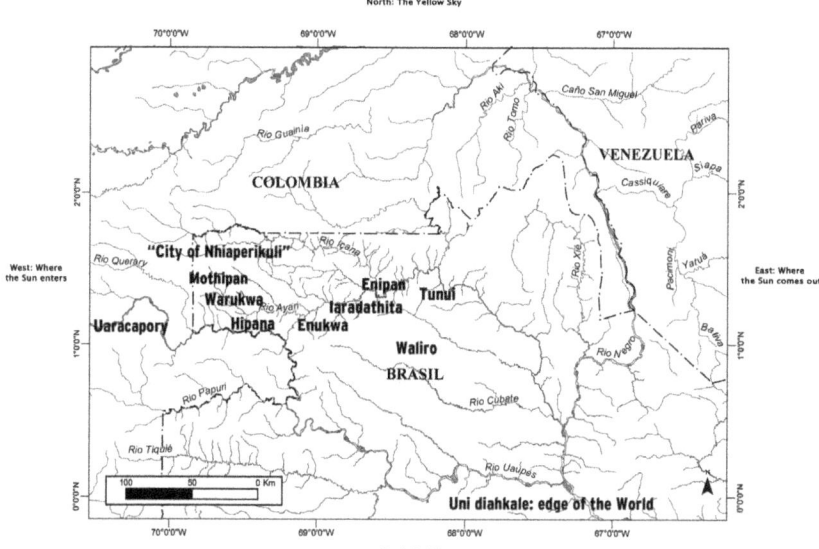

Key to Sacred Places
Uaracapory: Place of the Tree of Life, Kaali ka thadapan, origin of shamans' powers, malikai; **Mothipan**: fortress of the women, Amarunai, after they stole the sacred flutes from the men; place of origin of all waters; **Hipana**: center of the universe, 'navel of the sky' where Kuwai was born and ancestors emerged; **Enukwa**: ancestral emergence of the Walipere-dakenai phratry; *Iaradathita*: place of the animal souls; **Enipan**: place of the first initiation ritual; **Tunui**: place of origin of all fish; **Waliro**: place of the first plantation; *'City of Nhiaperikuli'*: stone house, where Mawerikuli's tomb lies; **Warukwa**: island of Nhiaperikuli's house. Numerous other places of importance for clan histories and ancestral soul-houses are located throughout the region.

Map 2 Mythscapes of the north-west Amazon (adapted from Wright 2009 and 2013)

or processions beginning and/or ending at these sacred places, during the course of which they celebrated the first rituals of initiation. These journeys are recalled in minute detail by elderly chanters who remember them in a lengthy series of chants performed in the course of these rites today.[2]

The creation stories of northern Arawak-speaking peoples are marked by multiple 'centres' at which major transformational events occurred in primordial times (the first birth, the first death, the first initiation rite, emergence of the first ancestors). These centres are described in minute detail by the religious specialists, the jaguar shamans, seers and savants, who – based on their direct experiences of the sacred – are capable of explaining holistically every shape and form, inscription, locations and inter-relations among elements of these sites. The 'centres' are also 'sanctuaries' in the sense that they

---

2   Similar, in some ways, perhaps, to the well-known 'Dreamtime' of the Australian Aborigines.

are highly charged sources of cosmic life force protected by the specialists. Their sacredness involves both a deep respect for their intrinsic significance, a strong taboo (enforced by sorcery) against disturbing any aspect or feature in them, and their connection with the invisible (except to the specialists) other world of the spirits and creator deities. Each centre is understood to be a unique portal to the sacred.

Sacred mythscapes

Each ethno-linguistic group has/had its own sacred mythscape. These mythscapes were 'multi-centric' (having one or more sacred centres where life-defining transformations occurred), with the capacity to expand centrifugally outwards to the furthest reaches of the known world and contract centripetally back inward. Expansive phases refer to the primordial 'opening up' of the world, which can have many meanings, such as historical exile from the world centre to the extreme peripheries (the boundaries with alterity) followed by a return home and regaining of power.

The idea of a multi-centred world resolves an apparent ambiguity of a world that was created at various points in space and through distinct world-opening acts. Although all peoples recognize the centre of the universe, where the universe began, as the place called Hipana on the Aiary River, each phratry has relations with the sacred spaces in its own territory that replicate all others. Near the headwaters of the Içana River, for example, the Koripako people also refer to a rapids called Hipana where, they say, there are 'holes at the bottom' and the dwelling places of the Yoopinai spirits. They say there could be a direct connection (through an underground tunnel) with the rapids of Hipana on the Aiary River, the place of origin of the universe. For the Koripako, the place is (or was, since most are now evangelical) an important place of animal souls, or *iaradathi*.

In both cases, Hipana is the name for a sacred centre and not a village settlement. There are other such names for sacred centres: Kaali ka Thadapani (great house or tree of sustenance), Warukwa (place of the creator), Ehnipan (place of the first initiation), Enúkwa (place of ancestral emergence) and Motípana (house of the first women), each referring to points on a 'map' of the primordial world where there are extensive petroglyphs or rock formations and other outstanding geographical features that are connected to the narratives of creation.

Not all of these 'centres' have the same importance nor qualities. Ehnípan (or Jandú Rapids on the Içana River downriver from Hipana of the Aiary) is a centre unto itself and yet, at the same time, a complement to the great world-centre on the Aiary River, as it is the origin place of the most important rite of initiation, when the world 'expanded' and 'contracted' with the sounds of the great spirit Kuwai, whose body became the sacred flutes and trumpets; and the place where he 'died', that is, left this world for the Other World of the ancestors.

While the sacred centres of the world, the sanctuaries and the ancestral emergence places of northern Arawak-speakers are the sources of new life, ambiguity is a feature that permeates their powers, insofar as they are also sources of primordial poison and sorcery. To visit any one of these places today, one must treat them with great respect, as places that 'have their own time' (DeLoria, 2011), where the power of the sacred events that took place there (and are often seen in every detail of these spaces) is still present and vibrant. The power of creation is inextricably tied to the power of destruction, as healing and sorcery, life and death, are two sides of the same entity. This is a common theme in the sacred stories of the northern Arawak-speaking peoples (Baniwa, Kuripako, Warekena and others), but it is especially evident in the sacred story of how the world came into being and was reproduced for all times, the story of Kuwai (see below).

The idea of a multi-centric world is also consistent with the disputes told in narratives between the sibs and ethnic groups. We include in this chapter a brief consideration of narratives of the historical ancestors, along with certain healing chants, insofar as they recall processes of forced exile to peripheral lands and return to the homelands, the centre of the world. Shamanic healing itself is largely focused on the epidemics and sicknesses that come from the external world, and healing or protection gained by returning to the world centre. The great shaman seers of the historic past created such sanctuaries or reinforced pre-existing ones.

In most cases, the world of alterity (the 'others', non-kin, affines or enemies) surrounds the world of 'people' (all those considered kin and who speak northern Arawak languages). Ambiguity inheres in the relation between kin (inside, at the centre) and non-kin (others, on the peripheries). In order for there to be continuity of the internal world of kin, there must exist the hostility of the external enemy, whose powers are nevertheless considered necessary for the reproduction of the internal world of kin.

Representations and interconnections

Considered altogether, the graphic representations of the primordial beings, chiselled in the distant past into the boulders of many rapids in the north-west Amazon, constitute a cultural memory of the primordial worlds, how they came into being and the world-changing events that made the contemporary world the way it is. (Gonzalez-Ñánez 1968, 1980, 1986, 2009; Wright 1998, 1999, 2009, 2013, 2014; Xavier Leal 2013) This cultural memory can be understood as a social history as well, in the most essential meaning of the term, as a view of how society is reproduced over time (Turner 1988). For, the elements comprising the sacred mythscape orient the peoples today as to the spirit powers that brought the world into existence, threatened it with destruction, or guaranteed its continuity over time.

Among northern Arawak-speaking peoples, furthermore, there is a strong belief in the association of primordial shamans and spirits with material places (large boulders in the rivers, caves, hills, depressions in the rocks of the rivers) in this world. Thus, there are numerous 'stone-houses' situated throughout each phratry's territory that are places of the 'first fruits' and their spirit owners, *yoopinai* spirits, the mountaintop sources of all fish. Several of these places require appropriate behaviour when they are approached, such as silence, avoidance of looks so as not to attract or disturb the spirits, because they may give humans sickness.[3] Others are 'stone houses' associated with primordial shamans, where people can solicit their protection from sickness or misfortune.

The different senses of connectedness amongst sacred sites in the northwest Amazon include: (1) through the petroglyphs illustrating fundamental themes of sustenance, birth, emergence and creation, initiation, death and the spirit world; (2) various kinds of movement in primordial time and space, of expansion outward and contraction inward, exemplified particularly in the voyages of the primordial women when they had sacred instruments in their power, and made the entire world a fertile space; (3) the narratives of exile and return of the historical ancestors from their homelands; and (4) places to which people today journey in order to leave offerings to the souls of past great shamans and wise people.

Thus, the site called Kaali ka Thadapani (Uaracapury, on the upper Uaupés River) is where the 'great tree of sustenance', the 'house of the earth-master Kaali' once stood. This 'house' existed in the miniature world prior to the birth of Kuwai. Then, there is the site called Hipana, where Kuwai was born and the first ancestors came out of the holes of the stone earth. Several sites mark places of the Creator's houses and world-transforming events. One of these 'houses of the Creator' is where death came into the world. All but the last of these places are marked by numerous petroglyphs, traces or reminders of primordial acts, beings and events; some even have apparently cosmologically significant arrangements of boulders. Altogether, the model

---

3   An example of inappropriate behaviour occurs when a person passes near a site where there are images of the 'lightning spirits' (perukali) chiselled into the boulders. If the person, in cooking a meal, allows a pot of boiling water to overflow into fire and the steam produces a hissing sound, the lightning spirits become alive as jaguars and attack the hapless traveller.

Multi-centric mythscapes

Figure 1 The centre (Kúwai) and four directions where sky and earth meet (Tsúwai) according to northern Arawak of the north-west Amazon (petroglyph located at Jurupary Falls, Inyaipana).

of a sacred 'mythscape' can be represented in the form of a quadrangle with a hole in the centre. Such a form delimits the universe for each northern Arawak-speaking society in the region.

Comparing the diverse mythscapes of the Arawak-speaking peoples in the north-west Amazon Region, one finds important concordances but also divergences. This can readily be seen in the chanting traditions called *kalidzamai* (for the Warekena, *kalidama;* for the Baré, *kariamã*) that recount the journeys of the primordial men and women to the ends of the world and back at the time of the first initiation rites (see Vidal 1987, for example, and Raffa 2003). These chants are of particular significance as frameworks within which all sacred sites are interconnected, expanding outward to the limits of the world, contracting inwards to the universe-centre, and connecting the upper layers of the cosmos with this world.

Among the Piapoco, Warekena, Dzauinai, Hohodene and probably other peoples, these chants are known as the 'Voyages of Kuwai', child of the creator and first woman (González-Ñáñez 1987; Hill 1993; Vidal 1987; Wright 1993/4). Among the Hohodene (Baniwa of the Aiary River), these complex chants invoke the *ipanai*, the house-spirits visited during a series of primordial processions made by the first women as they blew the sacred trumpets and flutes – the transformed body of their son, Kuwai. In doing so, they left the ancestral spirits of Kuwai *(kuwainai)* music in every place of importance in the world. These voyages are conceptualized as a 'pursuit' by the Creator to regain the flutes (Wright 1993/4) that the women had stolen from the men. At the end of these journeys, the chanters then 'bring back tobacco to the centre of the world, Hipana'. This return journey concentrates the spiritual power that filled the world with its sounds and sends it back upwards to the centre of the sky. Once the flutes were regained, the Creator sent the women on a 'mission' to the ends of the world (more exactly, to the four 'skies' – east, west, south, north), where they became the 'mothers of the whites'.

Whether 'pursuit' or 'mission', we see these world-expanding processions by and with the flutes as 'pilgrimages', because during them, the music of the sacred imbued the world with its power, and continues to do so every time an initiation rite is performed and the chants remembering the voyages are sung by the elders. These elderly, priestly chanters embody the primordial chanters, journeying in their thought, and with tobacco smoke, along the same routes as the first voyages. The task of the chanters is extensive and must be done in an exact order; otherwise their purpose – to protect the newly initiated boys and girls from potential harm that spirits anywhere in the known world could do to them – will not be fulfilled and the dangerous power of the sacred will ultimately bring tragedy to the living.

The first world

From the perspective of the Arawak-speaking peoples of the Aiary River (primarily Hohodene), the very first world was a ball of stone floating in empty space. The very first being, 'Universe Child', separated a piece of this stone ball and made it rise up in the sky to become the primordial sun, leaving behind a 'pot' (circular depression) in the stone ball. Shortly after, he went to look for the very first ancestors who emerged from the open hole left by the sun, at the place called Hipana, the 'universe navel', the 'celestial umbilicus' connecting the sky with the earth. As the first ancestors emerged from the hole, each singing its own song, the Creator sent them to their lands. At that time, there were no rivers, no riverbeds, no food for the first living beings.

At another centre-place, in the worlds that pre-existed the present earth, there was the primordial tree of sustenance, which contained all the original plant-foods and fruits, as well as the original shamanic powers, including *pariká* beans. The Creator and his people obtained these shamanic powers by cutting down this tree, called Kaali ka Thadapani, 'house of the earth-master'. The felling of the great tree opened up connections amongst all the communities of the world at that time, each of which could then obtain their shares of food to plant. These connections became the five principal riverbeds of the north-west Amazon; all of the riverbeds would, at a later moment, be filled by the fertile blood of the first woman. The felling of the tree brought all food and shamanic powers into the world; the latter, however, were 'stolen' by the tapir, creating a situation of chaos that the Creator had to set right

Multi-centric mythscapes

Figure 2   The great boulder (lower left) is the first earth and floated in infinite space, before there was any water flowing at the rapids; in the centre of the narrow passage is a perfectly round and deep depression in the rocks which is said to be where the first ancestors emerged. Photo: M.C. Wright 2009.

by reclaiming ownership of them. This was the beginning of the shamanic powers to heal; but it was also the beginning of the forest spirits into which tapir's companions, crazed by their inhaling of the sacred snuff, transformed. In Figure 3, each fallen tree becomes a riverbed:

The Creator Nhiaperíkuli (spelled in various ways: Naperúli, Iñiãperikuli, Ñaperikoli), according to the traditions of various northern Arawak-speaking peoples, lived in the primordial times, simultaneously in several different places of what is now known as the north-west Amazon region. For the Hohodene peoples, there is an island called Warukwa (see Figure 4) on the Dzukuali river, a short distance from Hipana, where Nhiaperikuli had a house. There, according to the stories, Nhiaperikuli and his brothers had many adventures with the fish peoples, the great anaconda, and others, but most importantly, using coca and incantations ,from there he shamanically fertilized the first woman with the child of his thought, heart and soul, Kuwai.

Sacred powers of the centre of the universe

Hipana is considered the centre of the universe in both a vertical and a horizontal sense. This most important place, situated on the Aiary River (at

Figure 3   Opening of the riverbeds of the north-west Amazon (which would later be filled by the rivers of blood from first woman). Drawing by Thiago Aguilar, Uapui, 2010.

Figure 4   Warukwa, Nhiaperikuli's House on the Dzukuali River, Upper Aiary. In this depiction the Creator performed shamanism over fish. Drawing by Thiago Aguilar, Uapui, 2010.

the rapids also known as Kupí), was where Kuwai, the child of the Creator (Nhiaperikuli) and the first woman (Amaru), came out into the world. The boulders and petroglyphs there illustrate (Figure 5 below) the following elements representing Kuwai's birth: (a) a line of boulders mark where Amaru 'sat' before she gave birth to Kuwai, and where girls at their menarche sit today so that their bodies may become strong; (b) a boulder with designs of the Pleiades constellation, visible at the time of plant growth, and others associated with Amaru; (c) a boulder that represents 'Kuwai', with petroglyphs of a serpent representing the 'pain of the whip',[4] and spirals that are the 'sounds of the flutes'; (d) another boulder, a short distance away, is said to represent the 'true Kuwai'; (e) a stone that has the shape of the 'placenta of Kuwai' after he was born, in the shape of a freshwater stingray; (f) several boulders representing the sacred flutes of Kuwai, and hawk feathers that empowered the original flutes to open the 'voice' of Kuwai; (g) a place of the ancient village where Nhiaperikuli made the Kuwai flutes; (h) stairway from the port.

In addition, the sacred place of Hipana is 'announced' to anyone approaching it from downstream by a large petroglyph of Kuwai on the face of one of the main boulders at the mouth of this portal to the sacred. In the reproduction below, a drawing of Kuwai by a shaman's apprentice and artist is juxtaposed with this petroglyph; the body of this spirit of sickness and sorcery, its 'shadow-soul' (*idanami*) is that of a sloth mixed with the teeth of a jaguar, and the face of a White Man. Kuwai was, after all, a univocal combination of alterity and identity, exceedingly dangerous to humans. The petroglyph, on the other hand, shows parts of Kuwai's segmented body along with rounded and swirl shapes that are the musical sounds emitted from his body.

Kuwai's sounds and singing created the world, that is, made it open up (expand) from its primordial, miniature size, to the huge territory and world that the Baniwa know today.

The first woman looks for a centre to give birth
According to one version of Kuwai's birth:

> Before Kuwai was born, his mother Amaru went looking for a place to give birth. She went to the Uaupés River, later the Içana River – at the place called Tsépan – and she lay down there. Later, she went to Puwedali, on the

---

4 At initiation and all rituals at which the sacred flutes are played, men and women whip each other, and elders whip the children. Whipping (*pakapetakan*) is done both for the purpose of 'making the children grow more quickly' and so that people will know how to resist the pain in this world (for, this world is known as '*kaiwikwe*', the 'place of pain').

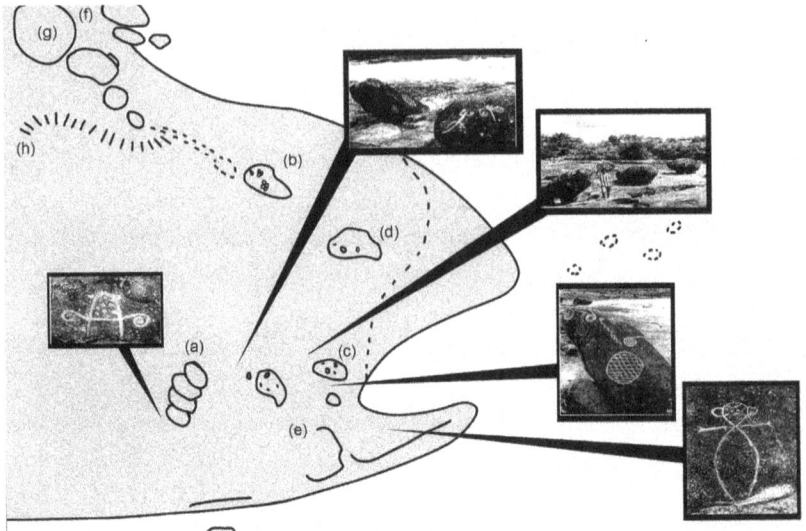

Figure 5 Sketch of petroglyphs and mythscape at Hipana, the World Center (adapted from Ortiz and Pradilla 2002 by M.C. Wright, in: Wright 2014:212).

Figure 6 Petroglyph and drawing of Kuwai-ka-Wamundana (Koch-Grünberg 1907; drawing by T. Aguilar, 2010).

Ucaiali (Uaupés) River, and went to lie down there. Later, Hipana (Uapui) and she stayed there. After Kuwai was born, he was hidden from her at a place downriver: at Dumalipekwa, three places below. Thuruapekwa, Thiripidapekwa. Nhiãpirikuli went after him.

Multi-centric mythscapes

Figure 7   Amaru Seated at the sacred boulders Of Hipana (drawing by T. Aguilar, Uapui, 2010; photo by I. Fontes, 2010). The drawing actually shows Amaru seated at Tsúwai, a place where 'the waters no longer flow', at the edge of the world.

Kuwai was conceived through a shamanic act in which Nhiaperikuli, sent his thought into the body of Amaru. Nhiaperikuli wanted to have a child through whom all of his knowledge and soul would be transmitted. The child, however, was an astonishing mix of creative sound and violent pain and destructiveness, who was banished to the 'end' of the world, then still miniature. The powerful and dangerous life force that Kuwai represented may be understood as the 'body of the cosmos', permeated with holes through which the breath of the Creator's heart-soul blows, which is capable of transforming into multiple spirit entities, embodying the forces of nature (the fertility of the forest and rivers, the devastating deluge of the rains, the fearful darkness of night), and the hidden source of all deathly ailments. The dangerous powers of his body were, in the end, harnessed by being transformed into the material shapes of flutes and trumpets, each representing at once a part of Kuwai's body, a first ancestor of a phratry, or a relation of alliance or antagonism that characterized the primordial way of life.

The life force that Kuwai represents includes society-in-time; that is to say, the entire story can also be understood as an explanation for how patrilineal heart-soul, or life force, came to be embodied in material forms (the sacred flutes and instruments) and reproduced over time and space. As long as there have been 'people' in this world, the belief in the Kuwai first ancestors has been the foundation for their organization into society.

Women's major role in the process of creation, besides containing this cosmic entity within her body, was precisely to introduce change in the midst of continuity. Shamans state that after the birth of Kuwai the first woman's blood overflowed the boundaries of the primordial, miniature world around Hipana, filling up the pre-existing riverbeds and making the rivers flow out, thus fertilizing the earth. This event was the second of the most important sources of change and motion in a new, dynamic and expansive universe (the first being the felling of the great tree of sustenance). Before this happened, the primordial universe was self-contained in a miniature area around the 'universe umbilicus', a still-spiritual connection between the first world and the new world that was coming into being.

The women's 'pilgrimage' with the sacred flutes and trumpets

Taking the story of Kuwai as a whole, there were actually three moments when the women 'opened up' the world: after the childbirth, when Amaru's blood trickled out of the miniature world and filled the pre-existing streambeds; at the end of the first boys' initiation ritual, when the women stole the sacred flutes and trumpets (the transformed body of Kuwai, consumed at the end of the first initiation rite in a great world fire that made the world contract to its miniature size) and paraded throughout the world playing them; and finally, after a war in which the men recovered the sacred flutes from the women, four of the women were sent off to the ends of the earth, while one stayed at the centre.

In the second 'opening', the men chased after the women and made omens to warn them of their pursuit. The Hohodene traditions remember a long sequence of five lengthy voyages made in primordial times by Amaru and the first women who had taken the sacred flutes away from the men after Nhiaperikuli had partially made them. The women fled from the men and played the instruments throughout the known world. The world opened up again from its miniature size to its present-day size, through the expansive power of the music and sounds of the flutes and trumpets (*limalia-iyu*). Amaru's father was the tapir, who had stolen the original shamanic powers from Nhiaperikuli. It was similarly the shamanic power and knowledge embodied in the instruments – the essence of Nhiãperikuli's 'heart-soul' – that Amaru and the women took away from the men.

The women went in four directions, expanding along the same riverbeds that Amaru's blood had filled. The map below traces the 'voyages of the women with Kuwai', beginning at the centre (Hipana), expanding in four directions outwards to the ends of the known world.[5] The first voyage actually traces a circular shape connecting the two sacred places that have the greatest power in the story of Kuwai: Hipana, where the child was born; and Ehnipan, where he was consumed in a great bonfire. This circle of the centre is called 'the shield of' (*liwapere*) the primordial shaman/chanter Dzuliferi (shamanic protection is the main purpose of the chants).

On the far upper Uaraná stream (Dzukuali), upstream from Hipana, is a place called Motipana with large stone formations that are said to represent Amaru and the first women's cave/fortress. There, the women performed the first initiation rites for their daughter. There also, Nhiaperikuli and his allies, the birds and animals, waged war against the women, took back the flutes, and sent four of the women to the ends of the earth. This sacred place is also said to be the origin place of all the water of the rivers in the region.

The remembrance of these events is performed in the sacred chants at all initiation rites, when every initiate is introduced to knowledge of the spirit world and the laws for living in society. When Kuwai transmitted the sacred initiation chants at the conclusion of the first ritual of initiation, humanity received the power to fertilize the world by means of shamanic protection ultimately neutralizing all potential harm. The sacred story and chants in no way annul time, but rather align change and continuity within the temporal and spatial coordinates of the universe.

Exile or diaspora? Ambiguity in the sacred journeys

At the end of the war, Nhiaperikuli dispatched the women to the four directions of the sky, sending them on missions to become the 'mothers of the white people' (the Portuguese and Spaniards in Portugal and Spain). Women became the conduits of openness to the external world and its alterity. The flutes which remained with the men are the 'body of Kuwai', the continuity of the primordial world for all future generations (*walimanai*). Identity will never be lost as long as power is maintained over its most potent, primordial symbol.

Women retained the ambiguous power of reproducing alterity, which can have both destructive and creative impacts on humanity. The women are,

---

5   In northern Arawakan (Hohodene, Dzauinai, Warekena, Piapoco, Baniva) ceremonial chants, the 'maps' of the primordial women's flight cover the whole of the Northern Amazon region and beyond, to the limits of their geographical knowledge. The chants re-create the flight and pursuit of the women in minute detail, consisting of hundreds of places where the music of the instruments was played. The primordial processions follow along the rivers and overland, eventually arriving at a very sacred place, a sanctuary, where initiation ceremonies are then held.

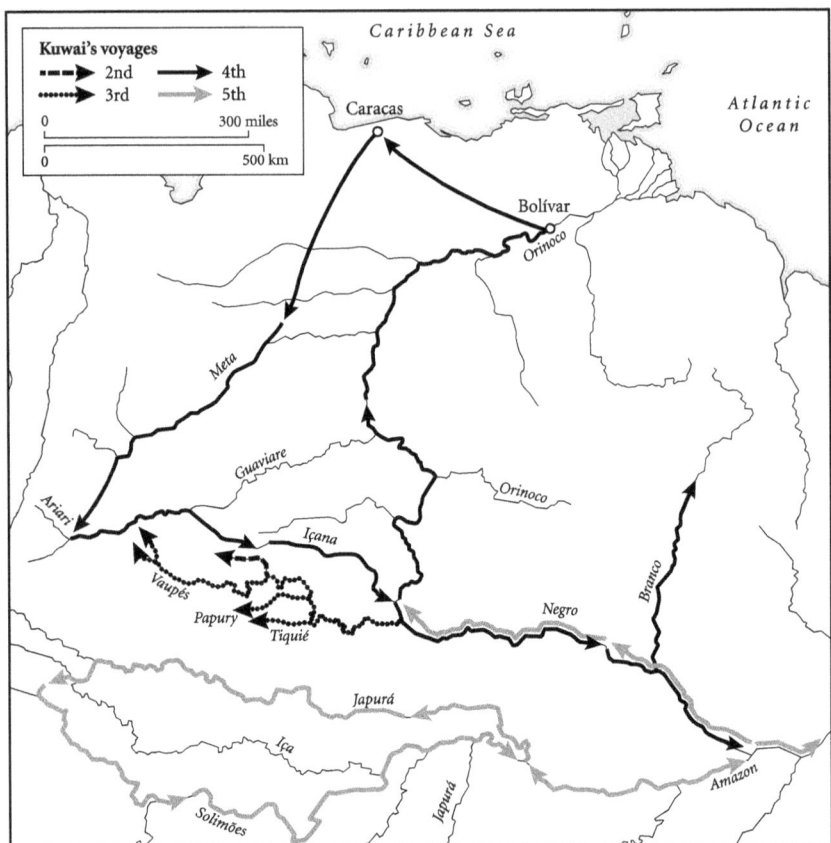

Map 3   Kuwai's second to fifth voyages (reproduced from Wright 1993/4).

according to the narrative tradition of Kuwai, shamanic intermediaries with the outside world, just as male shamans are intermediaries with the other world of the great spirits. Both therefore are locked in a kind of complementary opposition that is the moving force or dynamic of reciprocity and exchange, implying both marriage and sorcery.

Ancestral power embodied in the flutes and trumpets, known collectively as 'Kuwai', thus distinguishes one phratry's collective identity from another. As the law of exogamy (marital exchange) is a centrifugal force through which the external world (in-marrying women, non-indigenous peoples) penetrates the internal world of the sib/phratry, there is an extreme taboo on showing the flutes to the women, which we interpret to be an adaptive mechanism to preserve intact the internal continuity of phratric identity against the threatening powers that outsiders represent.

The 'Great City of Ñaperikoli' – where immortality was lost

For the Arawakan-speaking peoples of the far upper Içana River in present-day Colombia, there are mythscapes of major importance. One is called the 'Great City of Ñaperikoli', a site connected to another known as the 'Fortress of the Women', both located on the Yawiary stream. Both of these may perhaps be the same sites the Hohodene refer to as *motípana*, the fortress of the women, a cave where there are stone images of the primordial women. There are overland and riverine connections between the upper Uaraná and the Yawiary stream, as well as between the far upper Içana and the upper Uaupés Rivers in Colombia.

For the Koripako of this region, however, we cannot say that the 'Great City' is of 'their' traditions as a people. Unlike among the Hohodene, very few Koripako elders remember the meanings associated with this Great City, and we cannot affirm that what they remember comes from their ancestors. Another stream further up the Içana was of much greater importance for the Payoaliene sib of the Koripako as the location of their ancestral villages. While it is true that most of the inhabitants of the region in question are Koripakos who came from the upper Guainia River, there are also numerous descendants of the Cubeo, whose principal territory is further to the west, along the upper Uaupés and its tributaries.

A cluster of stone formations on the top of a hill at the headwaters of the Yawiary stream off the upper Içana is called 'the Great City of Ñaperikoli'.[6] Nothing similar to it has been reported in the literature on the Koripako or Baniwa (or other northern Arawakan peoples for that matter). It is an arrangement of massive boulders with hardly any petroglyphs on them, yet with an order and meaning attributed to the whole arrangement. The boulders are aligned along an east/west axis. Since Ñaperikoli is the sun deity, this alignment is surely significant. The site as a whole recalls a scene from the story of Mawerikuli, younger brother of Ñaperikoli who was the 'first person to die' and was buried underneath the house of Ñaperikoli, following the tradition of burials many generations ago. The tradition of Mawerikuli is said to be a 'Cubeo story', and it is possible that both Koripako of the upper Içana in Colombia and Guainia, and the Cubeo of the upper Uaupés, also in Colombia, may have had settlements in this region.

Underneath the huge 'stone house of Ñiaperikoli', perched at an angle on the slope of a mountain top, is a stone slab which appears like a stone coffin with a broken piece of an iron bell situated atop one end, similar to the carved

---

6   Leal's Master's dissertation, defended in 2013 at the Museu Nacional in Brazil, presents the most detailed report on his expedition with Kuripako guides to this site.

Figure 8   Four views of the Great City (photos by C. Xavier Leal 2013). The huge boulder upper left is the main house of Ñaperikoli perched on the edge of a granite slope at the top of a hill; the second photo (upper right) shows a slab of (apparently cut) boulder representing the stone tomb of the 'first person to die'; immediately below is a closer shot of the tomb which has a piece of an overturned iron bell at the tomb's head, possibly representing the 'death mask' of the first person to die; and the fourth photo (bottom left) is the massive stone 'kitchen' near the great 'house of the Creator'.

wooden masks the Baniwa put over the faces of their deceased in the past. It is certainly no coincidence that the piece was placed where it is – by whom and when is a mystery – and it is reasonable to suggest that the stone slab of the tomb may also have been placed deliberately (again, by whom is a mystery).

Behind the 'house' boulder is a 'kitchen' boulder (traditionally, all houses were longhouses, while today most houses have the main dwelling-place facing the river, and the kitchen construction behind the house). Behind it are several boulders representing 'sentinel posts', where, according to shamans' discourse, Ñaperikoli's pet birds (called Tchitchiro and Madoodo) could warn of approaching people. The whole arrangement is very reminiscent of the moment in the story told by the Baniwa of the Aiary River when death came into the world (see Wright 1998:pt. 3; ed. 1999), and Mawerikuli was laid in a stone coffin under the House of Ñaperikoli. On the eastern side of the site are

Multi-centric mythscapes 219

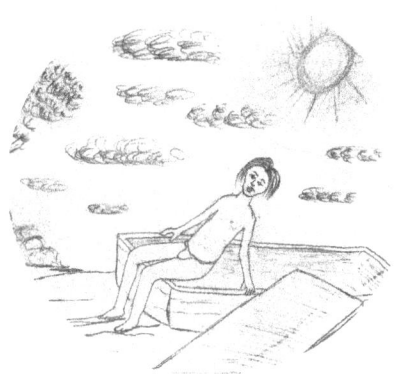

Figure 9 The tombstone of Mawerikuli, the first person to die in primordial times (drawing: T. Aguilar 2010; photo: C. Xavier Leal 2013).

the house and the tomb; to the west are the smaller boulders of the sentinel birds.

The image in Figure 9 shows the spirit of Mawerikuli rising from his stone tomb; this drawing, made by a shaman's apprentice in the year 2010, has been overlaid on the photo of the stone tomb. According to the story, Mawerikuli died from sorcery; but it was possible for him to return to life after three days of seclusion in the stone tomb, and thus all people would continue being immortal, had not an unfortunate incident occurred, the result of which was that he fell back down in the tomb, 'nothing but bones'. Despite all shamanic attempts to revive Mawerikuli, none of them could bring him back to life. So humanity lost its primordial immortality, which was only later regained through the creation of the sacred flutes and trumpets at Hipana. For with them, ancestral souls would be transmitted to all future generations. The paradox in this, of course, is that the same ancestral soul that transmits life also takes it away through sorcery and violent death, a powerful and ambiguous force that is the very heart of Baniwa, if not all of northern Arawakan religiosity.

Today, the shamans say that when they are seeking the answer as to whether a victim of sorcery will get well or not, they look for the image of Mawerikuli to see whether it is rising from its tomb, or falling inside. If it is rising, the sick person will return to life; if it is falling, the sick person will die. The image of Mawerikuli sitting on the edge of his tomb, halfway between life and death, aligned with the position of the sun (which is, in shamanic understanding, the body of the Creator Nhiaperikuli) dramatically illustrates the ambiguous situation of the victim of sorcery. Whether the ambiguity is resolved (that is, whether Mawerikuli will return to life) will depend entirely on the power of the shamanic cure.

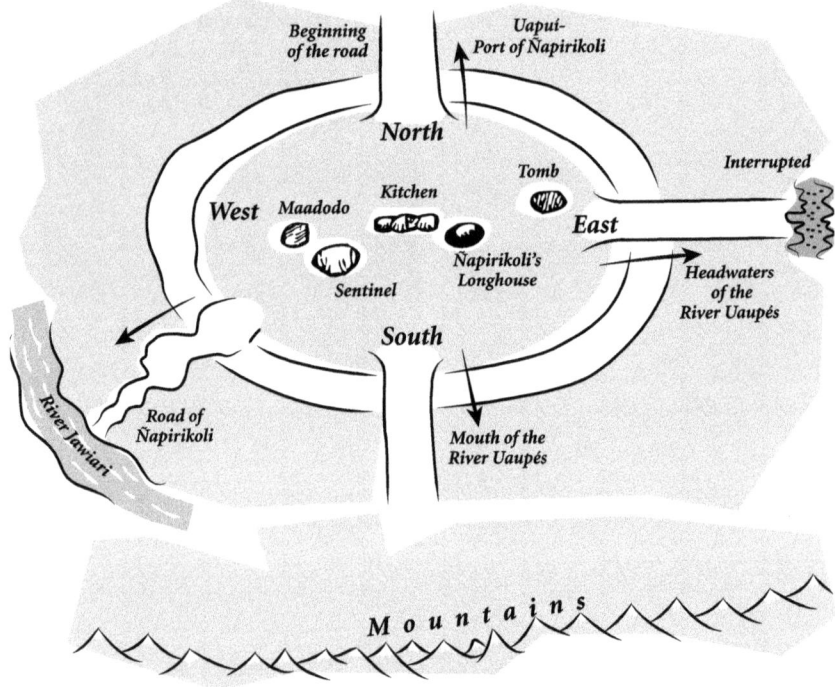

Figure 10   Sketch of the Great City (Xavier Leal 2013).

If there is a correlation, in the cosmovision of the Baniwa, between the sun's path across the sky and the arrangement of the boulders at the site, this would reinforce an association with themes of death and rebirth.[7] Like Hipana, the 'city' is part of a much larger and more complex site associated with other places, such as the 'cavern of the women', where, according to the Kuwai story, Amaru and the women hid after they had stolen the flutes from the men. This complex site contains a large number of rock formations and caves. Near the 'Great City' there is a place on the Surubim stream, deep in the forest off the upper Içana, where a large flat rock sits atop a hill overlooking the river and a vast expanse of forest – a place where, it is said, Ñiaperikoli 'sat and saw how the world would be' (Xavier Leal 2013).

In Figure 10 it is possible to see that the Great City is oriented in such a way that it leads to several of the main rivers of the region as well as other mythscapes. The site gives a perspective from the centre out over the vast terrain of rainforest and clusters of hills in the direction of other mythscapes such as at Hipana. This perspective would be distinct from that of a person

---

7   As, for example, one finds in the more elaborate constructions of sun and moon temples aligned with the avenue of the dead in Mesoamerica (cf. Carrasco 2013).

situated at Hipana, the universe centre at Uapui, connecting upriver to Warukwa (on the Dzukuali stream), downriver to Ehnípan, up to the sky umbilical cord, or down through the hole of emergence to the world below.

Historical exile and return

We briefly refer now to stories of the ancestors of a more recent past that tell of their forced exile from ancestral lands at the time of first contacts with the non-indigenous world (Wright 2005). Undoubtedly corresponding to the periods of indigenous slavery or *descimentos* (relocation downriver to colonial towns) of the eighteenth century, the Hohodene and other phratries remember how heroic chiefs fled from the colonies and returned to the phratric homelands, in the heart of their territory. Their return home coincided with a time of warfare and sickness in the colonies. The indigenous peoples had lost many of their ritual dance ornaments and instruments in this exile downriver, and had become extremely reduced in number by the time they fled and returned. Through the intermediation of the women from other phratries, the Hohodene ancestor was able to make alliances, and regain the phratry's social viability. Since then, the phratry has grown and prospered.

The end of these 'historical' traditions connects them directly with ancestors who probably lived in the last quarter of the nineteenth and beginning of the twentieth centuries. Today, those ancestors are remembered for their courage in returning to their homelands and reconstructing their society through marital and political alliances, empowering them to resist exile later in their histories.

Still, the relocation downriver created an ambiguity in the Hohodene vision of their society in a history that starkly represents the violence of contact: the descendants of the ancestors who sought refuge from the colonial situation claim that there is today a place downriver which is 'theirs' by virtue of their exile. The same descendants associate the downriver world with the transformation of those historical ancestors who remained in the colonies into 'white people', 'soldiers'. The downriver world represents loss of identity and transformation into 'others', the very enemy which forced them into exile, yet there is still a historical claim to a 'piece of land' that they consider 'theirs'.

Spiritual protection for the living

Indigenous history includes the pilgrimages that faithful believers make to the tombs of the great shamanic healers, savants, considered as 'saints' and 'saviours' of the past. The north-west Amazon has had a long history among Tukanoan- and Arawak-speaking peoples of such 'wise people', 'dreamers', powerful shamans and even gifted children who have demonstrated their direct connections to the creator-deities and souls of the deceased, and have initiated 'cross cults' associated with places of ceremonial dance.

In extensive field research along the tributaries of the upper Guainia, Omar González-Ñáñez and the Baniva elder Hernan Camico documented the burial site of the most famous of these prophet-seers, Venancio Camico, known popularly as the 'Christ of the Içana' (González Ñañez , O. and M. Camico 2013; see also Wright 1981 and 2005; Wright and Hill 1986), who is remembered today in numerous oral traditions of Arawak- and non-Arawak-speaking peoples of the region. He was a miraculous healer from the upper Guainia River with a great many followers, who came from afar to consult with him and follow his counsel. He was known as a *talisri* (dreamer or seer). The oral traditions about Venancio Camico state that his principal message was the elimination of sorcery and the installation of a society based on harmonious conviviality (that is, a reform in the collective heart/soul of the community). He began a tradition called the 'Song of the Cross' in which people would dance with or around a cross; as his fame grew, the local military government heard that he claimed to be a 'saint' and had a great following, so they went to test him and take him prisoner. Persecuted by the military from Venezuela, he sought refuge on the Âki River at a site called Mawáanali. He first lived at a settlement called Wayánatsi ('Guayana') on the Caño Âki, but with the spread of his movement, church and government officials began harassing him and his followers. So they fled to Mawáanali. There, indigenous people from the Xié River in Brazil joined up with Camico. He also had a settlement on the Caño Mâni. Finally, he moved to the village of Macareo (Caño Âki), where he died in 1903. There is a tomb in Macareo made in the Creole style where he was buried; many Baniva from Maroa, and Baniwa from the Aiary River continue their firm belief in Camico to the present day, visiting the tomb and leaving candles there asking for the protection of their well-being.

In a parallel fashion, the Hohodene of the Aiary River, who followed the seer/savant Kudui in the 1960s–70s, visit his grave at the cemetery on the island of Warukwa, sacred place of the House of Nhiaperikuli, for it is believed that his soul remains by the side of the grave to assist his kin and whoever seeks his protection. It was Kudui who had instructed the Hohodene that the true 'centre of the Universe' is the boulder of Dzuliferi, the primordial shaman, slightly above Hipana rapids. People today leave offerings at this boulder, asking for the protection and help of the great spirit of power, against sickness, or attacks by potential enemies.[8]

---

8   Since a greater part of the northern Arawak-speaking peoples converted to evangelicalism beginning in the 1950s, many of the pre-existing 'cross' cults' were

Multi-centric mythscapes 223

Figure 11 Mid-nineteenth-century savant and seer, Camico, 'saint' of the Baniwa (copy of lithograph from the Museu Nacional, UFRJ, Rio de Janeiro; reproduced in Wright 1999)

History is complemented by a genre of healing chants performed whenever a person has suffered a serious accident that has left him or her unconscious (being hit by a fallen tree, weakness and anaemia associated with sorcery). It is explained that, when that happens, the victim's soul has been engulfed by a giant water serpent and taken downriver to the periphery of the world around the first city of the White People (São Gabriel da Cachoeira, in

transformed into evangelical churches of 'crentes' (believers), whose predominant symbol of religious power became the de-territorialized New Testament.

Figure 12 The boulder of Dzuliferi at Hipana (photo by Isaias Fonte, 2010; with overlay of drawing by Thiago Aguilar, 2010).

the state of Amazonas, Brazil). The serpent is killed, its body ripped open, and the victim begins a long canoe journey from the peripheral world back to the world centre, a sanctuary or haven from the dramatic effects of epidemic diseases coming from the world of the Whites. Along the way, the soul is nourished by the healing power of honey from the bee spirits, and the sweet, healing nectar of tree fruits. The journey back to the centre coincides with the gradual healing of the person's soul and body, such that, by the time the chanter has finished, the victim should have recovered his or her senses, and come back into life. In the story to which the healing corresponds, the Creator asks his younger brother, 'so, you have exchanged your life for another?' – indicating reversal of death in the peripheral zone by complete revival at the world centre, having passed through the spirit worlds of the shamanic bees and drunk their remedies.[9]

Warekena mythscapes and pilgrimages along the upper Rio Negro-Guainia and the Cassiquiare basin

According to the Warekena tradition, the process of ethnogenesis (or, the beginning of ethnic groups) (González-Ñáñez & Camico 2013) occurred

---

9   Hill has argued (1993) that the descent to the east coincides with soul loss and the return to the centre, with healing. The chanting itself is sung through an 'art of microtonal rising' (ibid.), in which the slow, gradual rising tones correspond to the soul's return journey upriver and back to the centre, and the soul's return to health.

at Hipana (Uapui rapids), which is considered to be the 'world umbilicus'. Several peoples initiated their migrations from that site, with Iñápirrikuli-Ka-Kúwai as their leader, and began to expand and populate the world. Many of them crossed rivers, creeks and jungle roads until they settled in places in the Guainía and Orinoco basin. Each time they reached a place, they performed sacred rituals under the leadership of Iñápirrikuli, the Creator, and thereafter he and the 'Creator's people' founded new villages after each ritual of initiation (ibid.).

During Iñápirrikuli's world tour (also known as Kuwai's sacred voyages), he and his troop camped at Capihuara and made a ritual feast. They called it *kasíjmakasi* (a 'rite de passage' initiation ceremony). For the Warekena people, one of their most sacred places is at Capihuara on the Cassiquiare river, a riverine channel connecting the Orinoco with the Rio Negro river near San Carlos de Rio Negro, Amazonas state, Venezuela. They designed or painted many petroglyphs which can be seen today at this ancient place. One of the most sacred beings at Capihuara is Siwáli, an Arawakan ancestor.

Part of the myth-history explaining this is as follows:

THE PROCESSION OF THE KÚWE ACCORDING TO THE WAREKENA
TRADITION. STORY OF THE INITIATION OF THE DAUGHTER OF
GRANDFATHER SIWÁLI

At the beginning of Kúwe (Kuwai), who was born on the Aiary River, a branch of the Içana, the Creator of the Arawak commenced the partition of Kúwe for the entire world. The parts were divided amongst various lands. One part went to Brazil (in the south). The part of Kúwe which corresponded to the *warekena* (ancestors) went along the following route: it descended the Inirida River (Colombia) from the upper Içana and from there it continued on. On the Inírida it reached the rapids of Kubalé (Kúwaili). It formed this great rapids. It is believed that almost all fish go to lay their eggs at this rapids. This was the work of Nápiruli, who was the same Kuwai of the ancestors. He made it this way so that it would be easier for people to catch fish for the *kalíyama* (*kalidzamai* in Hohodene) ritual food for initiation. Kúwe and his procession continued on downriver to the Vichada.

One part of the group reached the mouth of the Vichada, but another part went to the Guaviare. There they divided and came back together. Some went by the upper Orinoco and others by the Atabapo River. They passed by the stone slab of *jabúa* (shining erisma tree) called by the Baniva '*îipane ûusru*'. There they gathered a collection of artwork for the initiation of the daughter of Átu (grandfather) Siwáli, an historic police official of the Cassiquiare who lived in Capihuara,. The various groups of Kúwe passed by each river. One of them arrived at the mouth of the San Miguel or Itíni-wíni River.

The other group went down the Atabapo to the Témi and soon passed by the port of Yavita (Aputsá). There, the traces of Kúwe can be seen on the stones. Soon after, they passed by a trail through the forest that led them to the banks of the Caño Pimichin (Pamitsìni). According to Baniva oral tradition, the trail from Yavita to Pimichín was opened in the times of the Creator, Nápiruli. The tracing of this trail was done when two groups of the procession of Kúwe and Nápiruli proceeded by going from side to side (several from the Pimichín and others from Yavita), following the 'sounds of the sacred animals'. This coincidence is important in that it reinforces the Maipure-Arawakan tradition and history of the creation (for further information see González-Ñáñez 1968).

There they brought together the Kúwe that they intended to take to the great festival of Capihuara where the daughter of Siwáli would 'partake of the *kalíyama*' (the sacred bread, fish and pepper). One of the groups that had divided in Yavita continued onward up the Témi and passed over to the Simakéni (tributary of the Caño San Miguel) by an abandoned trail and came out to a site on the San Miguel that they named 'Sapo' and which the Warekena call Duádua-nawi. There on the San Miguel they passed people who were fasting in preparation for the festival at Capihuara. There they gathered, at grandfather Atu Wichúwi-Chulínawi (owner of the whips or *kapési*). Further up from there, on the same San Miguel, both the group that came from the mouth of this Caño, and the peoples who had entered by way of Simakéni joined together in a site called Madénawi, where they broke the shells of many of the fruits that they had gathered for that *abálesi* (festival of fruits, or *dabokurí*), which in reality would be a ritual of initiation. All of them went on by the San Miguel, they made a journey that descended to the port of the 'painted rock', on the Cassiquiare, where they joined together other paintings or artwork. For their part, the others who came up to the Cassiquiare from the Río Negro passed by the site they called 'Esterita', on the Cassiquiare, from where they gathered together the artwork that was also for the festival of Siwáli. Finally, they all arrived at the gathering in Capihuara.

Once in Capihuara they went to where Depenáwe, the chief or lead dancer (*mádzaru*) for the initiation of the daughter of Siwáli, was. (Depenáwe is also a caño and site that is not very distant from Capihuara.) At this place, there was a great ceiba tree, where they found a pole for hanging the hammock of the girl who was fasting. Above Depenáwe, there was a small river, on the right bank of the Cassiquiare, called Dorotomóni, situated about four hours walking distance from Depenáwe. There was another point for the young girl's hammock, hanging from another pole. When they got there – in the early dawn – they passed by the mouth of another small river called Koromóni.

Multi-centric mythscapes

Figure 13   Petroglyphs at Siwiali (photographs by O. González-Ñáñez, 2009).

They passed by a curve of this river while the other group followed a curve on the Beripamóni river. There they stayed through the night until the morning.

For its part, the Siwáli group was already there in Capihuara. Finally, when the people from upriver arrived at dawn at Capihuara, Depenáwe was already there and the young girl had already partaken of the sacred food. Then, all the groups that had arrived from all parts came together in the morning and each one partook of the *kalídama* after the initiated girl and stayed the morning in Capihuara drinking, eating and dancing the '*gallinetica*' (the dance of the *Yúwiriru* [name of a flute] for the Warekena).

> Told by Pedro Francisco Bernabé – Warekena, Capihuara, Cassiquiare–
> 22 July 1987, text transcribed by González-Ñáñez.

In the Arawak mythical territory of the Guainia-Rio Negro we find many other mythscapes. For example, there is one on the San Miguel or Itini Wini stream, a traditional Warekena *caño* which is documented in *Mitología Guarequena* (González-Ñáñez 1980). But such mythscapes are not as sacred as that of Siwáli in the Cassiquiare.

We find sacred places on the upper Guainia, near the town of Victorino, Guainía-Venezuela, today a Kuripako community; very near to Victorino is an island named Tuwirimirrin where there are also important, sacred and mythical petroglyphs.

In the Atabapo river basin area, in the city of San Fernando de Atabapo barrio called 'La Punta de Lara', there was also an important mythscape possibly from the origins of the Maipurean Tsáse or Piapoko people. Archeologically, the petroglyphs were possibly made by the extinct Nerikawa (Nericagua) people, a Proto-Piapoko sib. According to Vidal (1993), La Punta was an ancient Arawakan ceremonial sacred place at the time of the Kuwai voyages. Zucchi (1992), Tarble (1985) and Greer (1995) have also studied the 'Nericagua complex' and the rock paintings of the Orinoco basin. Tarble further relates petroglyphs to the system of caves, since she interprets co-occurrence (both within caves and within larger geographic areas) as cultural association (Tarble and Scaramelli 1993). The asymmetrical designs, thought to fall into the sacred category above, are said also to occur on numerous petroglyphs associated with many sites in the middle Orinoco area. It should be noted that Tarble has recorded petroglyphs not only along the river, but also in more upland settings, including inside rock shelters (see also Tarble 1990). She sees these petroglyphs as representative of a ritual mode of Arauquinoid decoration (Tarble, cited in Greer 1995:205–7).

Conclusions

We have examined in this study several of the 'mythscapes' that northern Arawak-speaking peoples of the north-west Amazon have constructed and which they utilize as references to their primordial past, historical past and living present. Such mythscapes are 'multi-centric' – each can be understood from its own perspective, or from a collectively held view as elaborated in sacred stories. The stories of creation connect the centres; the powerful chants that accompany the same stories generate non-linear yet structured movements from the centre outwards to the limits of known space-time, followed by a return inward to the source of ancestral power. Centrifugal and centripetal movements are enacted in every initiation rite when the music of the instruments makes the world grow; at the same time the chanters create protective shields for the new generations of life. The primordial processions of the flutes and trumpets are like pilgrimages, in that they have sacred centres as their reference points, connecting themselves with the 'ends' of the world. This we saw in both the journeys described by the Hohodene chants and the Warekena sacred story, in which the primordial beings parade with the sacred flutes that leave from the great world-centre, disperse in various directions, and return to a place of gathering, renewal of life and rebirth from the dangers of the peripheral world. The peripheries are the spaces of alterity associated with spirits of the dead, other tribes who neither speak the same language nor follow the same ways of life as the northern Arawak-speaking peoples.[10]

The processions and returns to the centre of the world, the sources of ancestral emergence, are necessary to 'bring back' the soul from its centrifugal voyages, concentrate it collectively in a protected sanctuary, and re-connect

---

10   Such as the *Maakunai*, all peoples who do not speak the northern Arawak languages – speakers of Cariban, Makuan, and Tukanoan languages; as well as the non-indigenous peoples such as the Portuguese and Spaniards with whom the Hohodene, Baniva and Warekena have had the most historical contacts.

with the life force that generates all being. In referring to the cosmic significance of these ritual pilgrimages, Sullivan (1988:317) writes:

> Understanding the fully sacred meaning of the procession and obtaining this knowledge experientially offer[s] the [initiates and] community the chance for reflexivity and control over the meaning of change. [...] [T]he community not only grows in the form of future physical life but also regains contact with the sacred foundations of symbolic form itself, the distinguishing mark of human culture...

In the narratives and in the sanctuaries sacred forms are understood to be spatio-temporal portals to 'other' worlds, while in shamanic healing chants, the centrifugal and centripetal movements situate primordial identity in constant tension with historical alterity.

Ambiguity inheres in these sanctuaries, for they are of both worlds – this material world and the other, spirit world, at one and the same time. The sanctuaries were 'made' (the petroglyphs inscribed on the boulders, the boulders put into place, the sites brought into being) in the primordial time, when the events they symbolize took place; consequently, they all have times of their own. Nevertheless, the powers with which they were imbued are still vibrant and present, demanding appropriate respect and caution. Ambiguity resides in the context: when the two worlds mix during the rites and ceremonies, the extraordinary power inherent in such situations can result in disaster if the norms are not respected. Shamans regularly bring the two worlds together in their cures. When they do, they announce that they are bringing the 'new, other world' into 'this world'; which is to say, they exercise their 'world-making' powers (cf. Overing 1990; Wright 2014) to renew the primordial spirit-world in the healing of this (corporeal, material) world.

References

Carrasco, D. 2013. *Religions of Mesoamerica*. Long Grove, Ill.: Waveland Press.
DeLoria Jr., V. 2011 Interview in "In the Light of Reverence", produced and directed by Christopher MacLeod/Earth Island Institute. Sacred Land Film Project.
Gonzalez Ñáñez, O. 1968. 'La mitología baniva reflejada en su literatura oral'. *Economía Y Ciencias Sociales – Revista de la FACES-UCV* 3:87–96.
——— 1980. *Mitología Guarequena*. Caracas: Monte Ávila editores.
——— 1986. 'Sexualidad y rituales de iniciación entre los indígenas Warekena del Río Guainía-Rio Negro'. *Montalban* 17:103–38.
——— 1987. 'Los Curripacos: Un manual bilingüe'. *Revista La Iglesia en Amazonas* 37:34–49.

――― 2009. *Literaturas indígenas Maipure-arawakas de los Pueblos Kurripako, Waekenas y Baniva del Estado Amazonas.* Caracas: Editorial El Perro y La Rana.

González Ñañez, O. and M. Camico 2013. Expedición a las cabeceras del Caño de Âki: Toponimia de la cuenca del Caño de Âki, el Caño Peramán (Mâni) y otros afluentes hasta su desembocadura en el Guainía. Toponímicos del Cano Mâni, el afluente más importante del Aki. *UniverSOS* 10:73–92.

Greer, J.W. 1995. Rock Art Chronology in the Orinoco Basin of Southwestern Venezuela. Ph.D. thesis. University of Missouri-Colombia.

Hill, J.D. 1993. *Keepers of he Sacred Chants.* Champaign: University of Illinois.

Koch-Grünberg, Theodor. 1907. Südamerikanische Felszeichnungen. Berlin: E. Wasmuth A.-G.

Nimuendaju, C. 1950 [1927]. 'Reconhecimento dos rios Içana, Ayari e Uaupés'. *Journal de la Société des Américanistes de Paris* 39:125–83 and 44:149–78.

Ortiz, F. and H. Pradilla 2002. *Rocas y Petroglifos del Guainía.* Bogotá Fundación Etnollano. Museo Arqueológico de Tunja. Universidad Pedagógica y Tecnológica de Colombia.

Overing, J. 1990. 'The Shaman as a maker of worlds: Nelson Goodman in the Amazon'. *Man* (NS) 25:601–19.

Raffa, Manuel Romero 2003. *Malikai. El Canto del Malirri.* Bogotá: Cerec

Sullivan, Lawrence E. 1988. *Icanchu's Drum. An Orientation to Meaning in South American Religions.* Boston: MacMillan Press.

Tarble, K. 1985. 'Un nuevo modelo de expansión caribe para la epoca prehispánica'. *Antropológica* 63–4:45–81.

――― 1990. 'La cosmovisión orinoquense y el contexto arqueológico: un ensayo en interpretación'. Paper presented in the symposium 'Sacred Sites and Sites of Significance', World Archaeological Congress II, Barquisimeto, Venezuela, September 1990.

Tarble, K. and F. Scaramelli 1993. 'Una correlación preliminar entre alfarerías y el arte rupestre del Municipio Autónomo Cedeño, Edo'. Paper presented at the XV International Congress for Caribbean Archaeology, San Juan, Puerto Rico.

Turner, T. 1988. 'Ethno-ethnohistory: myth and history in native South American representations of contact with Western society'. In J. Hill (ed.) *Rethinking History and Myth. Indigenous South American Perspectives on the Past*, 235–81. Urbana: University of Illinois Press.

Vidal O., Silvia 1987. El Modelo del Proceso Migratorio Prehispánico de los Piapoco: Hipótesis y Evidencias. Master's thesis, Centro de Estudios Avanzados, Instituto de Investigaciones Científicas.

――― 1993. Reconstrucción de los Processos de Etnogenesis y de Reproducción Social entre los Baré de Rio Negro (siglos XI–XVIII). Ph.D. Thesis. Centro de Estudios Avanzados-IVIC.

Wright, Robin M. 1981. History and Religion of the Baniwa Peoples of the Upper Rio Negro. Ph.D. dissertation. Stanford University.

——— 1993/4. 'Pursuing the spirit. Semantic construction in Hohodene *Kalidzamai* Chants for initiation'. Amerindia. Paris, France: CNRS, v.18, 17-40.

——— 1998. *Cosmos, Self, and History in Baniwa Religion*. Austin: University of Texas Press.

———(ed.) 1999. *Transformando os deuses. Os múltiplos sentidos da conversão entre os povos indígenas no Brasil*. Campinas, S.P.: Editora da UNICAMP.

——— 2005. *História Indígena e do Indigenismo no Alto Rio Negro* [Indigenous History and the History of Indian Policy on the Upper Rio Negro]. Campinas: Mercado de Letras/Instituto Socioambiental.

——— 2009. 'Mythscapes of the northwest Amazon and their meanings'. Presented at the 2009 SE Conference on the Amazon and the Andes, UF-Gainesville, April.

——— 2013. *Mysteries of the Jaguar Shamans of the Northwest Amazon*. Omaha: University of Nebraska Press.

——— 2014. 'Mitagens e seus significados no noroeste amazônico'. In M.S.C. Martins (ed.) *Ensaios em Interculturalidade: Literatura, Cultura e Direitos de indígenas em época de globalização*, 133–72. Campinas: Mercado de Letras.

Wright, R.M. and J.D. Hill 1986. 'History, ritual and myth: 19th century millenarian movements in the northwest Amazon'. *Ethnohistory* 33(1):39–54.

Wright, R.M., ed. 1999. *Waferinaipe Ianheke. A Sabedoria dos Nossos Antepassados* [The Wisdom of Our Ancestors]. São Gabriel da Cachoeira: ACIRA/FOIRN.

Xavier Leal, C.C. 2013. Os Koripako Do Alto Içana – Etnografia De Um Grupo Indígena Evangélico. Ph.D. thesis. Museu Nacional-UFRJ.

Zucchi, A. 1992. 'Como ellos la cuentan. La ocupación de la Orinoquia según la historia oral de un grupo Maipure del Norte', 223-252. In M.E. Romero (ed.) *Café, Caballo y Hamaca. Visión histórica del Llano*. Ediciones Abya-Yala y Orinoquia Siglo XXI. Santa Fe de Bogotá.

CONTRIBUTORS

Dionigi Albera is a senior researcher at the CNRS (IDEMEC, Aix-en-Provence). He is carrying out anthropological research in the Mediterranean Basin on the interplay between different religions. On this topic he has published 'La Vierge et l'islam. Mélange de civilisations en Méditerranée', *Le Débat* (no. 137, novembre-décembre 2005); 'Pèlerinages mixtes et sanctuaires 'ambigus' en Méditerranée' (in S. Chiffoleau and A. Madoeuf (eds.), *Les pèlerinages au Moyen-Orient: espaces public, espaces du public*, Beyrouth: 2005); '"Why are you mixing what cannot be mixed?": Shared devotions in the monotheisms' (*History and Anthropology* 19:1, 2008). He has recently edited, with Maria Couroucli, *Sharing Sacred Spaces in the Mediterranean. Christians, Muslims and Jews at Shrines and Sanctuaries* (Bloomington: 2012).

Isabelle Charleux is a Senior Research Fellow (Directeur de recherches) at CNRS (National Centre for Scientific Research) – GSRL (Group Societies, Religions, Secularism). Her area of research is the Mongol material culture (especially architecture) and the interactions between Mongol and Chinese Buddhisms in the fields of social history and art history. Among her published works related to the volume theme are: *Temples et Monastères de Mongolie méridionale* (Paris: 2006); *Nomads on Pilgrimage. Mongols on Wutaishan (China), 1800–1940* (Leiden: 2015); 'Les "lamas" vus de Chine: fascination et répulsion' (*Extrême-Orient Extrême-Occident* 2002).

Jürgen Wasim Frembgen is Senior Curator of the Oriental Department at the Museum of Ethnology in Munich as well as Private Docent at the Institute of Near and Middle Eastern Studies of the University of Munich. Since 1981 he has been teaching anthropology and Islamic Studies at various universities in Germany; in addition he had been a visiting professor at Quaid-i-Azam University in Islamabad (National Institute of Pakistan Studies), National College of Arts in Lahore as well as Ohio State University in Columbus, USA. Since 1981 he has conducted annual ethnographic fieldwork in Pakistan (in the Karakoram, Indus Kohistan, Punjab and Sindh). He is currently researching the cult of Lal Shahbaz Qalandar and his devotees in Lahore. In addition, he has curated numerous exhibitions dealing with cultures of the Muslim world. Recently he published *The Friends of God – Sufi Saints in Islam. Popular Poster Art from Pakistan* (Karachi: 2006); *Journey to God. Sufis and Dervishes in Islam* (Karachi: 2008) and edited *The Aura of Alif. The Art of Writing in Islam* (Munich: 2010).

Omar González Ñáñez is a Senior Professor of Anthropology and Linguistics at the Universidad Central de Venezuela and at the Universidad de Los Andes, Mérida-Venezuela. In 1984 he was founder and first Director of the Escuela de Antropología. Facultad de Ciencias Económicas y Sociales, Universidad Central de Venezuela. Since 1970 he has been studying the ethnography, religions and languages of the Maipuran-Arawakan peoples Warekena, Baniva de Maroa, Kurripako and Piapoko of the Orinoco and Rio Negro basin in southern Venezuela. Amongst his publications are *Mitología Warekena.* (Caracas: 1980); *Gramática de la lengua Warekena (Maipure-Arawak): Una aproximación tipológica-relacional* (Caracas: 2009); *Las literaturas indígenas Maipure-arawakas de los pueblos Kurripako, Warekena Y Baniva del Estado Amazonas* (Caracas: 2009).

Angela Hobart is Honorary Reader at Goldsmiths College, having taught Applied Medical Anthropology (Cross-Cultural Therapy) there for many years; and Honorary Professor of Medical Anthropology, associated with the Health Humanities Department, at University College London. She also works as a therapist at the Helen Bamber Foundation for the survivors of cruelty and torture; and lectures at the British Museum on the art and culture of South East Asia. She is the Director of the Centro Incontri Umani, Ascona. Amongst her publications is *Healing Performances of Bali: Between Darkness and Light* (Oxford: 2003) and she has co-edited *Contesting the State: the Dynamics of Resistance and Control* (Canon Pyon: 2012), *Shamanism and Islam: Sufism, Healing Rituals and Spirits* (London: 2012) and *Aesthetics in Performance. Formations of Symbolic Construction and Experience* (Oxford: 2005).

Carlos César Xavier Leal received his M.A. in anthropology in 2008, from the Universidade Federal do Rio de Janeiro, Museu Nacional, programa de pós-graduação em antropologia social. His thesis was titled 'A Cidade Grande de Ñapirikolie Os Petroglifos Do Içana – Uma Etnografia de Signos Baniwa'. He recieved his Ph.D. from the same institution in 2013, with a dissertation on 'Os Koripako Do Alto Içana : Etnografia de um Grupo Indígena Evangélico'.

Pierre-Jean Luizard is a Senior Research Fellow (Directeur de recherches) at CNRS (National Centre for Scientific Research) - GSRL (Group Societies, Religions, Secularism). He has lived for long periods of time in mamy Arab countries in the Middle East, particularly Syria, Lebanon, Iraq and Egypt. A historian of contemporary Islam in his native country, he is especially interested in the impact of different manifestations of Islamic faith and the role some of them play within current political systems: the history of the Shi'ite clergy in Iraq; the history of Islamic reformism, particularly after the reform of Al-Azhar and popular Islam as carried through by Sufi brotherhoods in Egypt. His publications include *Histoire politique du clergé chiite, XVIIIe-XXIe siècle* (Paris: 2014) ; *La Question irakienne* (Paris: 2002) ; *La Formation de l'Irak contemporain* (Paris: 1991). He has also edited *Le Choc colonial et l'islam: les politiques religieuses des puissances coloniales en terres d'islam* (Paris: 2006).

Manoël Penicaud is a Junior Research Fellow (Chargé de recherches) at CNRS (National Centre for Scientific Research), based at the IDEMEC (UMR 6591 – Institute of European, Mediterranean and Comparative Ethnology). He has worked on several pilgrimages in Europe (Santiago de Compostella, Seven Sleepers in Brittany), North Africa (Daour of Regraga) and the Middle East (Holy Land, Ephesus). Among his recent publications are: *Lieux saints partagés* (ed. with D. Albera and I. Marquette, Arles: 2015); 'Le Père Paolo Dall'Oglio: otage volontaire par amour de l'islam', *Ethnologie française* (2016); *Le Réveil des Sept Dormants. Un pèlerinage islamo-chrétien en Bretagne* (Paris: 2016); 'Muslim pilgrims at the House of Mary in Ephesus', in M. Mignone (ed.), *The Idea of the Mediterranean* (Stony Brooks: 2017). He is also curator of exhibitions, such as *Shared Sacred Places* at the Museum of Mediterranean and European Civilizations in Marseille (2015), the Bardo Museum in Tunis (2016) and the National Museum of the History of Immigration in Paris (2017–18).

Yasushi Tonaga is Professor at the Graduate School of Asian and African Studies, University of Kyoto, Director of the Centre for Islamic Area Studies at Kyoto University and director of the Kenan Rifai Centre for Sufi Studies at Kyoto University. His field of expertise is the history of Sufism, of sanctity, and, particularly, the mystical thought of Ibn Arabi. His published writing on saint veneration and pilgrimages includes: 'Sufism in the past and present: based on the three-axis framework of Sufism' (*Annals of the Japan Association for Middle East Studies* 21(2):206); 'Sufi saints and non-Sufi saints in early Islamic literature' (*The Journal of Sophia Asian Studies* 22, 2004), and '"Polytheistic" Islam: Islam observed from the viewpoint of Sufi, Saint and Tariqa' (*Acta Asiatica* 86, 2004).

Robin M. Wright is Associate Professor in the Departments of Religion and Anthropology, and coordinator of the American Indian and Indigenous Studies Program at the University of Florida, Gainesville. He is former Professor of Anthropology and Indigenous Studies at the Universidade Estadual de Campinas (UNICAMP) in Campinas, Brazil. His field of expertise is indigenous religious traditions of the Americas and Pacific, especially the Northwest Amazon, and shamanism. He has published several monographic studies about Northwest Amazon shamanism and prophets; edited several volumes on indigenous peoples of the Americas and Christianity; and several articles on sacred geographies of the northern Arawak-speaking peoples of the Amazon.

Thierry Zarcone is a Senior Research Fellow (Directeur de recherches) at CNRS (National Centre for Scientific Research) - GSRL (Group Societies, Religions, Secularism), and a former visiting professor at Kyoto University (Japan) and Fribourg University (Swizerland). He also lectures at the School of Oriental Languages and Civilisations (Paris) and at the Institute of Political Sciences (Aix-en-Provence). His field of expertise is the history and anthropology of Islam in the Turco-Persian area (Turkey, Central Asia, Chinese Turkestan), especially Sufism, saint veneration and Islamized shamanism. His recent books include *Le Croissant et le Compas. Islam et franc-maçonnerie, de la fascination à la détestation* (Paris: 2015); *Poétesses soufies de la confrérie bektachie* (Montélimar: 2009); *Le Soufisme. Voie mystique de l'islam* (Paris: 2009); *Sufi Pilgrims from Central Asia and India in Jerusalem* (Kyoto: 2009); *La Turquie. De l'Empire ottoman à la République d'Atatürk* (Paris: 2005). He is also editor of the *Journal of the History of Sufism* (Paris) and has edited (with A. Hobart): *Shamanism and Islam: Sufism, Healing Rituals and Spirits* (London: 2012).

INDEX

Page numbers in *italic* refer to illustration captions.

'Abd al-'Al, Shaykh   59
Abd al-Malik al-Juwaynī   71
Abū al-Hajjāj, *mawlid* of   51–9, 65
Abū al-Hasan al-Hujwīrī   74
Abū al-Qāsim al-Qushayrī   73
Abū Bakr al-Bāqillānī   71
Abū Bakr Ibn Fūrak   71
Abū Hafs al-Nasafī   71, 72, 81
Abū Ishāq al-Isfarā'īnī   74
Abū Ja'far al-Kulaynī   77
'Adī, Shaykh   7, 19
'Adud al-Dīn al-Ījī   71
Afāq Khwāja   19
Afghanistan   131
Ahmad al-Badawī, *mawlid* of   59–62, 65
Ahmad al-Tahāwī   71, 73
Akya   113
Akyazili   8
Alayi Valley   145–6
Albera, Dionigi   1, 29, 233
Algeria   9, *10*, *70*, 191
Alī ibn Muhammad al-Jurjānī   71
Alley, R.   105
Alshqar, R. David   8
alterity   205
Amadou Hampāte Bā   191
Amaru   211, 213, *213*, 214, 215, 220
Amazonian Arawakan mythscapes   201–29
Amīr Khusraw   120
Amjad Husayn Shāh, Sayyid   123–6, *124*
Amon-Re   58
anarchism   167–8
Anatolia   1, 5, 8, 9, 10, 15, 20, 21, 31, 33
Anima   171
Anwar, Masuma   120
Arawakan mythscapes   201–29
architecture   19–20, 90
Arif Lohar   123
Arp, Hans   169
Arslankhan mausoleum   8, *14*
Artemis von Ephesos statue   157, *158*
Ascona   *see* Monte Verità
Ashkenazi, Daniel Hashomer   8
Assman, Ian   38, 41
Audouard, Olympe   60

Axial Age   37–8
Azerbaijan   4

Badī al-Dīn Nūrī   136
Bakunin, Michael   167, 168
Balkans   1, 20, 31, 33
Ball, Hugo   169
Bara, Charlotte   167
baraka   53, 56, 82
barques, sacred   57–9, 63, 64–5
Barrī Imām   121
Bastide, Roger   1, 8
Beautiful Festival of the Valley   58–9, 63
Beauvoir, Simone de   37
Bektashism   5, 11, *17*, 21, 29, 30–2
believing, act and process of   39, 44–5, 47
Bernbaum, Edwin Marshall   147
Black Madonna   161, *162*
Bloch, Morris   157
Brazil   8
Brittany   *see* Seven Sleepers pilgrimage
Bubastis, pilgrimage to   60, 61
Buber, Martin   170
Buddhism   6, 9, 13, 14, *16*, 19, 21, 40–1, 87, 92
   legends concerning Muztagh Ata   133–5
   pilgrimages to Wutaishan   13, 87–115
   superimposition of Islam on   131, 133, 135–49
Bulgaria   8
Bullhe Shāh   123
Busiris, pilgrimage to   60, 61

Cambodia   18
Camico, Hernan   222
Camico, Venancio   222, *223*
Capus, Guillaume   135, 136
Carazzetti, R.   160, 161
caves   4, 7, 9, 15, 18, *18*, 99–100, 101, 103, 105, 143, 183, 184, 217, 220, 228
Celtic influences and motifs   *160*, 160–3
Çengelköy church   8
Certeau, Michel de   38–9
chanting   223, 224
Charleux, Isabelle   87, 233

Chiara's rainbow trail 177–9
Chih, Rachida 63, 64
China 9, *14*, 15, *16*, *17*, 19–20, 40
    Wutaishan pilgrimage 13, 87–115
Christian-Muslim interactions 29
    ambiguous cults, practices and
        sanctuaries 30–6
    pilgrimages 7, 12, 13, 20, 183–98
Christianity 9, 10, 11, 13, 20, 42, 43, 138
Catholic pilgrimage sites *16*, 161–3,
    183–98
    disambiguity 46–7
*Christianity and Islam under the
    Sultans* 30
circumambulation rituals 13–15, *14*, 97–8,
    98, 114
Classical Antiquity, cults in 45–6
Coedes, George 178
Cohen, Eric 176
communitas 88, 103–12, 119, 196
Comoros Islands 191
Compagnons of the Cave, shrine of the 4
conferences and exhibitions 1–2, 169–71,
    172
Confucianism 40, 87, 92
Corbin, Henri 170, 172
Cortesi, Malu 179
creation myths 203, 204, 208–9
crocodiles, sacred 62–3
Cuba 8

Dall'Oglio, Paolo 189
Damballahwèdo pilgrimage 13
dance *121*, 123, 124, 126–7, 166, *166*, 167
Daoism 87, 92; *see also* Taoism
Dārā Shikūh 11
Daressy, Georges 52
Dātā Ganj Bakhsh 123
Dede Qorqut 12
Demavend mountain 141
demons *140*
dervishes 31, 119, 120, 121, 123, 124, 126,
    127, 128
Dilgo Khyentsé 113
disambiguation 39, 42–3
disputed sanctuaries 20–1
Disuq, Egypt 62–3
dreams 171–2
Duff-Gordon, Lucy 63
Dzongsar Khyentsé Rinpoché 113
Dzuliferi, boulder of 222, 224

Eade, John 106, 107, 108, 110, 180, 196, 197
earth deities 161
economic aspects of pilgrimage sites 21,
    61, 88, 94, 101, 102, 107, 108, 109, 112,
    176, 195, 196
Egypt 13, 79
    Pharaonic festivals and Sufi
        mawlids 51–65
Eliade, Mircea 170, 173
Elverscog, J. 107–10
Enipan 203, 204, 205, 221
Enukwa 203, 204
Ephraïm al-Naqava, Rabbi 9, *10*
equality 177
Eranos conferences 169–71, 172
exile and return 221

Fakhr al-Dīn al-Rāzī 71
Ferghana Valley 136, 144, 145
Five Dragon Kings Temple,
    Wutaishan 94, *94*
Foucault, Michel 128, 184, 191, 198
France *16*, 161
    Seven Sleepers pilgrimage 7, 12, 13,
        20, 183–98
Franscini, Stefano 174
Frégosi, Franck 115
Frembgen, Jürgen Wasim 119, 233
Fröbe-Kapteyn, Olga 171

Gao Henian 89, 111
gender ambiguities 13, 120, 121–4
Gennep, Arnold van 119
Germany 161, 169, 191
Gogā 19
Goldziher, Ignace 60, 61, 65
González Ñáñez, Omar 201, 202, 222, 234
Goodway, David 168
Gornenskij, I. 144, 146
Graeser, Gusto *164*, 164–5
Graeser, Karl 164, 169
Greece 8
Greek philosophy 37–8
Green, Martin 164

Haci Bektāsh 8, 15, *15*
Haiti 7, 8, 13
Hakim al-Tirmidhī 74
Hansen, Joerg 159
Hasluck, Frederick William
    reappraisal of article on 'ambiguous
        sanctuaries' 1, 29–47
Hayden, Robert 34

Index

healing 7, 14, 33, 161, 163, 222, 223–4
Hedin, Sven 132, 135, 136, 141, 144, 146
Hesse, Herman 165
Heydt, Eduard von der 169, 174, *174*
hidden and heavenly kingdoms, legends of 144–8
Hillman, James 173
Hindu mythology 147–8
Hinduism 7, 8, 9, 11, 14, 21
Hipana *203*, 204, 206, 208, 209–11, *212*, *213*, 214–15, 219, 221, 222, 224, 225
Hobart, Angela 1, 157, 234
Hofman, Ida 164
holes, ritual crawling through 13, 15, 18, *18*, 99, 100, 103
Hornell, James 63, 64
hybridity 47

Ibn 'Arabî 6
Ibrāhīm al-Dīsūqī, *mawlid* of 62–3
imagination, activation of 5–6
imām, term 76–7
Imam 'Ali 76, 77, 136–7, *137*, 149
imamology, Shi'ite 75–7, 80
India 8, 9, 11–12, 18, 19, 21, 133, 139, 147
Ingold, Tim 175
Iran 76, 78
Iraq 7, 19
Islam 5, 7, 8, 9, 11, 15, *17*, 19, 20, 42, 45
  practices of saint cults 80–3
  saints in Islamic thought 69–70
  spread of 64
  superimposition on Buddhism 131–49
  theory of saints 71–80
  see also Christian-Muslim interactions; Ismailism *and* Sufism
Ismailism 5, 7, 136, 137, 138
Israel 20
Italy 9, 161

Ja'far Tayran 9
Janaidar 144–7, 148
Japan 6, 18, 40–1; *see also* tea ceremony
Jaspers, Karl 37
Jawlensky, Alexej von 169
Jesus Christ 10
Jews *see* Judaism
Jikmé Püntsok 112, 113
Judaism 9, *10*, 14, 20, 35, 42, 43, 191
Jung, Carl Gustav 170, 171–2, *173*

Kabīr 12
Kashgar (map) *130*
Khan, Nusrat Fateh Ali 120
Khānifnāth 11, 18
Khatīb al-Baghdādī 71
Khejok Rinpoché 113
Khidr 8
Khotan, kingdom of 135, 147
Kohmari grotto 7
Kollmar-Paulenz, Karénina 148
K'ouen-Louen mountain 15
Kropotkin, Peter 167, 168
Kübler-Ross, E. 179
Kudui 222
Kugle, Scott 122
Kuwai *203*, 205, 206, 207, 209, 211, *212*, 213–14, 215, 216, *216*, 220, 225, 227
Kyrgystan 5, 131, 135, 144
  falcon hunter *142*
  see also Alayi Valley

Laban, Rudolf von 166, 167
Lacan, Jacques 43
Lake Maggiore *156*, 157
Lāl Shāhbaz Qalandar, Sufi cult of 13, 119–29
Lampedusa 9
language barriers 111, 114
Lapwood, R. 105
Larung Buddhist Institute 113
Legrain, Georges 52, 53, 57, 63
Levi-Strauss, Claude 43
Lieux saints partagés exhibition 1–2
light phenomena 104–5, 113
liminality 103, 119, 126, 167
Littman, Enno 65
Luizard, Pierre-Jean 51, 234

Madonna della Fontanna 162–3
magnetic anomalies 159, 160, 178
mandalas 171–2, *173*, 177, 178, 179
Manicheism 131
Manjushri 87, 90, 91, 95, 100, 101, 102, 103, *104*, 105, 113
Mary, mother of Jesus 82, 161, 186
Maspero, Gaston 52, 61, 65
Massignon, Genevieve 190
Massignon, Louis 65, 183, 184, *185*, 186, 187, 188, 189–92, *192*, 198
Mater Dolorosa 8
mausoleums 2, 8, 9, 11, 12, *14*, 19, 20, *83*, 134, 136, *138*, *139*; *see also* tombs
Mawerikuli 217, 218–19, *219*

mawlids in Egypt   51–65
Mayeur-Jaouen, Catherine   63, 64, 65
Mazdeism   138, 149; *see also* Zoroastrianism
McPherson, Joseph Williams   58, 63
Mecca, pilgrimage to   15, 64
métissage   47
Métraux, Alfred   7
miracles   7, 9, 10, 33, 62, 64, 71, 72–4, 75, 80–2, 184, 222
Miyvacir, Duke   88, 89
monasteries on Mount Wutaishan   18, 90, 96–7, 98, 100–2, *104*
Mongol Buddhists   87–115
monotheism   41–4, 46
Monte Verità   12, 20, 22, 157–81
Morimoto, Kazuo   77
Morocco   8, 191
Moses   136, 149
Mothipan   203, 204, 215, 217
mountain cults in Pamir Mountains   143–4
Mountain of Truth   *see* Monte Verità
mountains   4
    Demavend   141
    Muztagh Ata   7, *132*, 132–49
    Wutaishan   87–115
    see also under names of legendary mountains
multi-centred worlds   204
Mūsa Sāda Sohag   123
music   120, 166, 175
Muslih al-Dīn, Shaykh   136
Muslim Brotherhood   55, 61
Muslims   *see* Islam
Muztagh Ata mountain   7, *132*, 132–49
mythscapes in Arawak-speaking Amazon   201–29

Napier, David   161
Naquin, Susan   105, 106
natural settings and sites   4–5, 32–3, 99–100, 163, 201–29
    see also caves; mountains; trees *and* waterfalls
nature, reconnection with   157, 165, 166, 175
negative aspects of ambiguity   3, 36–7
Nestorianism   131
Newmann, Erich   170
Nhiaperikuli, City of   203, 217–21, *218*, 220
Nietzsche, Friedrich   163, 165
Nihilism   168

Nizām al-dīn Awliyā   120, 123
Nooran, Jyoti   120
Notre-Dame of the Carmel   13
Notre-Dame du Rosaire   8

Oedenkoven, Henri   164
offerings   *15–16*, 19
Omulû   9
Opet, Feast of   58–9, 63
Ottoman Empire   30, 33, 34, 35

Pakistan
    Sufi cult of Lāl Shāhbaz Qalandar   13, 119–29
Pamir Mountains
    mountain cults and saint veneration   5, 131–49
paradise gardens, legends of   144, *145*
paradoxical sanctuaries   20, 22, 157, 179, 194, 195
pardon, Catholic   183, 186, 190, 192, 193, 194, 196
Parveen, Abida   120
Peat, D.   159
Pénicaud, Manoël   1, 183, 235
petroglyphs   202, 204, 206, *207*, 211, *212*, 217, 225, 227, 228, 229
Pharaonic influences on Sufi *mawlids*   57–61, 63
pilgrimages
    to Bubastis and Busiris   60, 61
    communitas   88, 103–12, 119, 196
    to Mecca   15, 64
    to Monte Verità, Switzerland   12, 20, 22, 157–81
    sacred journeys in Arawak-speaking Amazon   215–16
    Seven Sleepers, France   7, 12, 13, 20, 183–98
    Tro Breizh, France   190
    to Wutaishan, China   13, 87–115
Pinguet, Maurice   134
Poland   161
polytheism   41
positive aspects of ambiguity   3, 36–7, 47
pre-religious sacredness   2–6, 12, 21
Preston, James J.   196

Qāf Mountain, legend of   141–3
Qalander Shah, Baba   9
Qing identity, forging of   108
Quranic verses   70, *70*, 79, 82, 184, *189*, 190, 191

Rabi'a Gul   126–8, *126*, *127*
Rachel, tomb of   20
rainbows   177–9, 180, *180*
rebirth rituals   15, 18, *18*
reform communities at Monte
   Verità   163–73
Reuss, Theodor   167
Rinpoché   113
ritual metonymy and metaphor   43–4
Rölpé Dorjé, Changkya Khutugtu   90, 101,
   102, 104, 105, 110
Rossetti, Claudio   175, 179
Rousseau, Jean-Jacques   163, 165

sacred places in Arawak-speaking
   Amazon   202, *203*, 203–28
Sa'd al-Dīn al-Taftāzānī   71, 72, 81
Sa'īd Sarmad   11, *11*, 12
Sain Mūmtaz 'Alī   121–3, *122*
Sain Saheli Sarkār   123
Sainte Barbe   8
saints
   dual saints   8–10
   in Islamic thought   69–70
   pre-religious saints   6–8
   syncretic and 'supra-confessional'
      saints   10–13
   tombs of   7, 18, 75, 81, 123, 136, 138
   see also under named saints
Sakyong Mipham Rinpoché   113
Sallnow, Michael   106, 107, 108, 110, 180,
   196, 197
Sari Saltuk   10, 12, 31
sayyid/sharifology   77–80, *78*, *79*
Schimmel, Annemarie   171
Scholem, Gershom   172
Sehwan Sharif, Pakistan   119, *120*, *121*, 124
Seven Sleepers pilgrimage, France   7, 12,
   13, 20, 183–98
Seven Sleepers shrine, Azerbaijan   *4*
Shāh Husayn   121
shamanism   12, 131, 206, *210*, 214, 216
Shambhala   147, 148
Sharaf al-Dīn Yahyā Manerī   7
shared sanctuaries
   categories of   2
   communitas at   88, 103–12
   hypotheses on   1–22
   reappraisal of Hasluck's article on
      ambiguity   1, 29–47
   and syncretism   195
   tolerance of   34, 40, 106
Sharīf, Muhammad   *139*

Shaw, Rosalind   194
Shi'ite imamology   75–7, 80
Shintosim   40–1
Simona, Giovanni   159
Siyāh Qalam, Muhammad   *185*
Siyah Qalam manuscript   *140*
Skorupski, Tadeusz   178
Song Yun   134
Sonognini, Lorenzo   175
South American myths   9
Spain   161
spirit kingdoms, legends of   140–3
spiritual protection   221–4
Stein, Aurel   135, 137, 148
Stewart, Charles   194
stones, sacred   4, *4*
Sufism   5, 7, 8, 9, 19, 20, 21, 71, 138
   cult of Lāl Shāhbaz Qalandar   13,
      119–29
   mawlids in Egypt   51–65
   walī theory of   73–5, 80
   see also Bektashism
Sullivan, Lawrence E.   229
Sunnite theology   71–3, 80
superimposition of religions   131–49, 196
Suzuki, Teitaro   170, 171
Switzerland
   Monte Verità, Ascona   12, 20, 22,
      157–81
Sykes, Ella C.   135
symbolic meanings, intermingling of   19
syncretism   8, 10–13, 47, 92, 92–3, 131, 133,
   184, 194–5
Syria   75
Szeemann, Harald   157

Tajikistan   5, *132*; *see also* Alayi Valley
Taki, Mohamed   *192*
Tanta, Egypt   59–62, 65
Taoism   13, 19, 20, 21, 40, 161, 165, 168, *173*,
   174, 175; *see also* Daoism
tea ceremony   175–7, *176*
Tibet   15, 146, 147
Tibetan Buddhists   87–115
Tillich, Paul   170
tolerance   34, 40, 45, 106, 119
Tolstoy, Leo   163, 165
tombs
   indigenous pilgrimages to   221–4
   of saints   7, 18, 75, 81, 123, 136, 138
   see also mausoleums
Tonaga, Yasushi   69, 235

tourism *see* economic aspects of
    pilgrimage sites
transposable rituals   13–19
trees   5, 6, *83*, 177
Tro Breizh pilgrimage   190
Tunui   203
Turgenev, Ivan   168
Turkey   *17*, 33, 137, 184, 191
Turner, Victor   14, 103, 119, 157, 167, 196
Tuttle, Gray   110, 111
Tuyuq mausoleum   19

Uaracapory   *203*, 205
ulamā'   72
UNESCO World Heritage sites   112
Uzbekistan   83; *see also* Ferghana Valley

Voegelin, Eric   38
voodoo   7, 13

Wachsmann, Shelley   63
walī, term   69–70
walī theory of Sufism   73–5, 80
Waliro   203
Warekena mythscapes   224–8
Warukwa   *203*, 204, 209, *210*, 221, 222

waterfalls   168, *180*
Way of Nine Palaces   92
Weber, Max   39, 40
Werefkin, Marianne von   169, *170*
white camel, legends of the   136–7, *137*,
    144
Wilheim, Richard   172
women in creation myths   214–15
Wright, Robin M.   201, 202, 235
Wutaishan pilgrimage   13, 87–115

Xavier Leal, Carlos César   201, 202, 235
Xuanzhang   133
Xuyun   89

Yarkand   15
Yazidism   7, 19
Yūsuf, Sayyid   54

Zarcone, Thierry   1, 7, 19, 20, 131, 236
Zayn al-Abidīn, Imam   121
Zen   175
Zhang Dungu   111
Zoroastrianism   7, 19, 21, 131; *see also*
    Mazdeism